# The Peasants of Marlhes

# The Peasants
# of Marlhes

Economic Development and
Family Organization in
Nineteenth-Century France

By James R. Lehning

The University of North Carolina Press

Chapel Hill

© 1980 The University of North Carolina Press
All rights reserved
Library of Congress Catalog Card Number 79-18707

Library of Congress Cataloging in Publication Data

Lehning, James R  1947–
   The peasants of Marlhes.
   Bibliography: p.
   Includes index.
   1. Marlhes, France—Economic conditions.
2. Family—France—Marlhes—History. I. Title.
HC278.M27L44   301.42'0944'581   79-18707
ISBN 978-0-8078-7412-7 (pbk.)

*For Joan and Amanda Lehning*

# Contents

# List of Tables

# List of Figures

# Acknowledgments

This book would be incomplete without an expression of gratitude to the people and institutions who provided support and advice during its research and writing. The staffs of the Archives Nationales de France in Paris and the Archives Départementales de la Loire in Saint-Etienne were helpful with suggestions of sources. M. Emile Aubert, mayor of the commune of Marlhes; his adjoint, M. Claude Chorain; and M. Louis Pouly, the *secrétaire* of the commune, welcomed me to the village and provided me with access to sources as well as glimpses of life in rural France. M. Pouly deserves special thanks for putting up with my frequent presence in his office for more than six months. M. Batut of the Direction des Services Fiscaux de la Loire kindly granted permission to use the Archives de l'Enregistrement for the period after 1875. In the final stages of writing, Penny Tadman, Priscilla Garcia, and Susan Parker helped type the manuscript.

Any project such as this also requires financial assistance at every step, and I have been most fortunate in this regard. Research grants from the Social Science Research Council and American Council of Learned Societies, the National Institute of Child Health and Development, the Northwestern University Office of Research, and the Department of History of the University of Utah helped support different aspects of the research reflected in this book. The College of Humanities of the University of Utah provided financial assistance for publication.

A more profound debt is due the scholars who have provided advice, criticism, and encouragement during the past five years. Foremost among these is Joan Wallach Scott, who introduced me to the study of social history and whose own work is a marvelous example to follow. Etienne van de Walle helped deepen my skills in historical demography and provided helpful criticism of the manuscript. The scholars associated with the Centre Pierre Leon de l'histoire économique et sociale de la region lyonnaise, especially Professor Yves Lequin, gave me the benefit of their knowledge of Stephanois history and access to unpublished studies of the region. Professor Lequin, as editor of the *Cahiers d'histoire*, granted permission to reprint in this book parts of an article published in that journal. Charles Tilly, James J. Sheehan, T. W. Heyck, Henry Binford, Drew Gilpin Faust, Theresa McBride, and John Modell also commented on parts of the manuscript. I of course remain responsible for any errors that may remain in the text.

The completion of this study of nineteenth-century families is above all due to the encouragement and love I have received from my own family. My parents, Thomas and Eileen Lehning, and my brother, Thomas Lehning, have provided much support along the way. Joan Mower Lehning, my wife, shared the trials of living in a small industrial city in France, assisted in gathering materials, and helped me through the worst moments of this project. Her contribution is as great as my own. Finally, our daughter Amanda, seven months old as I write this, has provided immeasurable help in furthering my comprehension at least of modern attitudes toward children.

Salt Lake City
April 1979

# The Peasants of Marlhes

# Chapter 1
# Introduction

Virtually continuous political, economic, and social turmoil dominates our view of European history during the nineteenth century. Political history describes the great age of revolution, the "rebellious century," with the people deposing monarchs and bringing governments under popular control. In economic history the Industrial Revolution dominates the century, marked by the reorganization of production into factories and the surge of productivity that followed this change. And in social history the movement from a rural society of nobles and peasants to an urban society of bourgeois and workers appears to be the most important facet of the period. Change much more than continuity was the watchword of the period from the French Revolution to the Great War.

For both contemporary observers and later scholars the age of industrialization, urbanization, and political revolution was also the age of profound change in the family. A prominent victim of the February Revolution of 1848 in France, François Guizot, blamed his fall from power on the disintegration of the traditional family as a result of the growth of cities and industry.[1] In a better-known lament on the influence of these factors on family life, Frédéric Le Play claimed in the early 1870s that by breaking the necessary link between the family and the workshop, urban and industrial development undermined the traditional patriarchal or stem family and led to unstable nuclear families and social disorder.[2] A third witness spoke from observation of the region with which this study is concerned, the low mountains south of the industrial city of Saint-Etienne in the Loire department of France. Writing in 1894, Pierre du Maroussem mourned the deterioration of peasant stem families; the result, he thought, was social instability. Family change summarized for him the problems of the nineteenth century: "Isn't this, at bottom, a description of the social question?"[3] While the image of social decay present in these nineteenth-century writings has largely disappeared from the sociology and history of the family, scholars remain convinced that industrialization and urbanization, the most obvious symbols of the sweeping changes of the century, were responsible for changes in family organization.[4] We remember with fondness the mythical secure family life of the world we have lost, and blame the factories and cities of the nineteenth century for taking it away from us.

The usual approach to the study of the transformation of family life has been to examine urban working-class families during the development of factory industry.[5] But while economic development certainly includes the large textile factory in a sprawling industrial city, it also must encompass greater participation in markets, increases in agricultural productivity, and the growth of cottage industry, as well as the mutations in mentality that accompanied these alterations in economic organization. Cities in nineteenth-century Europe were vital in each of these transformations, because of the city's role as a community that coordinated and controlled widely dispersed activities.[6] They cannot, however, be viewed in a vacuum: by its nature the growing city had an impact on the surrounding countryside, where many of the activities it controlled took place. The great expansion of the European urban population in the nineteenth century led to an expansion of the coordinating and controlling activity of the city. In the European countryside there took place a process I will call rural urbanization: rural because it involved the countryside and its residents, urbanization because it meant the extension of urban-based networks of trade, industry, and administration into the countryside. Virtually all European peasants encountered this form of urbanization at some time during the last three centuries, and it dramatically altered the ways they worked, organized their lives, and raised families. These changes, as they were experienced in the French village of Marlhes, are the subject of this book.

The economic influence of towns and cities on the countryside is as old as the towns themselves, but in the several centuries before the French Revolution this control was strengthened by the development of handicraft industries in the countryside, a process historians have recently termed proto-industrialization. The restrictive guild systems of medieval cities forced expanding industries into the countryside, where they found a supply of labor that enabled them to produce goods cheaply. Proto-industrial work expanded greatly during the seventeenth and eighteenth centuries, and a wide variety of products came to be produced in the countryside: textiles, of course, especially wool and linen, but also carved wooden vessels, iron products, pottery, leather goods, rush matting, and, in Russia, even icons were made by peasants during the slack agricultural seasons. Both natural and social factors explained the location of these industries: the ability to produce the raw material assisted the growth of many rural industries, while the existence of poor peasants and small farms and the absence of social controls on home building contributed to the spread of others. In many instances proto-industrialization depended upon rural entrepreneurs, but in virtually all cases the goods produced were intended for sale in urban markets, or even in international markets only the urban merchant could enter. The linen industry of Flanders provides a good example: its product found its largest market in the Americas, not in Europe.[7]

By the early nineteenth century this form of manufacture was in decline across much of western Europe as competition from factories undercut dispersed cottage industry in many parts of the continent. The plight of the handloom weavers of England or Silesia is only the best-known example of a decline that recurred in Flanders, Ireland, and other areas. Whether proto-industry was expanding or declining, however, it brought European peasants into an urban orbit: the peasant became part of a market that he could not control, but whose fluctuations affected his prosperity. The nearby city, with its merchants and contacts with the world beyond the local region, was his link to this market.

The peasant also began to find manufactured products available for his own purchase. Changes in peasant demand patterns in this period remain only imperfectly understood, but there are suggestions from seventeenth-century England and Holland that peasants began to want to purchase goods they could not make themselves. Peasant expenditures on buildings and equipment for his farm stimulated the production of metal goods, brick, tile, and wooden goods. The furnishings of peasant homes became more diverse and elaborate, spurring the manufacture of glassware, earthenware, and even clocks. These patterns of peasant demand may not have fueled industrialization, but they did encourage the peasant to participate in the market. This required cash, and this in turn altered the decisions the peasant made in agricultural production.[8] Increasingly, European peasants produced crops that could be sold rather than subsistence crops intended for family consumption.

This led the peasant back to the city, for it was in the city that he found an expanding market for his agricultural goods. Urban demand for agricultural products was a basic part of the preindustrial economy in Europe: a city could not produce its own food and depended on the surplus production of rural areas to feed its population. This usually meant the product of the immediate hinterland of the city, since transport of bulky agricultural goods was difficult and expensive. Coinciding with the increased interest of the peasant in producing for a market, the urbanization of western Europe and the development of an urban working class that purchased its food encouraged increased agricultural production and the adoption of the technological advances that made up the agricultural revolution of the eighteenth and nineteenth centuries. Enclosures, improved crop rotations, new implements, artificial fertilizers, and improved seeds and livestock were adopted by landowners and wealthier peasants.[9] Agricultural productivity grew, and the peasant increasingly produced for the urban market rather than for the consumption of his own family. This interaction of peasant consumption changes and growing urban demand for agricultural goods furthered the movement of the European peasant into an urban market system.

There were, therefore, a number of economic relationships between town and countryside that increased in strength in the eighteenth and nineteenth centuries. In many instances the increase in strength was pressed by the state, an urban institution that was itself increasing in power and authority during this period. The concerns of the preindustrial state were limited to war making, the administration of justice, diplomacy, and the maintenance of public order, but these led the king's ministers to an interest in the relations of town and country. Above all, agriculture and the distribution of food in the nascent market system of preindustrial Europe came to the attention of government administrators. Fighting a war required the feeding of troops, so in times of war the state apparatus worked to mobilize food supplies and transport them to the armies. The maintenance of public order required the provision of at least minimal food supplies to the cities, and even in peacetime the trade in foodstuffs of most European countries was wrapped in a substantial package of government regulations that controlled prices and distribution. The Jacobin Maximum and the revolutionary armies of the Terror are only extreme cases of the continuous preoccupation of eighteenth- and nineteenth-century governments with agriculture. This preoccupation forced the peasant into the food market and created national markets for agricultural products.[10]

The preindustrial state also needed money for its wars and palaces, and the tax collector became a symbol for the peasantry of the influence of the outside, urban world on his life. Governments established new administrative offices to assist in the collection of taxes. In many countries these officers were urban based, and all took their direction from a higher administration that used cities to transmit their orders down the bureaucracy until they reached the peasant. Taxes also had to be paid in specie, which the peasant could acquire only by selling the products of his farm to the urban market.

As industrialization and urbanization spread during the nineteenth century, the concerns of the central government, and its ability to act on those concerns, also increased. Victorious in their struggles with the nobility for political power, governments across Europe abolished serfdom and feudal bonds during the eighteenth and nineteenth centuries, altering the legal status of peasants. In France the revolutionary government took an interest in the ways peasants passed property to their children, and the Civil Code of 1804 made the wishes of the state a part of the family strategies of all French peasants. The state began to insist that the peasant educate his children, and nineteenth-century laws required rural communes to build schools, hire teachers, and use textbooks that communicated the views of urban society and prepared children to live in cities, where literacy was necessary, and not in the countryside, where the only required skill was knowing how to farm.[11] From around 1750 through the nineteenth century, there was an almost continuous spread of government influence over the actions of the peasant. In virtually every case this came from the city to the countryside, as the state bureaucracy communicated urban decisions to the peasantry.

By the multipronged process of rural urbanization, therefore, the European countryside lost its relative isolation, became part of national and international markets for agricultural and industrial goods, and felt the pressure of an urban-based government. The interlocked components of rural urbanization—proto-industrialization, agricultural development, urbanization, the development of markets, and state building—occurred throughout Europe. Different areas experienced it as early as the late seventeenth and early eighteenth centuries; most of western Europe felt the pressure only in the late eighteenth and nineteenth centuries; and in parts of eastern Europe it has occurred only during this century. Yet for the European country dweller the long period of social and economic change from the mid-eighteenth to the mid-twentieth century meant some experience with urban markets, industries, and governments, and this experience radically transformed the lives of the peasants of Europe.

These long-term processes of social and economic reorganization provide the background for this study of peasant families who lived in Marlhes, a village in the low Pilat mountains south of the industrial city of Saint-Etienne in the Loire department in southeastern France, sixty kilometers southwest of Lyon. In the middle of the nineteenth century, Marlhes was a commune of forty-five hundred hectares of land and more than twenty-eight hundred people living in the bourg and in the more than one hundred small hamlets that dotted the rolling mountain landscape. Its past was long even if not spectacular. It had been a parish in the diocese of Le Puy since at least the seventeenth century and probably long before that. One of the hamlets, La Faye, was the seat of a seigneury for which the seigneurs d'Argental rendered homage in the late thirteenth century. By the end of the Ancien Régime, La Faye was the seat of a barony. During the Revolution, La Faye, Marlhes, and two other large hamlets, Peybert and Prelager, were made communes by the revolutionary government, but by the end of the revolutionary period only Marlhes remained one. Its principal contribution to the Revolution itself was to serve as a locale for masses by a nonjuring priest during the Terror.[12]

Its long history did not convince outsiders that nineteenth-century Marlhes was worth an extended visit. Théodore Ogier, a traveler who passed through in 1850, found the bourg uninteresting: "This hamlet that forms Marlhes, properly speaking, is not large; it is composed of several houses spread over a fairly large piece of ground; a regularly formed Place has been prepared in front of the church; it is large [and] a mission cross has been placed in the middle; the houses which surround it are without regularity." He was more impressed with the home of the wealthy M. Colomb de Gast in Coin, a small hamlet where he spent the night, about five kilometers from the bourg: "One could place it in the category of chateaux."[13]

The historian who studies Marlhes in the last century is likely to agree with Ogier: there is little about the village that sets it apart from its neighbors in the Stephanois region. Marlhes was only one of twenty or thirty rural communes located on the lip of the Furens and Gier valleys. These interlocked trenches ran northeast to southwest across the southern third of the department and formed the central part of the region named after the principal city of the valley, Saint-Etienne. The valleys were walled in by steep but low mountains: Saint-Etienne was some five hundred meters above sea level, and the peak of Mont Pilat, south of the city in the Monts du Lyonnais and only fifteen kilometers from Marlhes, was the highest point in the region at fifteen hundred meters.

The geographical contrast between valley and mountain, however, is the key to the social and economic history of the Stephanois region and justifies a study of Marlhes. Since the eighteenth century, the valley has been urban and industrial and the mountains rural and primarily agricultural. Saint-Etienne first rose to prominence during the late seventeenth century, when two artisanal industries appeared in the town. Silk ribbon-weavers began working in the region, enjoying the absence of corporate restrictions on their work. Skilled light metalworking for lock making and firearms came to the city and its region at the same time. Until the nineteenth century these two trades were the basis of a prosperous provincial city of about fifteen thousand people. During the nineteenth century, however, Saint-Etienne and the other cities that stretched along the narrow floor of the valley experienced concentrated industrialization and urban growth. Two new industries came to the valley, coal mining and heavy steel milling. The population of Saint-Etienne grew by 700 percent during the century, absorbing its four small neighbors and reaching over one hundred thirty thousand by 1900. The other cities of the valley—Rive-de-Gier, Saint-Chamond, Le Chambon-Feugerolles, and Firminy—shared in this industrial development and population growth.

The new heavy industry and urban development of Saint-Etienne and other cities of the valley remained to a large extent the prisoner of the narrow coal deposit that ran from Rive-de-Gier to Firminy. The visible signs of the industrial and urban world—coal pitheads, factories, concentrated workers' housing—remained along the major road of the region, Route Nationale 88, which ran down the center of the valley. Only at Saint-Etienne, where the valley widened, did an extended city appear.

Marlhes and its rural neighbors to the south and north of the valley were not physically transformed by the industrial development of the nineteenth century. Even today there is a noticeable difference as one drives out of the valley into the mountains. The last view of the sprawling, smoking city disappears around a turn and one is immediately among steep mountain gorges and pine forests, with the only habitation an occasional small village featuring a country auberge.

The interest of Marlhes for the social historian is not, therefore, that it participated directly in the development of heavy industry in the region, nor that it grew from a small village into a major city, as did many villages in Lancashire. Rather, its fascination stems from the fact that it closely witnessed these changes as they occurred twenty kilometers away in the industrial valley, but remained a rural village. The immediate symbols of the modern world missed Marlhes. It entered the modern world through another route, through the impact of the development of the valley on its peasant inhabitants. In the first half of the nineteenth century the peasants of Marlhes wove ribbons for Stephanois merchants, and with those merchants they felt the strain as new factories in Germany, Switzerland, and the United States caused the decline and reorganization of the Stephanois ribbon industry in the last third of the century. The rapid growth of the valley's population increased the demand for agricultural products, and the peasants of Marlhes adapted their production to this market. Administrators collected taxes and enforced the inheritance and education laws of France. Life in nineteenth-century Marlhes depended increasingly on the nearby urban center.

The reactions of the several thousand peasant families who lived in Marlhes between the July Monarchy and World War I to the urbanization of their village provide an improved understanding of the tumultuous nineteenth century as well as the problems of social change in any society. The evidence available about these families suggests that the process of family change was not so firmly linked to economic development as Guizot, Le Play, du Maroussem, and later scholars have thought. Economic change did not cause immediate and direct change in the patterns of family behavior in Marlhes. Rather, the peasants of Marlhes pursued a consistent set of goals throughout the nineteenth century. They sought to maintain the family homestead as a basis for a limited kinship group and to support the family group through the contributions of all of its able-bodied members. The family, symbolized by the homestead, continued to be of central importance. The pressure of economic changes in the late nineteenth century, such as the increased importance of dairy agriculture and the decline in the availability of industrial work, altered the family strategies the peasants used to reach these goals. Pressure in one area led to a reallocation of family labor to another area. Neither economic changes in agriculture and industry nor the Civil Code's restrictions on property transmission altered the family goals. The peasant family in Marlhes adapted itself to rural urbanization, considering its alternatives in the context of its goals and drawing as much as possible on inherited strategies. The ability to adapt to economic development without altering fundamental family objectives clearly stands as the most remarkable aspect of the peasant family in Marlhes during the nineteenth century.

# Chapter 2
# The Growth of the
# Urban Economy

The dependence of rural villages in the Stephanois region on the urban valley was already established by the early nineteenth century. Most villages in the region, including Marlhes, produced some livestock for sale to the city, and many peasants supplemented their agricultural income by weaving ribbons for Stephanois merchants. The rural economy was thus tied to the city through a rudimentary market system and the decentralized organization of the ribbonweaving industry in the region. The half-century between 1850 and 1900, however, was a period of change in the economic structure of the region as these links to the city intensified. The impetus for change came from the urban region, itself rapidly industrializing, and was transmitted to the rural villages through the economic structures inherited from the Ancien Régime. One characteristic of the change was a tendency toward increased economic specialization in the villages. Ribbonweaving declined in importance and moved in the direction of factory organization, leading to greater emphasis on agricultural activities in the countryside. At the same time the rapid growth of the urban population of Saint-Etienne and other cities in the valley increased the market for agricultural products and pushed agriculture toward the production of dairy goods and livestock for sale. Throughout this period, the interaction of the rural and urban economies increased and intensified, bringing more rural residents into the urban economy.

Agriculture in Marlhes and the rest of the Stephanois region appears to have been largely an individual enterprise, free of any communal restrictions on cultivation. The Cahiers de doléances that have survived for parishes in the region do not mention traditional communal grazing rights such as *parcours, vaine pâture*, gleaning rights on freshly cut fields. Because the Cahiers probably represented the views of larger landholding peasants, who would most object to these "feudal" restrictions on their use of their property, this silence strongly suggests that even by 1789 these customs had died out in this area of peasant smallholding. Significantly, the only mention made of "feudalism" in the Cahiers is in reference to the feudal dues that remained in force and the privileged status of some members of the rural community that exempted them from taxation and increased the burden on those who were taxed.[1] Stephanois peasants in the late eighteenth century were more concerned with taxes and dues than with restrictions on cultivation. Certainly by the period with which we are concerned, the middle and late nineteenth century, the restrictions on cultivation typical of the Ancien Régime had disappeared completely from Marlhes and the rest of the region.[2]

The only remnant of the Ancien Régime that can be found in nineteenth-century Marlhes was the continued existence of communal landholding, long after it was nominally ended by the Rural Code of 1827. The commune of Marlhes itself did not own much land, but several hamlets which had been independent communities under the Ancien Régime did. The largest of these hamlets was Chaussitre, near the border between Marlhes and Saint-Genest, which in 1834 and 1851 owned 164 hectares of land. Several other hamlets also owned substantial amounts: La Faye owned 22 hectares, Montaron 10 hectares, and Peybert 2 hectares. Communal lands were, however, poor pastures located in the highest and coldest parts of the mountainous landscape. Their principal contribution was to provide those peasants with access to them with places in which to graze their livestock and, if the lands were wooded, with firewood and the material to make shoes. Therefore, their place in the family economy cannot be disregarded, but their overall importance in the scheme of agriculture in Marlhes was minor: in 1834 and 1851 they covered only 6 percent of the land in the commune, and by 1901 this had decreased by 2.2 percent.[3]

The cereal sector of the agricultural economy during most of the nineteenth century was characterized by low yields similar to those found in early modern Europe. Data from *Statistiques Quinquennales* and *Décennales* of agriculture indicate very low harvests in the first half of the century and only slight improvement by the end of the century in the mountain area south of Saint-Etienne. The commune of Saint-Genest-Malifaux, chef-lieu of the canton in which Marlhes was located, reported a harvest of 8.5 hectoliters per hectare of rye grain and 20 hectoliters per hectare of oats in 1837. The canton as a whole reported similar harvest levels in the *Statistique Quinquennale* of 1852: 8.4 hectoliters per hectare and 20 hectoliters per hectare for rye and oats respectively. In 1882 the canton averaged 18 hectoliters per hectare of rye grain and 20 hectoliters per hectare of oats. The rye figure is inflated by the probably erroneous 40 hectoliters per hectare reported for the commune of Planfoy;[4] if this figure is eliminated from the calculation, the average is 15 hectoliters per hectare. In 1892 the figures are 13.9 hectoliters per hectare for rye grain and 16.8 hectoliters per hectare for oats.[5]

The poor return from agriculture in the region and the absence of significant development in the cereal sector during the nineteenth century is also apparent in seed return ratios. Returns on seed at mid-century were three to one for rye and five to one for oats. By the end of the century the return for rye had increased to five to one, while oats had declined slightly to four to one.[6] These returns are lower than estimates for villages in early modern France and approach the low level of estimates for medieval France. In the Breton village of Quimper in the eighteenth century, for example, rye returned four grains for each sown and oats five for one.[7]

As the comparison with Ancien Régime production levels suggests, the canton of Saint-Genest and the entire department of the Loire remained far behind the rest of French agriculture during the nineteenth century. In 1840 the department was among the least productive departments in France, with its rye crop exceeding that of only five other French departments. At the end of the century, the 13.9 hectoliters per hectare reported for rye in Saint-Genest were still far below the average of 18 hectoliters per hectare reported in 1840 for the north of France. The cereal production of the mountain region south of Saint-Etienne was underdeveloped even in comparison with the largely traditional French agriculture of the early nineteenth century, and failed to develop during the second half of the century.[8]

The low cereal yields in the mountains were the result of poor climate, rocky mountain soil, and traditional methods of cultivation. The winters were cold, snowy, and long, in some years lasting well into May and frequently damaging or destroying spring crops.[9] M. Colomb de Gast, a large landowner of the commune of Saint-Sauveur-en-Rue in the mountain region and a member of the Société Industrielle de Saint-Etienne, reported in 1851: "The poor weather of the month of May has completed the destruction of the rye that the abundance of snow had severely damaged. They have been replaced, partly in oats, partly in spring rye, but the cold continues to hinder their proper growth." The same report indicated that during the month of May 1851 there were frosts from the first to the sixth of May, snow on the eighth and sixteenth, and cold again, after a week of good weather, on the last three days of the month.[10]

The poor quality of the soil in the mountains and the absence of chemical improvements assured low harvest returns under these weather conditions. An official report of the Year II divided the Stephanois region into three types of land. The smallest was along the Rhône River; this land was the best in the district but also the most restricted in area. Most land could not be tilled at all; some of this could be used as natural pasture in the spring and summer, but most was covered with forests. Other land could be sown every other year, provided it was well manured.[11] On this land one could grow "only rye, oats and potatoes," according to a report in the Year IX.[12] Little fertilizer was used to improve the quality of this soil. Joseph Duplessy indicated in 1818 that "the shortage of fertilizer is general . . . people have only the fertilizer from stables rarely holding enough animals to furnish the necessary improvements."[13] The plow used was the traditional *araire* of western Europe.[14]

Systems of rotation used in the region reduced the return from the land to the cultivator. In the mountains south of the city, where Marlhes was located, a biennial rotation was necessary: oats, rye, or potatoes were planted the first year, and the land was left fallow the second year. North of Saint-Etienne in the canton of Saint-Héand a triennial rotation system was used, with potatoes following rye or wheat and the third year fallow. Only a small portion of the land in the region could be worked in a five-year rotation: rye the first year, potatoes the second, spring grain the third, oats the fourth, and fallow the fifth.[15] The effect of the most common rotation systems was to cut by a half or a third the potential harvest for each farmer.

There can be little doubt that the cereal produced in the area was consumed entirely by the local population. A report of the Year II indicated that "the mountain villages barely supplied their own requirements, leaving the urban centers of Saint-Etienne, Saint-Chamond and Rive-de-Gier totally unprovided for."[16] It seems doubtful that the mountain area was even able to meet local demand for grains during most of the nineteenth century. Reports in 1837 and 1853 indicate that the canton had to import grain to supply the human, if not the animal, population. In 1837 the commune of Saint-Genest-Malifaux consumed 6,798 hectoliters of rye, while producing only 5,598 hectoliters. In spite of the fact that it produced little wheat (only 42 hectoliters in 1837), that grain was a part of consumption patterns and 800 hectoliters were consumed, almost all of which had to be imported.[17] The imbalance was even greater by mid-century: in 1854 the canton consumed 2,200 hectoliters of wheat, all of which was imported. Only 8,302 hectoliters of rye were produced, while 50,164 hectoliters were consumed.[18] Unfortunately, no further figures for consumption are available. It seems clear, however, that even in the second quarter of the century a large part of the population was buying its grain or bread.

The conditions of cereal production remained virtually unchanged even at the beginning of the twentieth century. The agricultural improvements of the second half of the nineteenth century came largely in the area of animal husbandry, a direction urged by agricultural reformers as early as the Second Empire. The members of the Société Impériale d'Agriculture de Saint-Etienne argued in 1863 that the climate of the region should "naturally lead the efforts of *agriculteurs* toward creating prairies and producing milk. . . . Such is the way all intelligent *agriculteurs* of the canton [of Saint-Genest-Malifaux] are moving with enthusiasm."[19] The Second Empire encouraged this shift in emphasis, providing monetary prizes through the Société d'Agriculture de Saint-Genest-Malifaux for those cultivators who made significant steps in this direction. Probably the most successful of these were the Baron de Saint-Genest, who improved part of his lands in the commune of Saint-Genest-Malifaux from wasteland to pastures; and Courbon La Faye of Marlhes, who also converted part of his holdings into meadow for livestock grazing.[20] The long lists of winners at the annual Concours Agricole, however, suggest that some improvements were being carried out by others as well.

Efforts at agricultural reform through increased production of dairy products built on a firm basis of animal husbandry that included most members of peasant society. A cautious examination of data in the *Statistique Agricole* indicates that an earlier husbandry of sheep was supplemented in the second half of the nineteenth century by increased emphasis on raising cows. Significant numbers of both animals existed in the first half of the century. The sizes of the herds follow different paths, however: the number of cows increased sharply, while the number of sheep increased only gradually. Between 1822 and 1892 the number of cows in the canton of Saint-Genest-Malifaux increased steadily, almost doubling from 1,965 to 3,874. The years of the July Monarchy and the early Second Empire, the period of strongest growth in the population of the industrial valley, appear most important in this increase. The increase from 1822 to 1857 was 73 percent, compared to the 14 percent increase from 1857 to 1892. In contrast to this strong expansion of the number of cows in the canton, however, sheep increased only gradually between 1822 and the end of the century: there were 3,043 sheep listed in 1822, 3,357 in 1857, 3,070 in 1881, and 3,518 in 1892. The commune of Marlhes shows a somewhat sharper increase, especially in the middle of the century, with 720 sheep in 1820 and 1,694 in 1881.[21] If cows were well suited to the climate and terrain of the mountain region, sheep were even more so, and the mountain peasants knew this before the members of the Société Impériale.

The increase in animal husbandry did not come at the expense of cereal cultivation, and the new artificial pastures that were encouraged by the Second Empire seem to have been the result of improving wastelands and clearing forests. This tentative conclusion may be drawn from cantonal data on the area planted in cereals. In 1856 the five communes of the canton of Saint-Genest-Malifaux planted a total of 2,570 hectares in grain; in 1892 the now seven communes of the slightly enlarged canton (the creation of the commune of Saint-Regis-du-Coin in 1858 drew land from both Marlhes and the commune of Saint-Sauveur-en-Rue in the canton of Bourg-Argental) planted a slightly lower total of 2,301 hectares; by 1905 this had increased to 2,703 hectares, higher than the 1856 acreage. There is therefore only a moderate fluctuation in the amount of land devoted to cereals, indicating no major conversion of land from cereal production to meadows. When the area sown is broken down among the different types of cereal crops, it becomes even more evident that the production of cereals for human consumption remained important. Rye, the principle human food crop, remained relatively stable, passing from 1,778 hectares in 1856 to 1,578 hectares in 1892 to 1,720 hectares in 1895. Potatoes were planted on 396 hectares in 1856, 417 hectares in 1892, and 569 hectares in 1905.[22] Thus there does not seem to have been any shift of land from grains consumed by humans to those consumed by animals. If meadow land increased, it had to have been at the expense of wasteland or forest rather than cereal land.

The livestock raised in the area provided food and other materials for the peasant farm as well as a cash crop. Cows produced the manure that was the only fertilizer known in the region. They also provided the motor force for plowing and hauling. The *Statistique Quinquennale* of 1852 indicated, for example, that all 154 cattle and 1,502 cows in the canton of Saint-Genest were used for agricultural work.[23] Sheep produced wool, which was spun, woven in the village, and made into clothes. In these capacities the animals were important contributors to the domestic economy of the family.

The greatest value of the livestock raised in the mountains lay in their marketability. The growing urban population of the region provided a large market for meat as well as for milk and related dairy products.[24] The canton of Saint-Genest-Malifaux was a major producer of milk for Saint-Etienne.[25] While sheep also produced milk that was made into cheese,[26] most of the sheep raised in the area were sold to butchers who came to the periodic fairs and markets held in the countryside around Saint-Etienne. The *Statistique Quinquennale* of 1852 indicates this pattern: of the 1,002 lambs born in the canton during the year, 910 were intended for slaughter, 52 were used for breeding, and 40 were killed accidentally.[27]

Therefore, the agricultural economy of Marlhes and the other rural villages of the mountains presents a mixed picture during the nineteenth century. The most dynamic sector of the agricultural economy was that of animal husbandry, which grew during the late July Monarchy and the Second Empire. The increase in livestock in the village did not, however, improve substantially the output of the cereal agriculture carried on in the poor mountain soil. This sector remained in 1900 as it had been a century before, stagnant and handicapped by traditional methods and equipment. The peasant farmers of Marlhes did not, therefore, experience an agricultural revolution such as occurred in seventeenth- and eighteenth-century England, with the increased availability of fertilizer from husbandry improving the output of the soil.[28] Agriculture in Marlhes was more compartmentalized, less cohesive than on the large estates of England. It was the movement of husbandry coexisting with a generally stagnant cereal agriculture that characterized the history of agriculture in nineteenth-century Marlhes.

        The development of husbandry in the Stephanois region was closely related to the market economy of the region. The growth of this urban market and the improvement of the mechanisms for marketing agricultural goods during the second half of the nineteenth century provided an important spur to the development of the village economy.

The growth of the market for rural products was directly linked to the rapid population growth of the city of Saint-Etienne in the nineteenth century. The city was one of the fastest growing cities in France during the century. Saint-Etienne added over 117,000 individuals to its population in the period between 1801 and 1891, a growth of over 700 percent. This growth was not constant throughout the century. It was most rapid in the first half of the century, averaging 3.4 percent per year between 1801 and 1851, and was especially strong between 1821 and 1851, when the population increased from 25,534 to 56,003, an increase of 3.8 percent per year. It slowed in the second half of the century, declining to 1.4 percent per year in the period from 1861 to 1891. In contrast to the relatively steady growth of the first half of the century, the second period was more intermittent, fluctuating from net declines in the 1856–61 and 1881–86 intercensal periods to increases of 2.9 percent and 2.3 percent in the 1866–72 and 1886–91 periods. In spite of these lower percentage increases, however, the increases in absolute numbers matched those of the first half of the century.[29]

The demographic growth of Saint-Etienne in the nineteenth century was in large part due to its development as one of the first industrial centers of France, and its fluctuations were controlled by the fortunes of its industries.[30] At the beginning of the nineteenth century the economy of the city rested on two traditional crafts: *passementerie*, the weaving of silk into ribbons; and *quincaillerie*, light metalworking. The first of these grew rapidly in the period between 1820 and 1850. These traditional trades were gradually supplemented, however, by two new ones—coal mining and heavy metallurgical manufacturing.

The coal industry developed through the exploitation of one of the most obvious resources of the valley in which Saint-Etienne was located, the coal basin that extended from Rive-de-Gier to the northeast to Firminy southwest of the city. The earliest pits had been placed in the early eighteenth century in Rive-de-Gier, and the industry developed slowly in that century.[31] The first half of the nineteenth century saw an increase in the pace of development, as forty-seven concessions were added to the ten granted prior to 1810. Production almost tripled in the 1826 to 1845 period, increasing from 559,000 to 1,405,000 tons.[32] This expansion continued in the Second Empire because of increased demand from railroads and the metallurgical industries. One economic historian of the region claims that the 1869 production of the Loire made up a quarter of the total French production in that year.[33] The last quarter of the century saw increasing competition from the Nord and Pas-de-Calais regions as well as exhaustion of some deposits in the Stephanois area, but production remained high to the outbreak of World War I. From the beginning of the Third Republic until 1913, the Loire region consistently produced between three and four million tons of coal each year and employed between fourteen and twenty thousand workers.[34]

The demographic impact of the coal industry was increased by the development in the nineteenth century of a heavy metallurgical industry. This began under the First Empire when James Jackson, an Englishman, founded the Fabrique d'Acier Fondu, the first steel mill of its type in the Loire and in France. The mineral resources of the region, the presence of coal for forges and coke making, and readily accessible iron deposits encouraged the industry.[35] By 1818 there were two slitting mills (*fenderies*) at Feugerolles, one at Unieux, Rive-de-Gier, Saint-Genis-Terrenoire, and Saint-Julien-Terrenoire, and five at Saint-Paul-en-Jarez, and *aciéries* at Trablaine and La Berardière in Saint-Etienne.[36] The industry continued to develop because of the presence of combustible material and industries such as light metalworking and nail making that could use iron.[37] In 1830 there were 379 heavy furnaces using wood charcoal, 29 using coke. Railroad construction and armament production in the period from 1840 to 1860 increased demand for the products of the industry, and by 1872 it was employing twelve thousand workers.[38] In spite of the increased competition from the Lorraine basin after 1870, the industry still employed fifteen thousand persons in 1901.[39]

During the nineteenth century, therefore, the valley that ran from Givors and Rive-de-Gier southwest through Saint-Chamond, Saint-Etienne, and Le Chambon-Feugerolles to Firminy developed into one of the major industrial areas of France. This development caused the growth of the population not only of Saint-Etienne but also of the other cities in the valley. Saint-Chamond and Rive-de-Gier, for example, were cities of five thousand in 1800; by the end of the century they were each approximately fourteen thousand. Firminy had over seventeen thousand persons in 1906 and Le Chambon-Feugerolles twelve thousand. The growth of Saint-Etienne was the most spectacular among the industrial cities of the Loire, but was by no means unique.

The population growth of the urban region created an important local market for the products of the countryside. For much of the first half of the century, however, access to this market was hindered by poor roads that made communication between the cities and the countryside almost impossible during bad weather. The road system of the department, as throughout France, was poor in 1800. The mountainous geography of much of the area accentuated the usual problems brought about by the absence of a well-developed national road system and the low sums expended on the maintenance of the roads that existed. The market system of the region was adapted to the weaknesses of this road system and was strongest in the *lieux de passage* along the existing major roads.

As figure 1 indicates, the arrondissement of Saint-Etienne was crossed by only two major roads at the end of the Ancien Régime. The most important of these traversed the Gier and Furens valleys on its way from Lyon through Saint-Chamond, Saint-Etienne, Firminy, and Le Chambon before turning south toward Le Puy and Toulouse. The other major route connected Saint-Etienne with Roanne, Moulins, and Paris. A secondary road made travel possible between Saint-Etienne, by Saint-Chamond, to Annonay in the Ardèche. In spite of their status as the principal royal roads of the region, all of these roads were in terrible condition at the end of the Ancien Régime.[40] The situation was even worse on those roads that served only local traffic. Colin Lucas cites a petition from the communes of Saint-Genest-Malifaux and Marlhes to the "department" of Saint-Etienne, dated 18 November 1787, that described the poor condition of the routes from those communes to Saint-Etienne: several narrow and poorly kept tracks led from Saint-Genest to the "major" road from Planfoy to Saint-Etienne. This road followed a sharp descent, marked by tight curves that made impossible the passage of a wagon loaded with a long load such as timber; the grade was so steep that a team of oxen could not restrain a load on the way down and could only pull up an empty cart. Each year many oxen collapsed from the effort required.[41]

Progress in improving this system was slow. Throughout the first half of the century funds were usually lacking for projects on *routes nationales*, while the improvement of local roads was left to the charge of communes that were unwilling to impose additional taxes to improve roads. The First Empire, in fact, saw a decline in the condition of the major roads that bore heavy traffic due to the lack of funds for maintenance.[42] In 1818 the route from Lyon to Le Puy by way of the coal basin was almost impassable and the entire road system around Lyon and Saint-Etienne was in poor condition, while the route from Lyon to Paris absorbed almost the entire subvention for road construction.[43]

During the remainder of the nineteenth century, however, an improved transport system was built on the foundations of Ancien Régime roads (see figure 2). Route Nationale 88, the principal road through the coal basin, was first built in the eighteenth century; during the nineteenth century it was improved by resurfacing and the realignment of several sections to better locations. The project was not finally completed until the years just before 1914, when the last section from Firminy to Le Puy was opened. Most other sections were completed during the Second

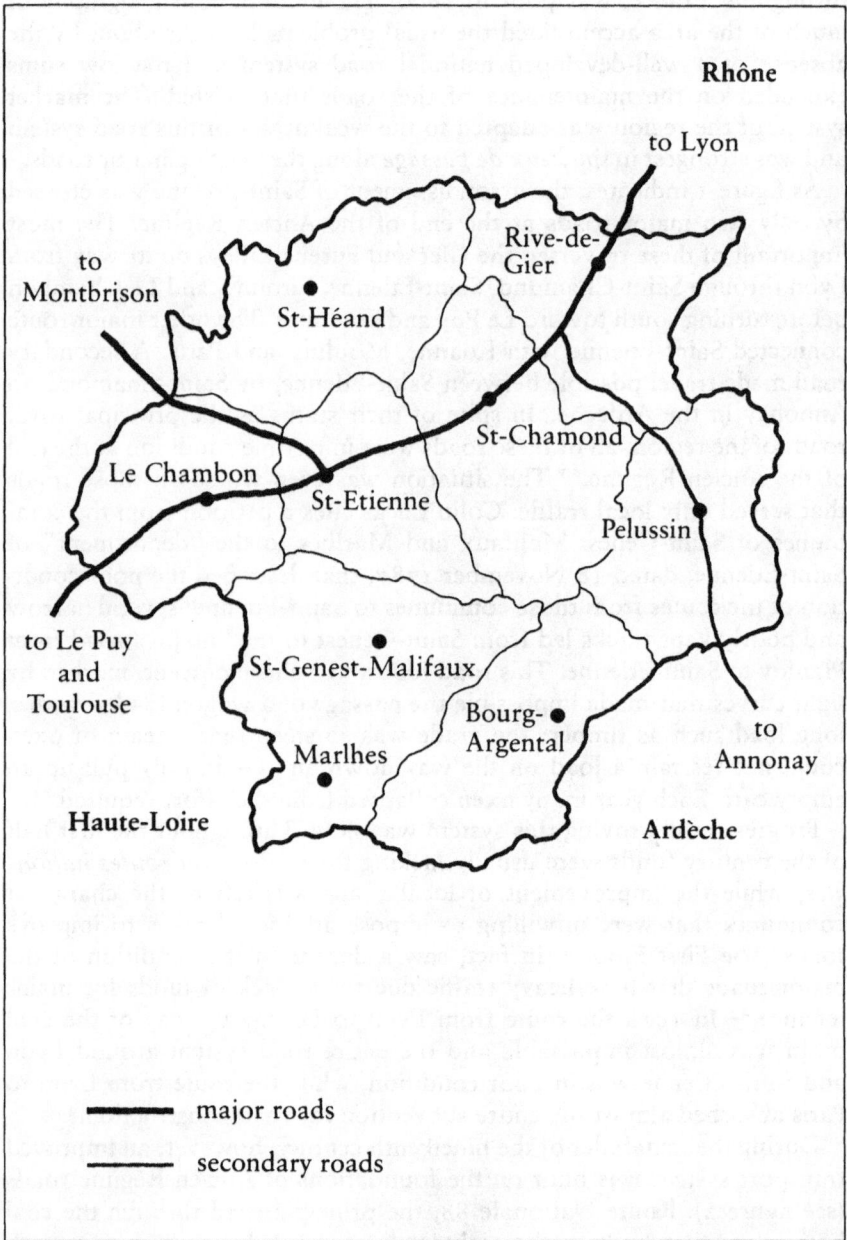

**Figure 1.** Principal Routes of Communication in Stephanois Region, End of Eighteenth Century

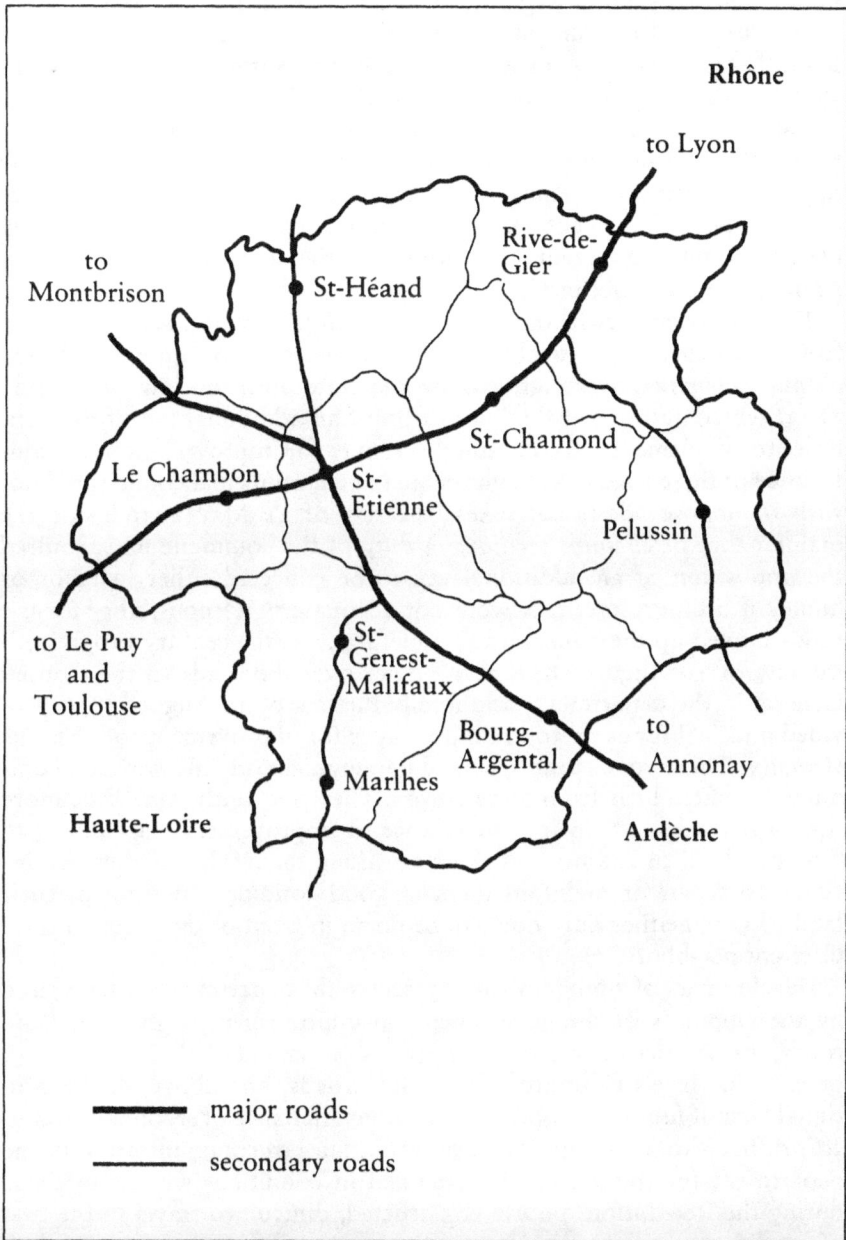

**Figure 2.** Principal Routes of Communication in Stephanois Region, End of Nineteenth Century

Empire and early Third Republic.[44] Other roads such as the route toward Montbrison and Roanne and several older tracks were improved to the point that they could bear steady traffic. Route Nationale 100, the north-south axis of the region, was opened in 1832. This road left the commune of Saint-Cyr-de-Favrières in the canton of Saint-Symphorien-de-Laye in the north of the department, entered the arrondissement of Saint-Etienne through the canton of Saint-Héand, traversed Saint-Etienne from La Terasse to Bellevue, then entered the mountains south of the city, passing by Planfoy and Bourg-Argental before leaving the department on its way to Annonay in the Ardèche.[45]

The improvements in the *routes nationales*, however, set them apart from lesser roads. The local roads that connected two communes, called *chemins vicinaux*, were ignored by the state until the law of 28 July 1824, which authorized the imposition of an additional tax of five centimes to supplement the communal revenues for improvement and maintenance of these roads. As might be imagined, municipal councils did not rush to impose additional taxes; the law of 21 May 1836 made the maintenance of *chemins vicinaux* a duty of the commune and required the imposition of an additional tax to be collected either in labor or money if ordinary revenues were not adequate.[46] Responsibility for the roads moved up the administrative hierarchy as the century progressed: the law of 10 August 1871 gave power over the roads to the Conseil Général in the department, and finally the law of 10 August 1879 provided national funds of 300 million francs for improvements of *chemins vicinaux*. Those roads that provided communication only within a commune benefited little from these efforts. They frequently were little more than dirt tracks and their maintenance or improvement was subject to "the goodwill of the property owners along them who, if they are inclined to repair or maintain them in good condition in front of their lands, know neither duty nor will to do so in front of the lands of their different neighbors."[47]

Development of a modern road system in the department was hindered by the emphasis of the government on improvement of existing main roads, the absence of concerted programs on the national, departmental, or cantonal levels to improve secondary roads, and above all the continual lack of funds for improvement or maintenance of secondary roads. It is difficult to avoid the conclusion that lines of communication in the department for the most part remained in conditions similar to those during the Revolution: poorly constructed, difficult to travel in the best of conditions, and almost impassable in poor weather.

With only this poor road system available, marketing of agricultural products and livestock depended heavily on a system of fairs and markets in the countryside. The sale of livestock took place in the rural commune itself through a system of fairs that brought butchers from the cities in search of animals for slaughtering. These fairs were not a creation of the nineteenth century in the Stephanois region, but reflected a centuries-old pattern of economic exchange between town and country. Several of the larger rural towns of the countryside, especially those to the north of the city, such as Saint-Galmier, Feurs, and Sury-le-Comtal, had traditional fairs reaching back to the late Middle Ages.[48] By the beginning of the nineteenth century, many rural towns in the arrondissement of Saint-Etienne held fairs several times a year.

The distinguishing characteristic of the fairs in the countryside was their infrequency: in most communes of the arrondissement they occurred four times per year. In contrast to weekly or biweekly markets they provided only infrequent opportunities for peasant participation in the market. The peasant's principal form of involvement was probably as a seller of livestock; only secondarily did he purchase small items such as farm tools or clothing sold by the traveling peddlers who frequented the fairs. The peasant's relationship to the system of exchange was almost entirely one-way, as a seller.

Figure 3, which presents the system of markets and fairs in the arrondissement in 1820, indicates that while there was a strong system of fairs in the countryside there were few weekly or biweekly markets. Rural communes that held both fairs and markets were rare and were exclusively chef-lieux of their cantons. While a total of fourteen communes outside the coal basin held fairs at different times during the year in the early years of the Restoration, only three of these communes also held weekly markets.[49]

The geographic orientation of the fairs is also important. Two centers may be discerned: first, the coal basin and the cities of Saint-Etienne, Saint-Chamond, Rive-de-Gier, and Le Chambon; second the Rhône River, which ran along the edge of the department by the canton of Pelussin and the northern section of the canton of Bourg-Argental. This impression is strengthened and refined by comments in prefectoral reports about these fairs. While the fair of Saint-Etienne was noted as being of mediocre significance, those in the other towns of the coal basin (Firminy, Le Chambon, Saint-Julien-Molin-Molette) were very important. The fairs of towns along the Rhône were considered vital, while those of other rural communes in the region were less so.[50] The system thus appears weak at its center, strongest in the first circle around that center, and then weakening again as one moves further away from the coal basin until reaching the system centered on the Rhône. Probably the small towns of the coal basin, which still included a substantial proportion of agricultural workers in their populations, were able to satisfy their needs within their own commune or canton. The larger, more heavily industrialized center, Saint-Etienne, had to go farther away for its purchases. Because the sale of animals for butchering to supply meat to the urban population

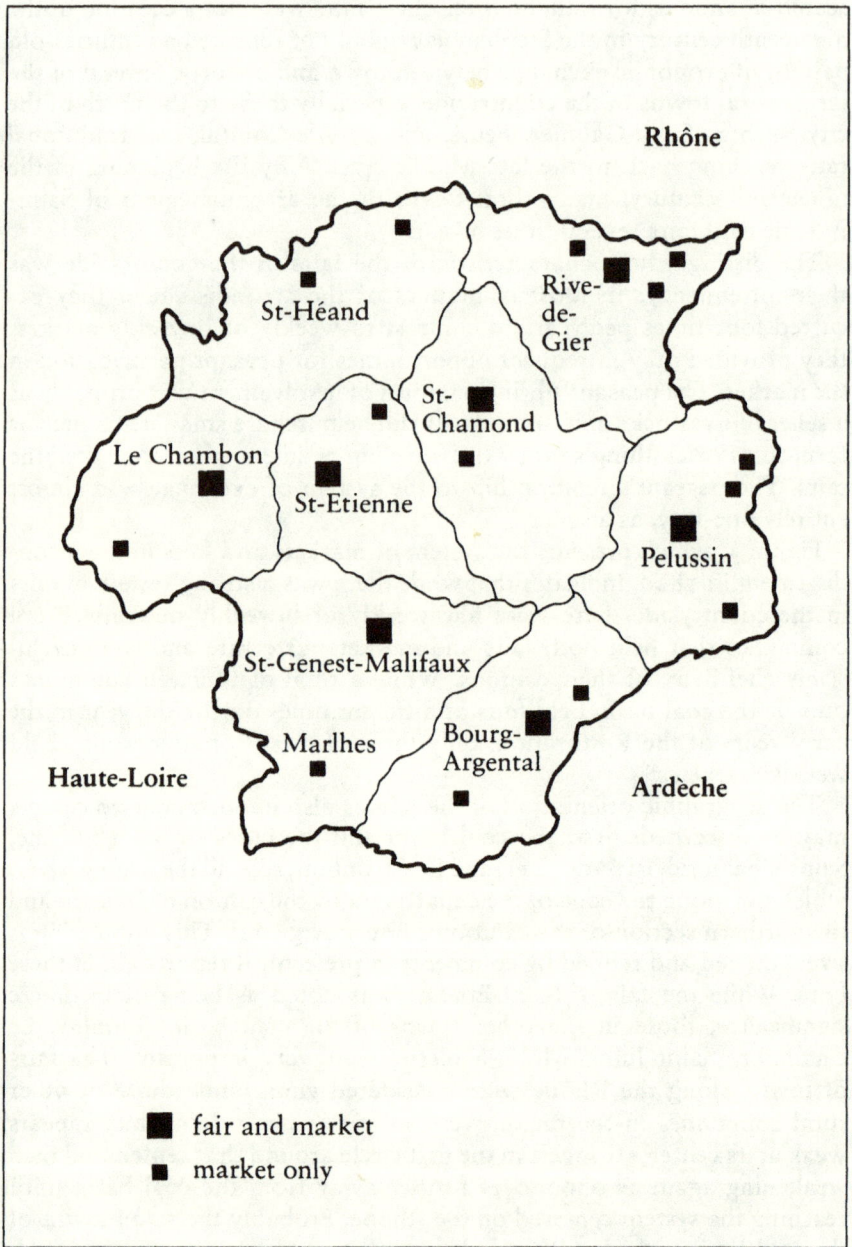

**Figure 3.** Fairs and Markets in Arrondissement of Saint-Etienne, 1819–1823
Source: A.D.L. 58 M 16.

did not take place in the city itself but in the surrounding countryside, the Saint-Etienne fair was seldom frequented, while those in the countryside bustled with activity.

The other major agricultural product of the region, dairy products, found no such easy system of exchange until the Second Empire. During the first half of the century, milk was probably marketed through individual merchants who purchased it from the peasant. An observer at the end of the century, Pierre du Maroussem, described the way these merchants operated: the merchant took care of the transportation to the market and preparation of the milk for sale,[51] and in return took as a commission a fixed amount of milk—initially 12.5 liters per week, later an additional 12.5 liters per month.

Only under the Second Empire was the marketing mechanism improved and systematized. In the late 1850s, under the encouragement of the Baron de Saint-Genest, nightly caravans of milk wagons began to move from the bourgs of the mountain communes to the city of Saint-Etienne.[52] The creation of this form of transport eased the marketing of milk and expanded during the remainder of the century. By the time he visited the canton in 1893, Pierre du Maroussem found three wagons loaded with milk leaving each night from Marlhes, the Pilat region, and even the commune of Riotord just over the border in the Haute-Loire. Miniature lines of transport extended out from the main roads, drawing the milk produced in the scattered hamlets of the region. Du Maroussem called the system "the stream that runs into the great river."[53] It is impossible to say what quantity of milk was transported in these nightly caravans, but the increased accessibility of the growing urban market made this area the leading producer of milk products for Saint-Etienne by the 1880s.[54]

Consumption habits in the countryside changed at the same time that the peasant was increasing his participation in the market system through the sale of livestock and dairy products. Until the late 1860s, most goods consumed in the countryside were produced either in the home or the rural village, by one of the artisans who combined farming with a skill such as weaving or iron working. Only rarely would a purchase of clothes or manufactured goods be made at a fair. Toward the end of the Second Empire this village and home-oriented system of exchange began to change. More and more peasants turned to a developing system of weekly and biweekly markets for clothing and manufactured goods.

The increase in peasant market participation as buyers may be inferred from the proliferation of frequent local markets during the last years of the Second Empire and the first decade of the Third Republic. This development is apparent in a comparison of figures 3 and 4. Most of the

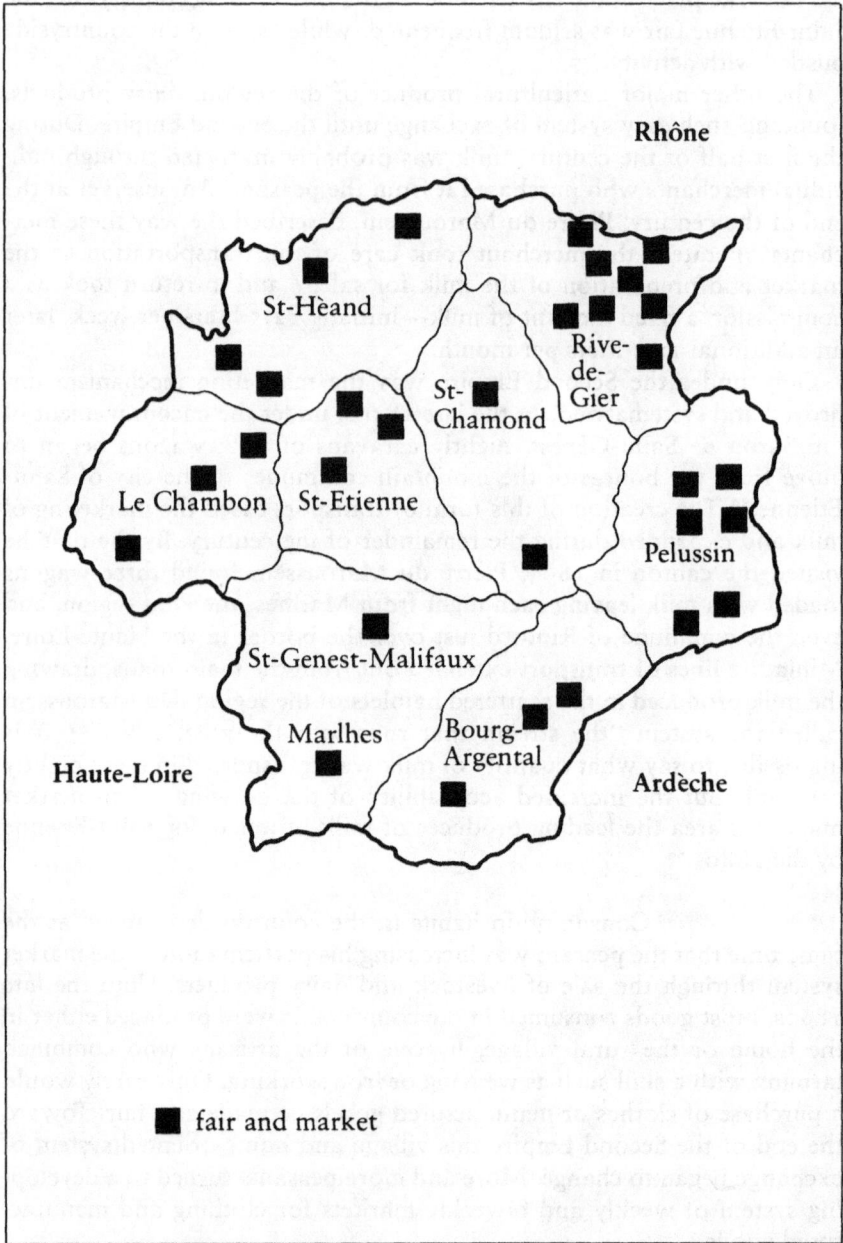

**Figure 4.** Fairs and Markets in Arrondissement of Saint-Etienne, 1876
Source: A.D.L. 58 M 17.

towns that held only quarterly fairs in 1820 had begun to hold weekly or biweekly markets by the Third Republic. Louis-Jean Gras contrasts the twenty-one markets in fourteen communes that Joseph Duplessy listed in 1818 with the following figures for 1909: seventy-nine weekly markets, three monthly markets, eleven weekly livestock markets, and fifteen monthly livestock markets in seventy communes.[55] By the beginning of the twentieth century nearly all of the communes of the arrondissement held a market of one form or another; most of these were weekly markets.

The weekly markets that developed in the third quarter of the century differed significantly from the quarterly fairs that were common in the first half of the century. While rural products and foodstuffs continued to be sold by peasants, weekly markets were also for the sale of manufactured products from outside the area to the peasant. These weekly markets sold not only food, animals, and dairy products but also pots, pans, other metal objects, and cloth.[56] Their frequency suggests that these markets were necessary for consumers in the rural villages rather than for sellers of livestock. No commune could support a weekly livestock market; there would not be enough animals to be sold each week for that to be the principal reason for a market's existence. The evidence of the new weekly or biweekly markets argues that at least a part of the rural population was beginning to supply itself with the necessities of life by purchase. Much of this increased consumption was probably confined to food purchases. Part, however, must have included the manufactured goods becoming increasingly available in France at this time.[57]

The development of the system of exchange and its implications for the peasantry can be seen more clearly in an examination of the fair and market organization of the mountain region south of Saint-Etienne. In the canton of Saint-Genest-Malifaux there were fairs in two of the communes, Saint-Genest, the chef-lieu, and Marlhes, the next largest commune, at the beginning of the century. Saint-Genest held seven fairs in 1807 and 1818, five in 1830, and six in 1837. These fairs sold primarily animals but also cloth, haberdashery, and light metal goods. Five fairs were held annually in Marlhes betwen 1806 and 1819 and four each year after that. These sold only animals and small amounts of cloth. There was no market in Marlhes: the only market in the canton was held each Tuesday in Saint-Genest. A prefectoral report of 1823 indicated that this market was indispensable for that commune and the surrounding countryside because of the general interest in it.[58] Given this structure of fairs and markets the peasants who lived in the five communes of the canton would have frequent opportunities to sell their livestock at the ten fairs held each year in Saint-Genest or Marlhes, as well as fairs within a day's journey in the canton of Le Chambon. These fairs also provided an opportunity to purchase a few items of consumer goods: cloth, hats, pots and pans, and farm implements. As far as items of regular food consumption were concerned, however, there was little opportunity to purchase them except through the weekly market in Saint-Genest, a long trip that would take a full day. The trip to the fair was likely to be a major event, caused by the sale of livestock, rather than a regular occurrence around which consumer habits were organized.

In the course of the nineteenth century, however, the pressure for additional and more frequent opportunities to purchase consumer goods increased. The Municipal Council of Marlhes petitioned in 1872 to be allowed to hold a biweekly market, stating that "given the importance of the population of the commune of Marlhes, the sale and provision of goods and merchandise occurs with a great deal of difficulty . . . [and] Marlhes by its central position would aid the small neighboring communes with this market."[59] The addition of the new market, made by prefectoral decree on 30 November 1874, expanded the opportunities for market participation in the commune and in the canton.[60] With the addition of this market to the weekly market in Saint-Genest, most residents of the canton were within close walking distance of at least a biweekly market selling food and manufactured goods. There are no existing records that indicate the extent of the business of these markets. Their frequency, however, and the products available there suggest that in the last quarter of the nineteenth century the peasant in the mountains was acting not only as a seller of livestock and dairy products but also as a buyer of food and manufactured products. These new consumption patterns further encouraged peasants to produce for the urban market to acquire the cash required for their own purchases.

The agriculture practiced in Marlhes and other mountain villages was complemented by an industrial sector, the weaving of silk ribbons. This industry reinforced the dependence of the countryside on the urban center of Saint-Etienne. Ribbonweaving had been the most important economic asset of Saint-Etienne since the early eighteenth century. A *Statistique de la République* dated 29 Thermidor An IX claimed that the *fabrique de rubans* had been in existence at Saint-Etienne for 150 years; the principal historian of the trade, Louis-Jean Gras, agrees in placing at some time in the late seventeenth century the movement of silk weavers from the commune of Saint-Didier-en-Seauve in the present department of the Haute-Loire to Saint-Etienne and the establishment of the *fabrique*.[61] In spite of difficult times during the Revolution, especially under the Terror,[62] the trade grew rapidly in the first several decades of the nineteenth century. A notice in the *Bulletin de la Société Industrielle* of 1828 indicated that ribbonweaving far outstripped any other industry in the area, employing 57 percent of the persons working in the arrondissement of Saint-Etienne.[63]

The size of the labor force engaged in ribbonweaving is less important for this study than the distribution of the work force in the hinterland of the city. In the Year IX the industry extended throughout most of the arrondissement of Saint-Etienne as well as the northern cantons of the Haute-Loire and a few cantons of the arrondissement of Montbrison that were close to Saint-Etienne.[64] It held to these limits through the first half of the century.[65]

The weaving of ribbons in the Stephanois region may best be described as a decentralized trade coordinated by an urban merchant, the fabricant. The fabricant received orders for ribbons at the beginning of each season from commissioners representing the fashion houses of Paris and other centers of fashion. He then acquired the raw silk—at the beginning of the century it was acquired from producers in the Midi of France and Piedmont, later from China—and arranged to have it processed through a number of preparatory operations: cleaning, spinning, dyeing, and carding. He designed the ribbon and arranged to have the design transferred by a skilled artisan into a pattern for raising and lowering the warp with each throw of the shuttle. The prepared silk for the warp of the ribbon was wound onto bobbins by other workers whom the fabricant employed. The wound silk was then ready to be given to the weaver.

If the ribbon to be woven was a complicated design known as a *façonne*, it would be given to one of the skilled artisans who lived in the city of Saint-Etienne itself. If it was a simpler pattern, a *unis*, the fabricant would give the wound silk for the warp, the silk to be used for the weft, and the design to a *commis à barre*. Usually a former weaver himself, this agent of the fabricant traveled through the countryside on horseback from village to village to place orders with weavers and to supervise the work as it progressed. The weaver wound silk for the weft onto bobbins; he or she also provided the loom. In the city these might be the most advanced looms of the day, mechanical looms operated entirely by the movement of the bar that drove home each thread of the weft. These were usually fitted with a Jacquard attachment, an arrangement of punched cards that determined the pattern by automatically raising and lowering the appropriate threads of the warp. In the countryside Jacquard looms were rare and most weavers worked on smaller looms. In contrast to the Jacquard looms that could weave a number of ribbons at one time, the looms used in the countryside could weave only one ribbon at a time and the raising or lowering of threads of the warp to form the pattern had to be done by means of foot peddles underneath the loom. The rural looms were therefore slower than those in the city. The Jacquard looms were able to weave both simple *rubans unis* and more complex *façonnes*, as well as *velours*, while the smaller looms could only weave *unis*. Duplessy indicates that men wove *façonnes* and *velours*, while both sexes wove *unis*. In 1836 Philippe Hedde, a local merchant, indicated that there were about five thousand looms in the city, with more than half equipped with the Jacquard attachment, and about eighteen thousand simple looms in the countryside. The weaver was paid the full amount of the order only when the completed ribbon was returned to the fabricant. It was then finished by pressing to remove the imperfections caused by uneven threads and packaged for shipment to the buyer.[66]

The principal features of the trade were its decentralized work force, which allowed it to employ large numbers of workers, each of whom performed only one specific task in the complex process that turned raw silk into finished ribbons, and its control by a single urban merchant, the fabricant. The weavers of the Stephanois countryside were concerned with only one part of the ribbon trade, the actual weaving of silk threads into ribbons. They bore no responsibility for the production of the raw material, nor did they have to purchase these materials. The marketing of the finished product was handled not by the weaver but by the fabricant. Stephanois weavers were not entrepreneurs but temporary employees of the fabricant, the true entrepreneur in the ribbon trade. The contact of the rural weaver with the entrepreneur was almost nonexistent, as the *commis* acted as a go-between for the fabricant and the weaver in their business dealings. The rural weavers of the Stephanois region were shielded from the full impact of their industrial work both by their place in the production process of ribbonweaving and by the mediation of their relations with the business world involved in the trade by agents such as the *commis à barre*.[67]

While the *rubannières* of the countryside were shielded from the discipline and pressure of industrial work, they were still linked to the urban economy and felt the effects of the changing position of the *fabrique* in the international market in the second half of the century. Indicative of this changing position are the violent fluctuations of the trade beginning in 1857, a sharp contrast to the steady growth of the first half of the century. A rough measure of these changes may be gathered from figure 5, which charts five-year moving averages of the amount of silk reported weighed in the Condition des Soies of Saint-Etienne.[68] The fluctuations of the trade between 1857, the end of the last real boom period of the nineteenth century, and the end of the century are readily apparent in this graph. The amount of silk used fell steadily throughout the 1860s, when the Stephanois *fabrique* permanently lost its American market to factories in Paterson, New Jersey. There was some recovery in the 1870s and again in the 1880s after a short crisis, but the 1890s and the first years of the new century were a period of stagnation and declining volume. While the overall consumption of silk by the *fabrique* increased in the second half of the nineteenth century, the sustained steady growth of the first half of the century clearly had ended.

Behind the violent fluctuations of the *fabrique* was a deterioration of

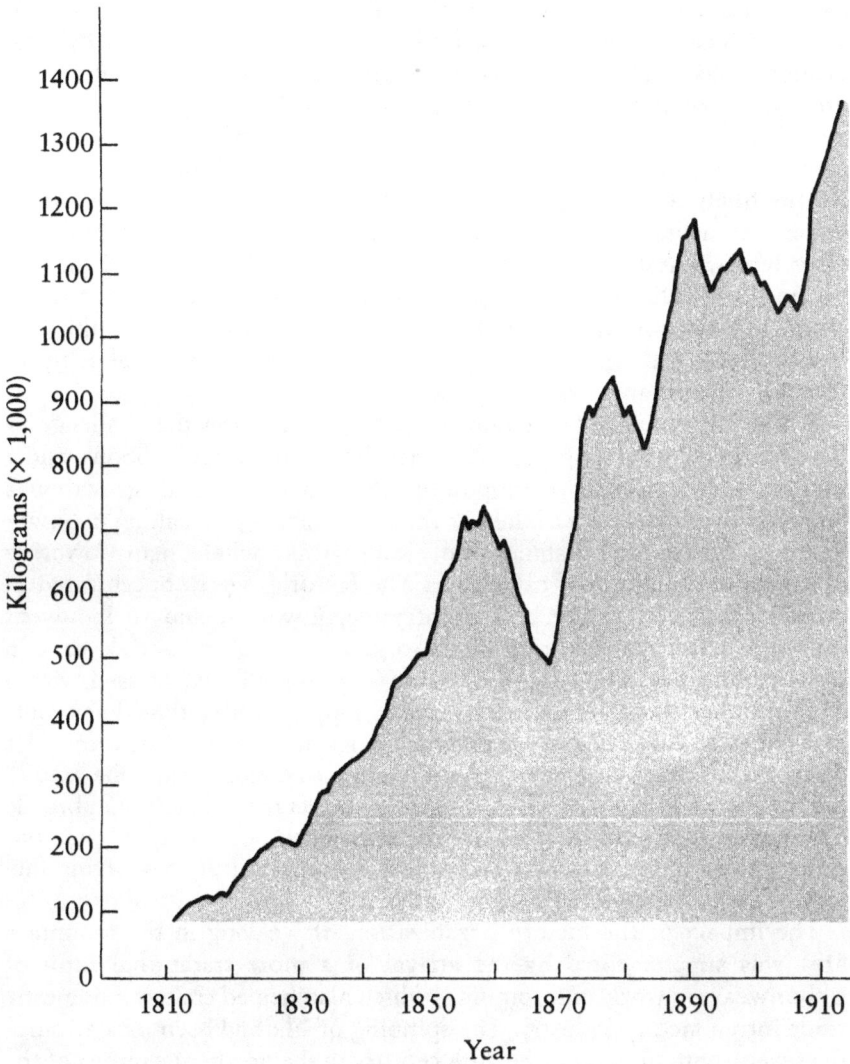

**Figure 5.** Weight of Silk Weighed at Condition des Soies of Saint-Etienne, Five-Year Moving Average, 1808–1913

Source: Lucien Thiollier, "Condition Publique des Soies," in *Association Française pour l'avancement des sciences, XVII Session, Août 1897* (Saint-Etienne, 1897), pp. 30–31; and A.D.L. Chambre de Commerce, Carton 89, Dossier 2, "Relève annuel des operations de la Condition Publique des Soies et du Bureau de Titrage des matières textiles de Saint-Etienne."

its position in the international market. The *fabrique* had built its reputation and business on the production of exquisite ribbons used by high fashion houses, but by the second half of the nineteenth century the growth of urban working classes who purchased not only their food but also their clothing created a new and much more important demand for cheaper, simpler ribbons. These new consumers had little money or use for the finely designed and executed ribbons that were the pride of the Stephanois artisans, and they were supplied by factories built in Paterson, New Jersey, Basel, Switzerland, and the Prussian Rhineland. By the end of the nineteenth century the *fabrique* of Saint-Etienne dominated the world market only in the production of *façonnes*; it stood in third or fourth place in the production of *unis* and *mélangés*, the ribbons preferred by the urban working classes.

A few fabricants in Saint-Etienne attempted to meet the challenge to their markets by creating small factories that would weave ribbons, and a small factory sector did develop in the 1880s and 1890s. Its growth was hindered by the delicacy of the silk thread, which kept breaking in power looms, as well as the resistance of the industry as a whole to any lowering of artisanal standards of excellence. The factories were concentrated in certain areas of the city and countryside, however, and their advent caused a major restructuring of the organization of industrial work in some rural areas. The canton of Saint-Genest-Malifaux, blessed with a large number of running streams and a supply of abandoned sawmills that could be converted to weaving factories at little expense, received a disproportionately large number of the score of factories that operated in the 1880s and 1890s. Lucien Thiollier, secretary of the Chambre de Commerce, indicated the presence of factories in both Marlhes and Jonzieux in 1893,[69] and factory inspection reports indicate a weaving factory in Saint-Genest-Malifaux in that year.[70]

The impact of the factory organization of weaving in the mountain area was supplemented by the arrival of a more traditional form of ribbonweaving work, silk spinning, which also helped change a domestic trade into a factory industry. The spinning of silk had been located since the seventeenth or early eighteenth century in the northern cantons of the department of the Haute-Loire, directly south of the canton of Saint-Genest.[71] Spinning does not seem to have come to the canton of Saint-Genest until the late Second Empire or the first years of the Third Republic, although it is difficult to be precise about the foundation of any spinning establishment. There are indications in the landholding records of the commune of Marlhes that a *moulin à soie* was established in the 1870s by Pierre Granger in a sawmill. Granger seems to have initially rented a mill from François Barrallon at Rivet, a hamlet of the commune, then near the end of the decade purchased a mill at La Fabrique, which he improved to make it more suitable for spinning silk.[72] By the end of the 1880s there were spinning mills operating in the communes of Jonzieux, Marlhes, and Saint-Genest-Malifaux in the canton.[73]

These attempts to mechanize the production of ribbons were unsuccessful in the long run. The factory sector remained a small part of the industry as a whole: in 1904 the Conseil des Prudhommes pour les Tissus of Saint-Etienne estimated that of thirty thousand looms, twenty-seven thousand were in family workshops and only three thousand in factories.[74] In the same year the Chambre Syndicale des Tissus of Saint-Etienne estimated that a similar total of thirty thousand looms was divided between twenty-six thousand in small workshops of two or three looms while four thousand looms were in factories.[75] The Chambre de Commerce of Saint-Etienne also estimated thirty thousand looms, with twenty-seven thousand in domestic shops and three thousand in factories.[76] The absence of a genuine census of looms makes these estimates no more than guesses, but their import is clear: factory organization had made only slight inroads into ribbonweaving by the beginning of the twentieth century. The position of the *fabrique* remained uncompetitive against the factories of Paterson and Basel, unable to meet its foreign competitors.

Thus, the second half of the nineteenth century witnessed two changes in the traditional rural industry of ribbonweaving, both the result of decisions made outside of the villages. The importance of ribbonweaving in the rural economy declined dramatically even as the trade moved towards factory organization. The stagnation of the trade and the decline in the production of the simpler types of ribbons struck the countryside harder than the city: in 1851 there were 1,976 persons working in the trade in the canton of Saint-Genest-Malifaux, but by 1881 this had dropped to 876 and by 1911 it was down to 573.[77] The availability of industrial employment shrank fourfold, therefore, in the sixty years from 1851 to 1911. The unsuccessful attempt by a few fabricants to reverse this decline through the concentration of production in factories restructured the weaving trade in Marlhes and other villages of the area, replacing domestic work with factory work. All of the weavers in 1851 had been domestic weavers; the vast majority of those still working in the trade in 1911 worked in small factories that had been built in the countryside.

The economy of the rural villages in the Stephanois region was characterized by a complexity that belies any simple view of peasant economy and society. Both agriculture and industry were vital to the rural economy, and had been so since the late seventeenth or early eighteenth centuries. During the period from 1700 to the 1860s, this economy mixed two sectors. There was diverse agricultural production, with farmers growing cereals for local consumption and raising livestock for both local use and marketing. Next to this was an industrial sector featuring domestic weaving of ribbons for the *fabrique* of Saint-Etienne.

The period from the middle of the nineteenth century to the outbreak of World War I was one of economic restructuring in Marlhes and the other villages of the Stephanois region. The balance between agriculture and ribbonweaving characteristic of the economy of the earlier period was replaced by a primarily agricultural economy, with a growing sector oriented toward production for the urban valley. The industrial sector lingered, but its importance was reduced and its fortunes affected a much smaller group in the rural population. Behind this economic change lay realignments of the links that existed between the countryside and the urban valley. The phenomenal demographic growth of the industrial cities in the Stephanois valley was felt in the rural villages of the region through the system of markets and fairs that already existed in the region. As the nineteenth century progressed, the means of communication between city and countryside were improved. Individuals such as the Baron de Saint-Genest improved the mechanisms for bringing rural products to the urban market, while the French state contributed to the slow evolution of a modern economic infrastructure by repairing major roads. These developments in turn further spurred the development of the market sector of agriculture. At the same time the ribbonweaving industry entered a period of stagnation and crisis. This began in the late 1850s and was relieved only intermittently between then and the beginning of World War I. Its impact on the rural economy was twofold: the availability of ribbonweaving as a rural occupation sharply decreased as the trade employed fewer people; further, its organization changed, from a domestic to a factory industry. Because of its proximity to the growing urban center, the village of Marlhes experienced a half-century of economic change that continually altered the expectations and perceptions of the peasants living there.

# Chapter 3
# The Experience of
# Economic Change by
# the Rural Community

It would be a mistake to think that all families living in late nineteenth-century Marlhes were socially equal or felt the changes caused by the nearby urban and industrial expansion in the same way. Before taking up the subject of the peasant family directly, therefore, we must consider these differences of experience and their implications for the village community.

One indication of social differences in the Pilat region comes from Pierre du Maroussem, who in 1892 visited a peasant family living in Saint-Genest-Malifaux, near the border between that commune and Marlhes. In his report on the family, du Maroussem described two types of farm characteristic of the region. There were large ones, with twenty to thirty hectares of land. About seven hectares of this was arable, devoted to growing rye, potatoes, and oats; the remainder was divided between pasture and field, used to graze about fifteen cows. A second, smaller type of farm covered only two or three hectares, perhaps even less, and raised at most three or four cows and a little grain.[1]

In du Maroussem's account the difference between the two types of farm seemed to be only the number of cows raised by each farmer. The economic changes of the previous forty years, however, had made differences in size of exploitation important criteria for social distinctions within the village community. At mid-century most of the residents of Marlhes had the same experiences with the economy as their neighbors, but by the last decades of the nineteenth century families with small holdings lived and worked differently from those with large landholdings. This changing social structure was the direct result of the growth of the urban center near Marlhes.

Because agriculture was an important part of the economy of Marlhes throughout the nineteenth century, the stratification of the rural community during this period was largely determined by access to land. The most enduring form of access was, of course, landownership. In Marlhes the structure of landowning may be examined using the *matrice cadastrale*, the register of the land tax, created in 1834. It listed each landholder in the commune, each parcel he owned or acquired, and its size and assessed value. The register was continually updated to reflect acquisitions or sales of property. Tabulations of land-holding in Marlhes have been made from this source for the years 1834, 1851, 1881, and 1901 and are presented in table 1.

The cadastre of the early nineteenth century has several limitations as a source for landholding information. It was created not as a record of landholding itself but as a tax register. There was no formal verification of ownership of land, and the creation of the *matrice* may have been an opportunity for those who occupied the land of others to transform this into ownership. The effect of this on tabulations from the register should be minor. Except in the case of long-absent heirs to property, a false declaration of ownership of a parcel was likely to be quickly challenged by the true owner. In any event, the declarations of ownership in the cadastre probably reflected very accurately the pattern of cultivation of the land, and this is more important for the purposes of this study than legal ownership.

A second problem with the cadastre is less easily discounted. The *matrice cadastrale* for Marlhes only registered lands owned by an indi-vidual within the commune itself; it took no notice of land the same individual may have owned in neighboring communes such as Saint-Genest or Jonzieux. This is a serious problem, especially as the nine-teenth century progressed and the equal inheritance provisions of the Civil Code gave land to sons and daughters who moved from their native

**Table 1.** Distribution of Land in Marlhes

| Hectares | 1834 | | 1851 | | 1881 | | 1901 | |
|---|---|---|---|---|---|---|---|---|
| | N | % | N | % | N | % | N | % |
| .01–1 | 283 | 48.5 | 265 | 43.7 | 224 | 40.9 | 195 | 37.8 |
| 1–4 | 141 | 24.1 | 172 | 28.3 | 176 | 32.1 | 179 | 34.7 |
| 5–9 | 55 | 9.4 | 57 | 9.4 | 55 | 10.0 | 48 | 9.3 |
| 10–19 | 46 | 7.9 | 52 | 8.6 | 40 | 7.3 | 41 | 7.9 |
| 20–29 | 19 | 3.3 | 19 | 3.1 | 28 | 5.1 | 22 | 4.3 |
| 30–39 | 16 | 2.7 | 16 | 2.6 | 6 | 1.1 | 21 | 4.1 |
| 40–49 | 7 | 1.2 | 9 | 1.5 | 7 | 1.3 | 2 | 0.4 |
| 50–99 | 11 | 1.9 | 13 | 2.1 | 9 | 1.6 | 6 | 1.1 |
| 100+ | 6 | 1.0 | 4 | 0.7 | 3 | 0.6 | 2 | 0.4 |
| Total | 584 | 100.0 | 607 | 100.0 | 548 | 100.0 | 516 | 100.0 |

Source: A.D.L. Série P Non-Coté, *Matrice cadastrale de la commune de Marlhes*.

commune to Marlhes at their marriage. The problem unfortunately cannot be solved simply by expanding the geographical area examined and exploiting more cadastres, for there would always be property held in neighboring communes not included in the area studied. A second possible solution—searching in the cadastres of neighboring communes for property owned by landholders in Marlhes—would be deserving of a study in itself; it is not feasible for a study such as this. In any event, this approach could run aground on the frequent duplication of names in the canton. The data presented here therefore reflect only the land owned in Marlhes by each individual, and must be accepted with that reservation. However, it would require a major difference between the landholding patterns of neighboring communes and those of Marlhes to alter significantly the results of this analysis, and such a change does not seem likely.

The data presented in table 1 suggest both the wide distribution and the great fragmentation that characterized the ownership of land in Marlhes throughout the century. In each year examined, about two-fifths of the landholders owned less than one hectare; more than 70 percent owned less than five hectares. There were, therefore, many landholders; it seems probable that in one-third to one-half of households some family member owned some land. But even with several landholders in the same household, such as a husband and wife who each owned land, few families would own very much.

The absolute amount of land owned by a peasant has little meaning in itself. The distributions of land in table 1 must be compared to the amount of land required for subsistence before their meaning will become fully apparent. For this we may borrow the definition of medium property holding used by Gilbert Garrier in his study of the Beaujolais and the Lyonnais, a mountainous area very similar to the Stephanois region. Garrier defines medium property holding as that which is able to guarantee the autarchy of the family group, assuring in a normal year their own consumption needs as well as a small excess for sale, capable of employing the entire family yet requiring additional labor only in exceptional situations. Other categories of landholding follow from this basic definition. For the mountainous zones of the Beaujolais and the Lyonnais, Garrier gives the following criteria:[2]

| | |
|---|---|
| Very small property | 0–1 hectares |
| Small property | 1–10 hectares |
| Medium property | 10–50 hectares |
| Large property | 50–150 hectares |
| Very large property | 150+ hectares |

The fragmentation of landownership in Marlhes throughout the nineteenth century becomes apparent when these definitions are applied to the data in table 1. The overwhelming majority of landholders held less than the self-sufficient level defined as medium property. In each year studied here, only about 18 percent of the landholders were above the minimum of ten hectares necessary to guarantee a viable, independent family farm. Only about 3 percent owned more than the fifty hectares needed to place them in the category of large landholders. The only variation noticeable during the century in this pattern of landholding is a slight movement at the end of the century from the smallest category, less than one hectare, into the next higher category, from one to five hectares. This modest concentration of land did little to improve the economic situation of landholders, for even with five hectares a family was still well below the minimum subsistence level of ten hectares.

The small size of landholding led to heavy dependence on the cultivation of land rented from others, in many cases probably kin who no longer lived in Marlhes. The farming of rented land is, unfortunately, less amenable than landowning to detailed study by the historian. Most leases in Marlhes were oral, not written, and no records exist that would allow the reconstruction of amounts of land rented by individuals. We must be content with an estimate of the extent of farming in nineteenth-century Marlhes that is made from a few scattered sources.

The available evidence suggests that the rental of land was widespread and that such land significantly raised the amount of land available to each cultivator. In the 1862 *Enquête Agricole Décennale*, the following figures are given for the entire canton of Saint-Genest-Malifaux:[3]

| | | |
|---|---|---|
| Cultivating by *maître-valet* | 26 | 2.9% |
| Proprietors cultivating only their own land | 431 | 48.3% |
| Proprietors cultivating their own land and land of others | 160 | 17.9% |
| Farmers not proprietors | 275 | 30.9% |
| Total | 892 | 100.0% |

These figures reflect the importance of cultivation of land rented from another by the cultivator as well as widespread landownership in the region. They also suggest the frequent combination of types of landholding. Almost one-half of those in agriculture cultivated only their own land. Another third were not themselves landowners but farmed the land of others. A significant group, however, combined both landownership and farming: almost one-fifth worked their own land and expanded their production by renting land from others. The small size of most holdings and the frequency with which owners added to their holdings by renting the land of others suggest that the line between landowner and farmer may not have been sharply drawn in the mountain region.

This impression is reinforced if we attempt to estimate how much those who rented additional land were able to add to their holdings. This is not made clear in the 1862 data, and the only data available for the region on this problem date from the end of the century, 1892–93. Pierre du Maroussem claimed that at that time in the commune of Saint-Genest-Malifaux there were 114 proprietors cultivating 2,638 hectares and 223 farmers cultivating 1,860 hectares.[4] Using these figures we may calculate an average holding for landowners of 23.1 hectares and an average of 8.3 hectares rented by farmers. These probably overstate the case, and take no account of differences in the amounts rented and owned by different individuals. It seems likely, however, that most land was rented by those who either owned no land or very little. If this was true, renting land provided a substantial portion of the agricultural population with sufficient land to form an agricultural basis for the family economy. If we assume that the average amount of land rented was five hectares, slightly more than half the amount given by du Maroussem for Saint-Genest, the data given in table 1 appear in a different light. A substantial majority of the landholders remain below the minimum of ten hectares needed to secure independence: around 70 percent in each year are below this level. Farmed land, however, places another 9 or 10 percent of landholders into the category of medium landholders.

The above is, of course, only an estimate based on extremely fragmentary evidence and a number of assumptions. It does little to change the initial impression of Marlhes as a rural society in which most members did not own or rent sufficient land to be independent of nonagricultural activity for subsistence. The data do suggest the importance of agriculture in this rural community. Through outright ownership, direct rental, or a combination of the two, virtually every family in nineteenth-century Marlhes held some land—perhaps no more than two or three hectares, sometimes as much as thirty or forty hectares. Agriculture was, in spite of the fragmentation of landholding, an almost universal economic activity.

The wide distribution of landholding in Marlhes, the small amounts owned by most individuals, and the stability of the landholding structure throughout the nineteenth century provided a broad basis for social equality in the village. This peasants' republic was further unified during the first two-thirds of the century by the traditional agriculture of the region, which tended to blur the distinctions between large and small-holders as well as between landowners and farmers. With returns on land so small, it required very large amounts of land to place a family clearly above its neighbors in individual wealth. As is evident from table 1, few families were able to reach the level of fifty hectares or more that might allow this clear preeminence. At best some families reached a tenuous kind of independence, frequently based on rented land. Most families shared the same situation as small, diversified producers of cereals and livestock. Their participation in the market for agricultural goods was limited by their productive capabilities. Gilbert Garrier has estimated for the neighboring department of the Rhône that two hectares of meadow could not produce quite enough straw to feed an average cow during the winter. The situation was probably worse in the mountains, since Garrier's average production of eighteen to twenty-two quintaux of hay per hectare seems high for the canton of Saint-Genest.[5] Smallholders could raise only a few cows, and their most significant participation in the market came through the sale of lambs that required less land. Agricultural activity acted to bind the village community together at mid-century, with more than three-quarters of the households in the village experiencing similar conditions in this sector of the economy.

The levels of agricultural production for each household in mid-nineteenth-century Marlhes indicate clearly the need each family felt for income beyond that provided by agriculture. This need was filled in Marlhes by the ribbonweaving industry until the organizational changes and stagnation of the industry in the last quarter of the century. In contrast to rural villages in other parts of Europe that were divided by the presence of domestic weaving industries, such as those in the West of France described by Paul Bois and Charles Tilly,[6] the Stephanois weaving trade recruited widely in the village during its domestic phase and provided another unifying factor for the rural community. Only with the decline of domestic weaving and the advent of factory work did weaving become a factor dividing the community.

Data on the recruitment of the labor force of ribbonweaving are presented in tables 2 and 3. For the present we will be concerned only with the 1851 data, indicating the recruitment patterns of the trade in the middle of the nineteenth century. Part A of table 2 clearly indicates that weavers were recruited from all ages of the female population in the canton of Saint-Genest-Malifaux. Work as a ribbonweaver became important in the fifteen to twenty-four age group for both men and women, and continued to be strong until relatively old age, remaining high even at age forty-five to fifty-four in both groups. Only above the age of fifty-five do the proportions working as weavers fall to very low levels.

Part B of table 2 indicates the strong presence of women in the weaving work force. Only 12.2 percent of the 1,976 weavers in 1851 were males. Clearly weaving was a trade almost exclusively reserved for women. Yet this table shows that almost all types of women participated in the trade: single women make up almost half of the total work force, but married women add another third, and widows—given their small place in the entire population—also show large numbers. Weaving, while generally limited to the female population, was spread throughout that population without regard to age or civil status.

At mid-century weaving was also practiced without regard for the amount of land held by the family. This is apparent from table 3, based

**Table 2.** Age Structure and Civil Status of Weaving Population in Canton of Saint-Genest-Malifaux

A. AGE STRUCTURE

| | 1851 | | | | 1911 | | | |
| | Males | | Females | | Males | | Females | |
| Age | N | % | N | % | N | % | N | % |
|---|---|---|---|---|---|---|---|---|
| 0–14 | 23 | 9.5 | 80 | 4.6 | 1 | 0.4 | 41 | 13.3 |
| 15–24 | 83 | 34.2 | 635 | 36.6 | 31 | 11.7 | 165 | 53.4 |
| 25–34 | 68 | 27.9 | 356 | 20.5 | 67 | 25.4 | 63 | 20.4 |
| 35–44 | 37 | 15.2 | 316 | 18.2 | 59 | 22.3 | 17 | 5.5 |
| 45–54 | 21 | 8.6 | 201 | 11.6 | 31 | 11.7 | 11 | 3.5 |
| 55–64 | 8 | 3.3 | 107 | 6.1 | 31 | 11.7 | 8 | 2.5 |
| 65+ | 3 | 1.3 | 38 | 2.2 | 44 | 16.8 | 4 | 1.4 |
| Total | 243 | 100.0 | 1,733 | 100.0 | 264 | 100.0 | 309 | 100.0 |

B. CIVIL STATUS

| | 1851 | | | 1911 | | |
| Civil Status | N | % of Total | % of Same Sex | N | % of Total | % of Same Sex |
|---|---|---|---|---|---|---|
| Single males | 145 | 7.3 | 59.7 | 111 | 19.4 | 42.0 |
| Married males | 94 | 4.7 | 38.6 | 145 | 25.3 | 54.9 |
| Widowers | 4 | 0.2 | 1.7 | 8 | 1.3 | 3.1 |
| Single females | 957 | 48.4 | 55.2 | 293 | 51.1 | 94.8 |
| Married females | 654 | 33.1 | 37.8 | 4 | 0.7 | 1.3 |
| Widows | 122 | 6.3 | 7.0 | 12 | 2.2 | 3.9 |
| Total | 1,976 | | | 573 | | |

Source: A.D.L. 49 M 85, 49 M 387, *Listes nominatives de recensement du canton de Saint-Genest-Malifaux*, 1851, 1911.

on census and landholding records. The first column of this table clearly indicates the dependence of the poorer members of the rural community on weaving. More surprising is the continued importance of weaving as one moves across the table, into groups owning larger amounts of land. More than half of those with from one to four hectares of land had a

**Table 3.** Landholding of Household Head and Presence of
*Rubannière* or *Ouvrière en Soie* in Household

A. 1851

|  | Number of Hectares Held | | | |
|---|---|---|---|---|
|  | Less than 1[a] | 1–4 | 5+ | Total |
| *Rubannière* present in household | 187 47.1% | 85 59.0% | 23 37.7% | 295 49.0% |
| *Rubannière* not present in household | 210 52.9% | 59 41.0% | 38 62.3% | 307 51.0% |
| Total | 397 65.9% | 144 23.9% | 61 10.2% | 602 100.0% |

B. 1901

|  | Number of Hectares Held | | | |
|---|---|---|---|---|
|  | Less than 1[a] | 1–4 | 5+ | Total |
| *Ouvrière en soie* present in household | 44 13.4% | 5 15.1% | 6 9.5% | 55 12.9% |
| *Ouvrière en soie* not present in household | 285 86.6% | 28 84.9% | 57 90.5% | 370 87.1% |
| Total | 329 77.4% | 33 7.8% | 63 14.8% | 425 100.0% |

[a] Includes nonlandowners.

Source: A.D.L. 49 M 85, 49 M 353, *Liste nominative de recensement de la commune de Marlhes*, 1851, 1901; Série P Non-Coté, *Matrice cadastrale de la commune de Marlhes.*

family member working at weaving. More than a third of those owning above five hectares of land also had a member working in weaving. Since some families would not have a family member who could work in the trade, these figures suggest wide distribution of weaving throughout the rural community. It formed an important complement for the entire population to the limited agricultural production of the region during the first part of the nineteenth century.

The result of these patterns of agricultural and industrial work was a village community remarkably unified in its economic experiences. The united community of mid-century was not, it should be stressed, the result of isolation of the community from outside forces. The economy of Marlhes provided frequent opportunities for the Stephanois peasant to participate in economic structures that extended far beyond the borders of the community. The nearby urban region, both as a market and as a focal point for the weaving industry, strongly influenced the economic experiences of those living in Marlhes. The unity of the community came from the fact that almost all members of it participated in the same way and to the same extent in these exogenous structures. Most households of Marlhes produced agricultural goods for the urban market, although to a limited extent at this time. Similarly, many households had one or more members working in domestic weaving. Participation in these two sectors was not limited to a particular group within the rural community. The market for agricultural goods and the weaving industry provided a unifying, not a divisive, factor in the village at this time.

The growth of the market sector in the agricultural economy of Marlhes in the last half of the nineteenth century proved to be an important factor in creating social differences in Marlhes. The landowning differences that characterized the village throughout the nineteenth century became more important as the expanding urban market led to specialization in animal husbandry and dairy production. This specialization required the conversion of wasteland into artificial meadows, and the expense of improving land and the capital required prevented many peasants from converting their land to grazing lands for cows. In the 1860s the Baron de Saint-Genest estimated that this cost 375 francs per hectare for labor alone and a total of about 600 francs per hectare.[7] Such an investment was virtually impossible for the average peasant even if he could have been convinced that it was desirable to do so.

The development of agriculture in the last half of the nineteenth century placed increased emphasis on the quantity of goods that could be produced by the peasant. The improved system for marketing milk, above all the nightly caravan from the mountains down to Saint-Etienne, required a certain level of production. Du Maroussem indicates that four cows were required to produce the daily *biche* of 12.5 liters for the caravan. Such production required the ownership or control of at least five hectares of meadow. Between one-half and three-quarters of the peasants in the mountains did not control this much land. Their participation in the sale of milk, the most important and dynamic factor in the agricultural sector, was limited. They probably kept one or two cows but were forced to sell the milk of these cows through a merchant, a less efficient and regular form of marketing. The perishable nature of milk, which could not be stored for several days to accumulate a full *biche*, also denied smallholders participation in the urban market. The introduction of the new system of marketing milk was important only to the one-quarter of families who were able to produce large quantities of dairy products. It benefited landholders such as Courbon La Faye, with his herd of eighty cows in 1884, rather than the hundreds who worked small farms of only a few hectares.[8]

Agricultural development in the late nineteenth century, with its emphasis on increased specialization of production and dependence on the sale of dairy products to the rapidly expanding urban market, affected different rural groups in different ways. The larger landholders were able to expand their production of dairy products to be sold in the urban market: the second half of the century saw not only the continued expansion of that market but also the growth of communications systems that facilitated transport of goods to the market. The small landholders in the rural community were constrained by their limited ability to produce agricultural products to limited market involvement as sellers. Rather than drawing increasing numbers of peasants into market agriculture, the expansion of the urban market during the nineteenth century allowed a small part of the community to expand its production and participate in the market to a greater extent than before. The effect of the expansion of the market was to emphasize the differences inherent in the landholding system of Marlhes. The increased productivity of improved land made these differences in the amount of land owned by a family much more important than they had been at mid-century. Two groups began to diverge in the rural community: those limited by their landholding to a modest level of production for the market and those whose holdings were sufficiently large to allow them to expand production and specialize in market dairy production.

The decline of domestic ribbonweaving and the development of factory organization also fostered divisions in the rural community. The changes in recruitment between 1851 and 1911 are indicated by the distribution of the work force by age and civil status given in table 2. It is immediately apparent that men and women experienced entirely different forms of participation in the trade. The men who worked in the trade were primarily heads of household, skilled artisans with more in common with the *passementiers* of Saint-Etienne than with the *rubannières* and *ouvrières en soie* of the mountain area. This group aged slightly during the century, as male artisans became more and more important and began to outweigh the few boys who worked in the trade. The twenty-five to thirty-four age group replaced the fifteen to twenty-four group as most important and the overwhelming majority of the males in 1911 were above twenty-five—that is, adults intending weaving as their life's work.

The majority of the work force continued to consist of women. The decline of domestic weaving and the rise of factory work affected the female population most. The factory work force, though still largely female, was different from that of the domestic trade. While more than half (58.7 percent) of the female work force in 1851 was older than twenty-five, the progress of factory work reduced this older part of the work force: in 1911 only 33.3 percent of the women were above this age. Instead, factory workers came from the young adult age group, between fifteen and twenty-four years: in 1851 this category included 36 percent of the workers; by 1911 it had risen to 53 percent.

The figures given probably understate the extent to which the age structure of the female work force was changing. The size of the work force itself was decreasing and this reduction should have occurred most in the earlier age groups, as young women entered other trades but older women continued in ribbonweaving. The increasing importance of younger women therefore testifies to the considerable extent to which working in the weaving trade had become the preserve of young women who worked in the trade until they married or had their first child.

A similar conclusion may be drawn from the civil status of the weavers. The married proportion of the work force declined steadily in the course of the half-century, and by 1911 almost every woman who worked in the trade was single: 94.8 percent. Only 1.3 percent were married and only 3.9 percent widowed. These data suggest that unmarried women worked in the weaving factories or *moulins à soie* but left the trade when they married to take up the duties of a *ménagère* on the farm of their new family.

The changes in the composition by age and marital status of the weaving population seem to be the result of the shift from domestic to factory organization. Domestic work could be interspersed with the duties of the farm and childraising, since within the household there was no apparent conflict between the industrial work of the woman and her agricultural and domestic duties. Domestic work could also be carried out with the assistance of other members of the family, and doubtless male farmers assisted during the slow winter months. Factory labor, on the other hand, required the presence of the worker from early morning until late at night and left little time or strength for agricultural work. An unmarried daughter might take up this type of work in order to supplement the income of her parents' household or collect a dowry; when she married and became responsible for a household of her own, she was forced to leave the weaving work force and assist her husband on the farm. The structural changes of the ribbonweaving trade in the mountain region therefore seem to have introduced a significant change in the life cycles of the women of the area. Different kinds of work were now associated with different stages of life. Single women worked away from home in factories while married women did agricultural work at home.

Factory labor also changed the social groups from which the labor force was recruited. As the lower matrix in table 3 shows, the wide social distribution of weaving characteristic of 1851 had changed significantly by 1901. The overwhelming majority (80 percent) of those households with a weaver held less than one hectare or no land. The change is even more dramatic in the group of households owning between one and five hectares of land. While more than half of this group had a weaver present in 1851, only 15.1 percent included an *ouvrière en soie* in 1901. Those households with larger landholdings, over five hectares, also moved away from weaving as a complementary occupation: while 37.7 percent of these households included a weaver in 1851, only 9.5 percent included one in 1901. Factory weaving became concentrated not only among young single women, but also among those members of the rural community who owned little or no land.

The concentration of weaving among the poorer, landless portion of the population was probably also associated with the increasing demands of market agriculture: married women were needed to prepare the agricultural products such as milk and cheese that provided cash income by the end of the century. Participation in the weaving trade became limited to the unmarried daughters of those without land and who therefore did not need their work on a farm. As with the agricultural changes of the second half of the century, the changes in the organization of weaving and its decline in numerical importance also created differences of experience between large and small landholders. The daughters of larger landholders were employed at home in the production of agricultural products. Families with little or no land, on the other hand, were unable to employ their daughters at home; the advent of factory organization meant that their daughters had to leave the household and work in the factory. As with market participation, the pattern of development in the ribbon industry created two groups in the rural community, characterized by different types of participation in the economic structure. That these two factors both distinguished groups on the basis of the amount of land held meant that they reinforced each other and strengthened the divisions between the two groups.

Thus, the development of the rural economy in the last half of the nineteenth century had extensive implications for the organization of the rural community. Village society at mid-century was characterized by the similarity of experience of most of its members: with the exclusion of a handful of very large landowners, every peasant household supported itself with a combination of diversified agricultural production oriented to a limited extent toward the urban market and domestic industrial work for the ribbonweaving *fabrique* of Saint-Etienne. The fluidity of work roles in this economy encouraged the complementary nature of these two types of work: because all work was done either on the farm or in the household, labor could easily be shifted from one sector to another, from agriculture to weaving or vice versa, depending on the needs of each sector. The heavy labor demands of agriculture during sowing and harvesting could be met by female members of the household who normally worked in weaving. Similarly, a pressing order for ribbons could be met with the assistance of male members who normally worked in agriculture.

In the last half of the century, the development of a large market for dairy products and the decline of domestic weaving encouraged landowning families to concentrate on agriculture and withdraw their labor from weaving. Women's work in these landowning families became concentrated on the preparation of agricultural products for sale. The new factory organization of ribbonweaving strengthened this tendency by requiring the presence of the weaver for twelve hours a day, six days a week, a rigid schedule that did not allow the fluid movement of labor characteristic of the earlier domestic economy. In this situation of forced economic choices, many families decided that opportunities were greater in the production of dairy goods for the urban market than in ribbonweaving. The result was the progressive division of the rural community into two groups: one, those owning land, specialized in agriculture for the urban market; the other, those without significant amounts of land, continued to balance agricultural and industrial income.

The division of the rural community that characterized the last third of the nineteenth century was, therefore, a result of the combination of that most basic of rural goods, land, with the changing influence of the growing urban-industrial economy of the valley. It is true that land was the most important variable determining membership in one or the other of the social groups in Marlhes at the end of the nineteenth century. In the context of the regional economy, however, it is apparent that the influence of land was magnified by the development of a growing market for agricultural goods and by changes in the availability and organization of industrial work.

The rural community in nineteenth-century Marlhes was diverse, with internal differences in landholding magnified as the century wore on by the external factors of market participation and industrial work. The valley was a major cause of the deepening of social divisions in Marlhes during the second half of the nineteenth century through the process that I have called rural urbanization. Dating these changes is difficult, because the urbanization of Marlhes was not an event but a process, continuing over time, advancing almost household by household through the village as families made economic choices. The growth of the urban market occurred most strikingly in the twenty years after 1840; the development of communications routes to this market began in the early years of the Second Empire and continued into the Third Republic; advances in animal husbandry also began under the Empire. The ribbon-weaving industry began to decay in the late 1850s, with fitful recoveries throughout the remainder of the century; factory work began in Marlhes in the 1870s, when Pierre Granger opened his silk spinning mill, while factory weaving did not appear until the 1890s. The entire half-century from 1851 to 1901 was one of gradual but continuous change in the economic structures of the Stephanois region that by the end of the century had created a new, divided village community in the place of the earlier village unified in its economic experiences.

# Chapter 4
# The Framework of Family Life:
## Seasonality and Mortality

The peasant families that lived through the economic and social change of the second half of the nineteenth century in Marlhes were, on one level, the products of the vital events of birth, death, marriage, and migration. These events were a part of the rhythm of family life, marking the stages in the development of the family and creating the framework for residence patterns, economic arrangements, and emotions within the family. In nineteenth-century Marlhes the rhythm and framework were those of traditional Europe, with demographic patterns providing more of a link to the past of the Ancien Régime than to the future of the twentieth century.

The histories of two families provide useful illustrations of the influence exercised on the family by the vital events of birth, marriage, death, and migration. In February of 1847, Jacques Courbon married Catherine Riocreux in the village church in Marlhes. Jacques was twenty-six and worked on his father's land in Marlhes before his marriage. Catherine was twenty, the daughter of landowners, Jean-Baptiste Riocreux and Marie-Anne Chavannat, both deceased. Jacques Courbon and Catherine Riocreux were married for more than twenty-eight years and had thirteen children, two of them twins, in that period. The first, Claude-Marie, was born nine months after the wedding, at the end of October 1847. The last, François Marius, was born in 1870, when Catherine was forty-three years old. Between these children came eleven others at intervals of between sixteen and forty-three months. The Courbons were fortunate and lost only two of their children in infancy. Until Jacques died in 1875, Catherine Riocreux bore, on the average, one child every twenty-seven months.

The year before the Courbons were married, in February 1846, Jean-Claude Servie, aged twenty-six, married Catherine Cheynet, aged eighteen. Their marriage lasted eighteen years and in that period Catherine had eleven children, three of whom died in infancy. During her eighteen years of married life, Catherine Cheynet had a child every twenty months, on the average.[1]

Each of these families grew quickly: after five years of marriage the Courbons had three children, the Servies four. The growth continued for both families, with both Catherine Riocreux and Catherine Cheynet bearing children well into their late thirties and early forties. When the last child was born to each couple, their oldest children were already adults.

This growth was balanced by deaths and migrations that reduced the size of the family. First came the deaths of children, most frequently in the first year of life. The ninth child of the Courbons, Jean-Baptiste Marius, died in 1864 at the age of six months, and their last child, François Marius, died in 1870 four days after his birth. Three of the Servie children died in infancy: Marie-Anne in 1849, Catherine in 1859, and Claude Remy in 1864. Much less frequent were the deaths of children after they passed their first birthdays, but this still occurred. Catherine Riocreux lost one of her twins, Marie Philomène, in 1879 at the age of twelve.

The most important deaths, however, were those of the partners themselves. Jacques Courbon was fifty-four when he died in 1875, leaving Catherine with eleven children between the ages of seven and twenty-eight. Jean-Claude Servie had died eleven years earlier, in 1864 when he was only forty-four years old. Catherine was the widowed mother of seven children ranging from Jean-Claude, aged seventeen, to Françoise, aged two. Another child, Marie-Marguerite, was born in 1865, eight months after the death of her father. Both women remained widows until their deaths in the 1890s.

Emigration also reduced the size of these families. In 1881 only the two youngest Courbon children were still living in Marlhes; the older children had at least temporarily left the commune, many of them probably for jobs as farm domestics. The Servie family held together better, with six of the eight living children still residing in Marlhes in 1881. Five of these children were living with their widowed mother, who remained the head of the household. Two of the older children, however, had emigrated from Marlhes.

The demographic histories of the Courbon and Servie families were relatively similar. Both families were very large, with the births of children spread over several decades. Both families lost several children in infancy or childhood, and the deaths of both fathers left their widows with young children to raise. Both families contributed to the stream of migrants heading from the commune to the industrial valley.

The implications of these family histories differed, however, because of the different social and economic status of each family. Jacques Courbon was a member of one of the wealthiest families in Marlhes, and soon after his marriage he received a large donation of land from his parents, making him one of the largest landowners in the village; in 1851 he held 29.6 hectares of land, enough to support his large family adequately if not in great luxury. Catherine Riocreux was listed on her marriage certificate as a landowner, and probably had inherited some land from her deceased parents. The large family of Jacques Courbon and Catherine Riocreux no doubt placed heavy burdens on their family income, but their landed wealth assured a high standard of living.

Even for the Courbons, however, a large family created problems. Each of the children who survived to adulthood had an equal right to the inheritance of their father, and his large holding of twenty-nine hectares would quickly disappear when divided into twelve shares. The satisfaction of the demands of twelve children born over a period of twenty-three years could lead to arguments within the family. The large number of children certainly made it difficult for each to receive individual attention from the parents, and the younger children were probably raised more by older brothers and sisters than by their parents.

The situation was different for Jean-Claude Servie and his family. Jean-Claude owned no land and worked as a farmer, renting land from other landowners in the commune. His tenancy on this land probably lasted for nine years, the usual length of leases in the region. While there is no indication of how much land Jean-Claude was able to rent and farm, competition for available land was strong in the region and it is doubtful that he could rent more than a few hectares. His wife Catherine supplemented the family income as a ribbonweaver, probably providing the difference between survival and disaster for the family. The large family and Catherine's frequent pregnancies, which reduced her ability to work as a weaver, placed heavy strains on the limited resources of the family economy.

The Courbons and Servies are, of course, only two of the hundreds of families who lived in Marlhes in the second half of the nineteenth century. Their brief histories, however, suggest the central role of the demographic events of birth, marriage, migration, and death in shaping the family as a social and economic unit. The combinations of these events in Marlhes had ramifications for many other aspects of the family system: the domestic economy, the transfer of land and property to children, the relations beween family members, and the ways in which children were raised.

The vital events of birth, death, and marriage each experienced seasonal and annual variations in nineteenth-century Marlhes. Annual variations will not be discussed here but are presented in appendix 1. Seasonal indices for deaths have been calculated for two periods, 1841–60 and 1891–1910, and are presented in table 4.[2] The two periods show similar patterns of seasonality, with identical troughs in July and peaks in mid-winter, in March and January respectively. The secondary peaks in April and March show that high mortality characterized the first four months of the year rather than any one month in that

**Table 4.** Seasonality of Deaths in Marlhes

| | 1841–1860 | | 1891–1900 | |
| Month | Total | Proportional Index | Total | Proportional Index |
| --- | --- | --- | --- | --- |
| January | 138 | 110 | 83 | 129 |
| February | 140 | 123 | 70 | 119 |
| March | 173 | 140 | 81 | 124 |
| April | 160 | 133 | 66 | 105 |
| May | 131 | 105 | 69 | 105 |
| June | 92 | 78 | 53 | 86 |
| July | 87 | 71 | 49 | 76 |
| August | 93 | 75 | 60 | 91 |
| September | 109 | 90 | 52 | 82 |
| October | 99 | 80 | 54 | 82 |
| November | 102 | 85 | 57 | 91 |
| December | 137 | 110 | 72 | 110 |

Source: A.C. de Marlhes, *Registres de décès*, 1841–60 and 1891–1900.

period. The months from June through November were months of relatively low mortality in both periods. The latter period shows less dramatic fluctuations than the first, with a difference of fifty-three between peak and trough compared to sixty-nine for the earlier period.

In both periods, therefore, the first four months of the year were the deadliest. This reflects the severity of winters in the mountain region, which increased mortality among children and the aged. The healthiest months were those of summer: the deaths during the winter of the most susceptible members of the population, infants and the aged, reduced the vulnerable population, and health conditions improved as the dangerous wetness of the winter and spring dried in higher temperatures. This calendar of death corresponds closely to that noted in previous studies of rural France, which have consistently shown peaks in the winter and modulation in the summer.[3]

The normal seasonal pattern of births and conceptions is presented in table 5. In the middle of the century there is a principal peak in the spring and early summer (May to July) and a secondary peak six months later in November and December in conceptions. The intervening troughs reach their lowest points in September and March. At the end of the century, a slightly different pattern of conceptions appears, with the principal peak in August, a secondary peak in December, and troughs in the autumn (September to November) and January. The seasonal variation of con-

**Table 5.** Seasonality of Births and Conceptions in Marlhes

| Month of Birth | Month of Conception | 1840–1859 Total | 1840–1859 Proportional Index | 1880–1900 Total | 1880–1900 Proportional Index |
|---|---|---|---|---|---|
| January | April | 157 | 98 | 108 | 106 |
| February | May | 151 | 102 | 92 | 98 |
| March | June | 205 | 127 | 105 | 104 |
| April | July | 163 | 104 | 92 | 95 |
| May | August | 157 | 98 | 121 | 119 |
| June | September | 137 | 89 | 93 | 95 |
| July | October | 150 | 93 | 96 | 95 |
| August | November | 160 | 101 | 95 | 95 |
| September | December | 169 | 108 | 108 | 110 |
| October | January | 148 | 93 | 77 | 75 |
| November | February | 151 | 96 | 101 | 104 |
| December | March | 145 | 91 | 107 | 104 |

Source: A.C. de Marlhes, *Registres de naissances*, 1840–59, 1880–1900.

ceptions was not so violent in either period as variations in deaths, with ranges of thirty-eight and forty-four in the indices of conceptions compared with sixty-nine and fifty-three for deaths. This pattern of deaths fluctuating more than conceptions is not unusual: in eighteenth-century Meulan, for example, the range of the seasonal index of deaths was fifty-three, compared with a range of twenty-seven in conceptions.[4]

The moderate fluctuations in conceptions and their spacing through the year suggests only a slight relationship to harvests. The coincidence with harvests is most noticeable in the seasonal patterns of mid-century, with the months of the heaviest agricultural work, the harvest month of September and the plowing and sowing month of March, appearing as low points in the level of conceptions. Similarly, the peaks in conceptions appear in the period immediately following spring sowing (May through July) but before harvests begin, and in November and December, when winter snows had put an end to most agricultural work.[5] At the end of the century, peaks in conceptions again appear in slack agricultural months, August and December. Also, there is a trough in the harvest month of September, although it continues through November. Missing, however, is the spring trough that at mid-century coincided with the sowing of the new crop.

The seasonal variations in conceptions seem to be the result of a combination of economic and demographic factors. The postharvest peaks may be attributed to both additional confidence by couples in their future after the harvest and return of husbands after temporary harvest employment in other areas, particularly the Plaine du Forez north of Saint-Etienne, where harvests were earlier than in the mountains. The peaks themselves also produced a response in the total level of conceptions, however, since they removed a portion of the female population from risk of conception. The level of conceptions was therefore bound to decline after a peak.

The effect of this seasonal pattern of conceptions was to produce minor peaks in the seasonal pattern of births in the winter months. This seasonality of births partially explains the seasonal peak of deaths in winter and early spring, as newborn infants succumbed to the rigors of the mountain winters. This explanation is also consistent with the failure of the secondary peak of births in late summer and early fall to be followed by a peak of deaths until December. The effect of the cold, damp winter weather of Marlhes seems to have been particularly harsh upon the youngest, weakest members of the population.

The seasonal curve of marriages, presented in table 6, followed that of deaths, with maximums in January–February and November. Two explanations are possible for this: one is that high mortality of the aged during the winter created opportunities for younger adults to obtain holdings and marry. While this may have had some effect, an attitudinal

**Table 6.** Seasonality of Marriages in Marlhes, 1841–1898

| Month | Total | Proportional Index |
|---|---|---|
| January | 117 | 160 |
| February | 201 | 300 |
| March | 19 | 25 |
| April | 41 | 59 |
| May | 80 | 110 |
| June | 63 | 89 |
| July | 48 | 63 |
| August | 38 | 52 |
| September | 66 | 93 |
| October | 55 | 76 |
| November | 105 | 148 |
| December | 19 | 25 |

Source: A.C. de Marlhes, *Registres de mariages*, 1841–98.

factor seems more important: the peaks immediately preceded the religious seasons of Lent and Advent, when the Catholic church did not allow marriages. The sharp decline in March and December, the months of Lent and Advent, and the reputation of the Stephanois region as a particularly devout area support this explanation.

The general correspondence between Marlhes and pre-nineteenth-century populations in the seasonality of vital events marks the village as firmly rooted in the population patterns of the Ancien Régime. Deaths, births, and marriages followed the seasons, creating an annual rhythm of family life. To a remarkable extent these events were concentrated in the winter, a season of frequent marriages and births, and also a season full of dangers for newborns and older people. As had been true for generations, the seasons meant more to the peasants in Marlhes than a change in weather: the coming of cold weather and snows meant both the celebrations associated with marriage and birth and the grieving that came with death.

The most important determinant of mortality in Marlhes was age. This is illustrated in life tables based on deaths at the middle and end of the century (see tables 7 and 8).[6] In both tables mortality is highest among infants, young children, and those over age fifty. There is of course nothing surprising about this: these rates reflect the physical strength of those between ten and fifty and the inability of the very young and the aged to resist the hazards of weather, malnutrition, and disease in the mountain region during the nineteenth century.

More interesting are changes in age-specific rates and life expectancy between the two tables. There is improvement in infant mortality rates ($_1q_0$), which declined from 223 to 216 per thousand. This improvement, however, is slight, and even at the end of the century infant mortality remained at a level similar to that found in many eighteenth-century villages. In Crulai, Louis Henry found an infant mortality rate of 205 per thousand for those born from 1688 to 1749, lower than in Marlhes. In Jean Ganiage's *Trois villages de l'Ile de France*, the rate was 212 per thousand. A recent survey of thirty-five reconstitution studies found a mean infant mortality level of 212 per thousand.[7] The infant mortality rate in Marlhes a century after these studies, therefore, marks the commune as a relatively dangerous place for infants to live.

However, Marlhes does exhibit lower child mortality rates than those of Ancien Régime France. In Marlhes $_4q_1$ decreased from 98 to 80 per thousand from the middle to the end of the century. The mean of twenty-four village studies in the eighteenth century was 177 per thousand; the level in Crulai, 122; that in the Ile-de-France villages, 142.[8] The rates in Marlhes are therefore relatively low, although they are not so low as to cast doubt on the results. Rather, these rates suggest an extreme case of the West

**Table 7.** Life Table for Marlhes, 1849–1853

| Age $x$ | Alive at age $x$ $l_x$ | Probability of dying in interval $q_x$ | Deaths in interval $d_x$ | Central death rate $m_x$ | To be lived in interval $L_x$ | To be lived in this and subsequent intervals $T_x$ | Expectation of Life $e°_x$ |
|---|---|---|---|---|---|---|---|
| 0 | 1000 | .223 | 223 | .274 | 815.1 | 40040.0 | 40.04 |
| 1 | 777 | .098 | 76 | .026 | 2884.3 | 39225.3 | 50.48 |
| 5 | 701 | .014 | 10 | .003 | 3480.0 | 36341.0 | 51.84 |
| 10 | 691 | .009 | 6 | .002 | 3440.0 | 32861.0 | 47.55 |
| 15 | 685 | .004 | 3 | .001 | 3417.5 | 29421.5 | 42.95 |
| 20 | 682 | .024 | 16 | .005 | 3370.0 | 26003.5 | 38.13 |
| 25 | 666 | .063 | 42 | .013 | 3225.0 | 22633.5 | 33.98 |
| 30 | 624 | .058 | 36 | .012 | 3030.0 | 19408.5 | 31.10 |
| 35 | 588 | .058 | 34 | .012 | 2855.0 | 16378.5 | 27.85 |
| 40 | 554 | .093 | 52 | .019 | 2640.0 | 13523.5 | 24.41 |
| 45 | 502 | .053 | 27 | .011 | 2442.5 | 10883.5 | 21.68 |
| 50 | 475 | .095 | 45 | .020 | 2262.5 | 8441.0 | 17.77 |
| 55 | 430 | .219 | 94 | .049 | 1915.0 | 6178.5 | 14.37 |
| 60 | 336 | .144 | 48 | .031 | 1560.0 | 4263.5 | 12.69 |
| 65 | 288 | .277 | 80 | .064 | 1240.0 | 2703.5 | 9.39 |
| 70 | 208 | .456 | 95 | .119 | 802.5 | 1463.5 | 7.04 |
| 75+ | 113 | 1.000 | 113 | .171 | 661.0 | 661.0 | 5.85 |

Note: each person dying between 0 and 1 lived an average of 0.171 years; each person dying between 1 and 5 lived an average of 1.057 years after exact age 1; each person dying at age 75 and over lived an average of 5.852 years after exact age 75. The rates for $_1q_0$ and $_4q_1$ have been calculated from births and deaths for the years 1841 to 70.

Source: A.C. de Marlhes, *Registres de décès*, 1841–70; A.D.L. 49 M 85, *Liste nominative de recensement de Marlhes*, 1851.

relationship between $_1q_0$ and $_4q_1$ described by Coale and Demeny in which child mortality rates are much lower than infant mortality rates.[9] This pattern appears most frequently in reconstitution studies in north-western France,[10] while the rest of France exhibited a North pattern of high child as well as infant mortality under the Ancien Régime. By the second half of the nineteenth century, however, mortality in France had declined, particularly child mortality, and the pattern began to conform most closely to West model tables.[11] The improvement in Marlhes from 1849–53 to 1899–1903 in $_4q_1$ suggests this transition and foreshadows a significant lowering of both infant and child mortality in the twentieth century.[12]

**Table 8.** Life Table for Marlhes, 1899–1903

| Age x | Alive at age x $l_x$ | Probability of dying in interval $q_x$ | Deaths in interval $d_x$ | Central death rate $m_x$ | To be lived in interval $L_x$ | To be lived in this and subsequent intervals $T_x$ | Expectation of Life $e°_x$ |
|---|---|---|---|---|---|---|---|
| 0 | 1000 | .216 | 216 | .257 | 839.5 | 42656.5 | 42.66 |
| 1 | 754 | .080 | 63 | .021 | 2928.6 | 41817.0 | 55.46 |
| 5 | 721 | .024 | 17 | .005 | 3562.5 | 38888.4 | 53.90 |
| 10 | 704 | .024 | 17 | .005 | 3477.5 | 35435.9 | 50.18 |
| 15 | 687 | .034 | 23 | .007 | 3377.5 | 31848.4 | 46.36 |
| 20 | 664 | .063 | 42 | .013 | 3217.5 | 28470.9 | 42.88 |
| 25 | 623 | .039 | 24 | .008 | 3055.0 | 25253.4 | 40.53 |
| 30 | 599 | .024 | 14 | .005 | 2960.0 | 22198.4 | 37.06 |
| 35 | 585 | .044 | 26 | .009 | 2860.0 | 19238.4 | 32.89 |
| 40 | 559 | .072 | 40 | .015 | 2695.0 | 16378.4 | 29.30 |
| 45 | 519 | .049 | 25 | .010 | 2532.5 | 13683.4 | 26.36 |
| 50 | 494 | .024 | 12 | .005 | 2440.0 | 11150.9 | 22.57 |
| 55 | 482 | .095 | 46 | .020 | 2295.0 | 8710.9 | 18.07 |
| 60 | 436 | .183 | 80 | .040 | 1980.0 | 6415.9 | 14.71 |
| 65 | 356 | .165 | 59 | .036 | 1632.5 | 4435.9 | 12.46 |
| 70 | 297 | .239 | 71 | .054 | 1307.5 | 2803.4 | 9.44 |
| 75 | 226 | .439 | 99 | .113 | 882.5 | 1495.9 | 6.62 |
| 80+ | 127 | 1.000 | 127 | .207 | 613.4 | 613.4 | 4.83 |

Note: Each person dying between ages 0 and 1 lived an average of .0257 years; each person dying between ages 1 and 5 lived an average of .0708 years after exact age 1; each person dying above age 80 lived an average of 4.833 years after exact age 80. The rates for $_1q_0$ and $_4q_1$ have been calculated using births and deaths for the years 1871 to 1901.

Source: A.C. de Marlhes, *Registre de décès*, 1871–1903; A.D.L. 49 M 353, *Liste nominative de recensement de la commune de Marlhes*, 1901.

The differences between infant and child mortality rates are reflected in differences of life expectancy. At birth this is low in both tables; it improved only slightly in the half-century. This measure was similar to estimates for the female population of the entire department in 1849–53, but improved more slowly than in the department: 40.04 versus 40.0 in 1849–53, 42.66 versus 47.4 in 1899–1903.[13] It was however higher than Gautier and Henry's estimate for Crulai.[14] At age one, both tables for Marlhes show significant improvement, increasing life expectancy 10.44 and 12.80 years respectively. The most dangerous part of a person's life was the first year; after the first birthday chances of survival and expectation of life improved greatly.

Even with these improved expectations, adult mortality in Marlhes was high. As can be seen in figure 6, $m_x$ in Marlhes was only slightly lower than that in a model life table reflecting infant mortality rates similar to those prevailing in Marlhes and with a life expectancy at birth of 34.8 years.[15] However, the sharp rise in mortality characteristic of older ages occurs earlier and more sharply in the tables for Marlhes than in the model table. This is especially true in 1849–53, when the increase is first noticeable at age fifty-five. At the end of the century the increase took place five years later, at age sixty. The model table begins its more gradual increase at age sixty, and follows a path between the tables for Marlhes. Mortality is lower in Marlhes than in the model table until the older age groups, when the rates in the model table and the rates for Marlhes become very similar.

The relatively high adult mortality rates in Marlhes in both the middle and the end of the century should not obscure the fact that there was some improvement in mortality during the period. We noted earlier the modest improvements in both infant and child mortality rates, and there is a similar improvement in adult mortality rates, reflecting better chances of life for older age groups. The 1849–53 adult mortality rates are lower than those for 1899–1903 until ages twenty-five to forty and again from ages sixty to seventy. The rates at all other ages show that the later period was less dangerous than the middle of the century. Differences between the values for $e°_x$, plotted in figure 7, increase steadily from age ten to age thirty, and remain substantial until age sixty. Although improvements in mortality were modest, they were nonetheless real, and the differences between these two tables suggest that the second half of the nineteenth century, probably the last quarter, witnessed some amelioration of the impact of health conditions on the population of Marlhes.

The absence of firm evidence makes any conclusions as to either cause of death or reasons for the decline in mortality in the period between mid-century and 1900 mere speculation. Several points, however, should be made about mortality at this juncture. In the first place, the principal component of mortality in Marlhes in both years was infant and child mortality, as in any high mortality population, and mortality of the very young improved only slightly from one period to the next. While high mortality in these age groups may be linked to the influence of the conditions of life in this rural village and the constant threat posed by the harsh climate of the mountain region to these most vulnerable parts of the population, there is some evidence that these dangers were heightened by patterns of child care in the village, especially among the poorer members of the community. Marlhes was an

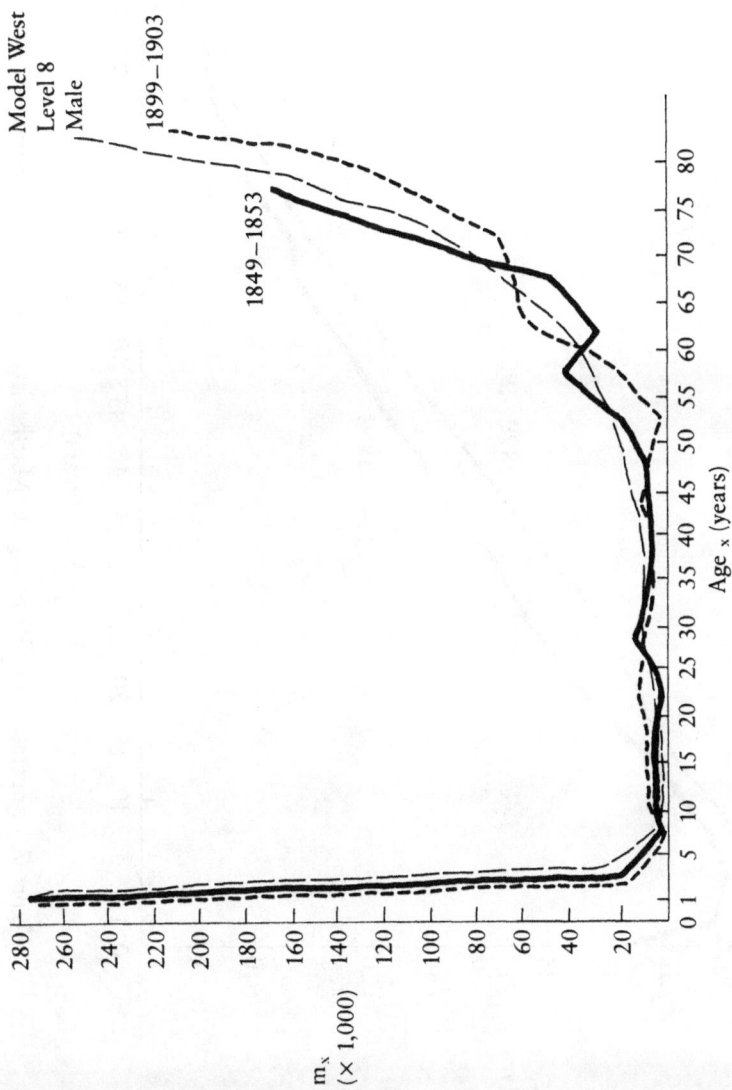

**Figure 6.** Mortality Rates by Age in Marlhes, 1849–1853 and 1899–1903, Compared with Model West Level 8 Male Mortality Rates

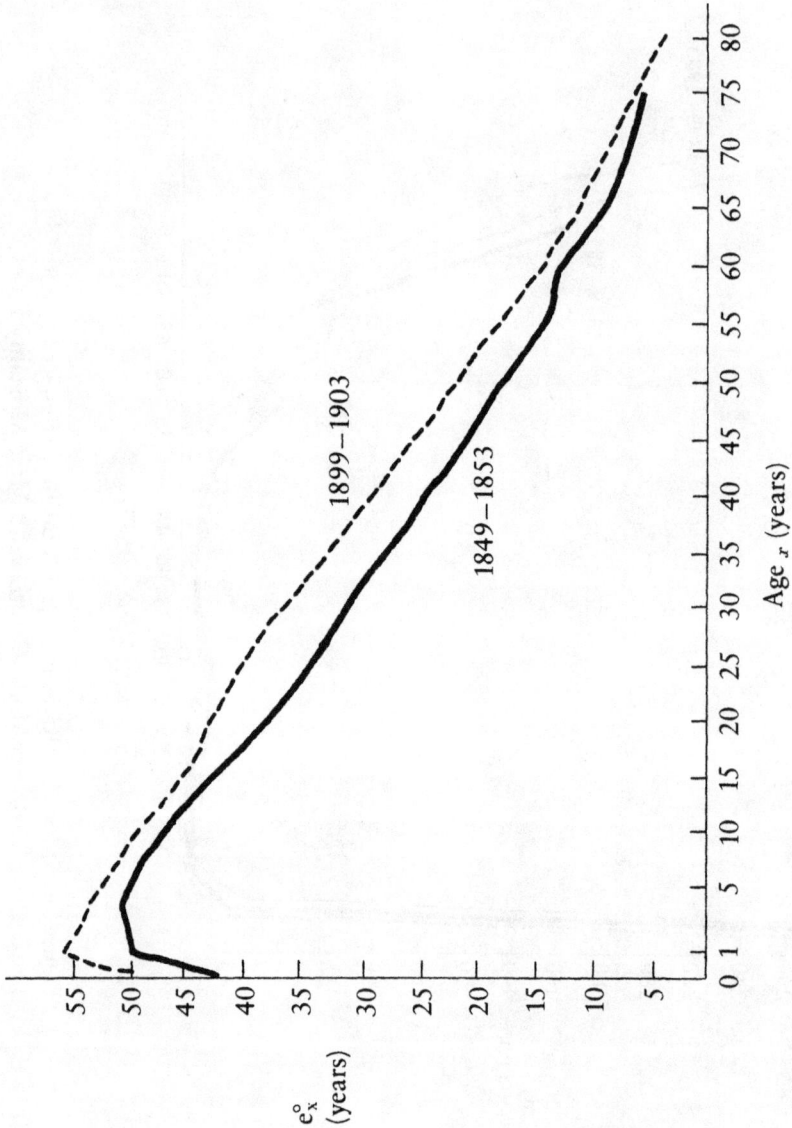

Figure 7. Expectation of Life by Age in Marlhes, 1849–1853 and 1899–1903

active participant in the wet-nursing business of nineteenth-century France, and it is common to find the deaths of nurslings listed in the death registers of the commune. These nurslings were taken into the family soon after the birth of a natural child, leading to the weaning of that child before his first birthday. The absence of adequate and healthful substitute foods for the natural child increased exposure to malnutrition and death from hypothermia or disease. These patterns of childrearing continued at least until the end of the century and are reflected in the persistence of mercenary wet-nursing and the continued high level of infant and child mortality.[16]

What improvement there was in mortality was largely in the chances of survival for adults, although even here the improvement was slight. It is possible that improved nutrition, the result of an increased standard of living, was at work here. Yves Lequin has found a significant increase in the height of conscripts in the rural areas of the Lyonnais, Beaujolais, and Roannais during the second half of the nineteenth century, suggesting improved nutrition, especially in childhood, as the century progressed.[17] These improvements may have led to increased ability on the part of adults to resist the dangers of the mountain climate and, for women, the threat of childbirth. This is, of course, only speculation; but it is more likely that this was the reason for improvement, rather than other factors, such as medical care. Doctors still remained rare in the mountains at the end of the century, and their influence was probably very small.[18]

The influence of different social conditions on mortality in Marlhes is not clear. It has proved impossible to obtain any quantitative measure of the mortality of landowners and nonlandowners from reconstituted families because of the small number of cases available.[19] Without quantitative measures of mortality for different social groups, it is difficult to ascertain whether wealthier members of the rural community were better protected than their poorer neighbors. On the whole, however, it seems likely that any differences in mortality were not great enough to have created significant differences in the family patterns of various social groups. Certainly all members of the community were threatened by the loss of infants or young children, the highest mortality age groups in the population. Because mercenary wet-nursing was concentrated among the poorer members of the village community, this group may have experienced higher levels of infant and child mortality. But ownership of large farms does not seem to have been a safeguard against the death of infants. Bartelemy Chirat and Catherine Bayle, for example, owned over fourteen hectares of land, but four of their eleven children died before their first birthdays.[20] If a family such as the Courbons lost only two children instead of the three lost in the Servie family, infant mortality remained an important fact for both families. The high infant mortality rates in Marlhes threatened the children of all families, and modest differences between social groups would not create two different life cycles.

In adult mortality the differences also do not seem to have been significant between social groups, although wealthier adults probably enjoyed better nutrition than poorer ones. If adults in landowning families lived longer than those in poorer families, at least one parent probably still died while some children were young and before the parents reached old age. Even though Jacques Courbon lived ten years longer than Jean-Claude Servie, both still left their widows with young children to raise. The longer life of Jacques Courbon did not mean that his family grew to adulthood before he died; it only meant that he and Catherine Riocreux had more children before his death.

There seem to have been few aspects of life in Marlhes during the nineteenth century that could create significantly different mortality rates between social groups. Larger landowners may have had more to eat and been better nourished than their poorer neighbors, but this advantage probably was canceled out by the poor protection from the elements provided by housing in Marlhes. With the few exceptions provided by the "chateau" of M. Colomb de Gast in Coin and the large house of the Courbons at La Faye, most dwellings in Marlhes provided little protection from the worst effects of the region's weather. Duplessy noted in 1818 that few dwellings had more than two floors and many had only a single floor, with the largest room serving as bedroom, kitchen, and workshop for weaving. Houses were of stone, but floors were dirt and the doors and windows provided little protection from wind, rain, and snow.[21] Ulysses Rouchon, at the end of the century, described conditions in the Haut-Velay that indicated little improvement in conditions in which people lived: there was minimal separation of stables and houses, and men and animals lived almost together.[22] Most families could not afford to construct a better dwelling and most members of the population lived under the same physical conditions.

The one condition likely to lead to differences in mortality was participation in ribbonweaving, but this affected only a part of the population. No evidence exists for the physical conditions of ribbonweaving in the countryside, but a report prepared in 1848 by a *passementier* in Saint-Etienne, Antoine Limousin, cited a report of a doctor that noted two great dangers to the weaver from his craft. The need to maintain humid air in the workshop led to pulmonary diseases and generally poor health. Further, the habit of leaning on the frame of the loom while fixing broken threads led, he claimed, to cancer of the stomach and circulatory ailments in the legs and lower body.[23] The latter danger might have increased the danger of death during childbirth or of stillbirths for the women who wove in Marlhes. If so, this would have caused a difference in mortality among women at the end of the nineteenth century as women from poorer families worked as weavers in factories while others, the daughters of larger landowners, began to work on their families' farms rather than as weavers. At mid-century, however, when almost all women worked as weavers, this would not have led to differences between social groups, although it may have contributed to the overall level of mortality. Without specific quantitative data, of course, it is impossible to do more than speculate about the influence of these factors.

If there were no significant differences in mortality between social groups in Marlhes, the limitations placed on the family group by mortality were similar for most families in Marlhes. Infant children died frequently in all families, and most marriages were broken while husband and wife were in their forties or fifties by the death of one partner. Children were frequently raised by only one parent or were orphaned, and the family economic problems caused by the loss of a parent were felt by virtually all families. It is probable that mortality did not create different family patterns in nineteenth-century Marlhes; its heavy toll placed severe limitations on the development and stability of the family group for all members of the rural community.

# Chapter 5
# The Framework of Family Life: Nuptiality and Fertility

The mortality of nineteenth-century Marlhes found its counterweight in the reproductive events of marriage and birth. Only through high fertility could the heavy losses from mortality in the village be replaced. The most important characteristic of reproductive behavior in Marlhes was the absence of any attempt at limiting the size of families, a type of fertility behavior that led to the eleven or twelve children in the families of Jacques Courbon and Jean-Claude Servie and many other families with five or more children. This pattern was common for all families in spite of differences of wealth and landownership. Again the Courbons and Servies may be cited as examples. Jacques Courbon was a wealthy man for Marlhes, owning more than twenty-nine hectares of land, one of the largest farms in the village. Jean-Claude Servie, in contrast, owned no land and depended on rented land and the ribbonweaving of his wife Catherine to maintain the family. In spite of this difference in material resources, both families were very large and showed no tendency toward family limitation. Similarly, in the village population there were few significant differences in the nuptiality or fertility of different social groups.

To provide an overview of fertility and nuptiality in Marlhes, I have calculated the indices given in table 9 of total fertility $(I_f)$, marital fertility $(I_g)$, illegitimate fertility $(I_h)$, proportion married of the female population $(I_m)$, and female age at first marriage $(SMAM)$ for 1851, 1881, and 1901.[1] These measures describe both the progress of overall fertility and its demographic components.

Table 9 shows the preponderant role played by marital fertility $(I_g)$ in the total fertility of the population. This is particularly true in 1851 and 1881, when marital fertility is greater than 80 percent of the performance of the Hutterite population. This high rate suggests that there was little conscious limitation of family size in Marlhes, at least until after 1881, and that the rates are an expression of natural fertility[2] on the part of most of the married population. There is a decline in marital fertility between 1881 and 1901 but the index remains high. If this decline in $I_g$

Table 9. Indices of Fertility and Nuptiality in Marlhes

| Year | $I_f$ | $I_g$ | $I_h$ | $I_m$ | SMAM |
|------|------|------|------|------|------|
| 1851 | .338 | .880 | .008 | .378 | 27.3 |
| 1881 | .379 | .820 | .009 | .457 | 26.1 |
| 1901 | .307 | .676 | .004 | .450 | 26.3 |

Source: A.D.L. 49 M 85, 49 M 260, 49 M 353, *Listes nominatives de recensement de la commune de Marlhes*, 1851, 1881, 1901; A.C. de Marlhes, *Registres de naissances*, 1849–53, 1879–83, 1899–1903.

indicates the beginning of family limitation in Marlhes, it was very late in the period and probably occurred only among those married during the 1890s. During the period under examination, most of the population followed the traditional pre-Malthusian fertility behavior already noted for the Courbon and Servie families.

It is also apparent that illegitimate fertility ($I_h$) was insignificant throughout the period. In this absence of significant illegitimate fertility, the mediator between marital fertility and total fertility is the nuptiality of the population, and particularly the proportion of the female population that marries. This proportion is expressed in the measure $I_m$, which indicates that a comparatively low proportion of women married in Marlhes at mid-century, with an increase in the period from 1851 to 1881. This increase is accompanied by a decline of slightly over one year in the estimated female age at first marriage. All three sets of figures for Marlhes, however, remain well within the limits of the western European marriage pattern that John Hajnal has described, characterized by high age at first marriage and low proportion ever married.[3] Thus, while there is a tendency toward lower age at marriage and increased proportion married in Marlhes, there do not appear to be major changes in the nuptiality patterns of the population as a whole.

The changes in nuptiality and marital fertility that occurred in Marlhes conform to the inverse relationship that has been found in other studies between these variables, with high marital fertility coinciding with low proportion married and increasing control of fertility coinciding with earlier, more frequent marriage.[4] Marlhes seems, therefore, to fit a pattern of delayed marriage limiting overall fertility and, when family limitation does begin, of limited family size allowing earlier marriage.

These are, of course, general relationships referring to long periods of time. In the short term in Marlhes the effects of these changes on overall fertility followed the timing of the changes in its two components. In the period between 1851 and 1881, when the proportion married increased the most, while marital fertility declined only slightly, overall fertility increased. In the last twenty years of the century, marital fertility decreased, while the proportion married stayed relatively stable or declined slightly. The result was a decline in overall fertility. The long-term pattern, however, showed only a slight decrease in overall fertility and the level remained relatively high.

Following the vital rates of the population of a commune of two thousand people over fifty years provides some insight into the workings of that population, but the implications of these vital rates become more evident when they are compared with a larger population. Table 10 provides comparative data for the entire department of the Loire. These allow us to set the commune of Marlhes in the context of the larger population of which it formed a small part. The contrasts between tables 9 and 10 show that the population of Marlhes experienced both a different pattern of development and a significantly different level of fertility and nuptiality than did the entire department. Marital fertility in Marlhes, for example, never reached the low level of the department in 1851: it is evident from the departmental figures that the movement toward family limitation in the department was both earlier and stronger than in Marlhes. As in Marlhes, the most important advance of contraception in the department came in the period after 1881; even prior to that period, however, the marital fertility level of the department suggests that a substantial proportion of the population was consciously limiting family size.[5]

A similar conclusion may be drawn by comparing the proportions married. Again, indices for Marlhes are never as high as those of the department in 1851. Although both sets of figures show an increase in the proportion married, the timing differed: in Marlhes, the major increase took place between 1851 and 1881; in the department as a whole, the increase from 1851 to 1881 was minimal, while a more substantial increase occurred between 1881 and 1901. In fact, even in 1831, the

Table 10. Indices of Fertility and Nuptiality in
Department of the Loire

| Year | $I_f$ | $I_g$ | $I_h$ | $I_m$ | SMAM |
|------|-------|-------|-------|-------|------|
| 1851 | .332 | .646 | .027 | .492 | 25.5 |
| 1881 | .306 | .592 | .027 | .494 | 25.5 |
| 1901 | .225 | .414 | .023 | .518 | 25.8* |

*SMAM for 1896; data not available for 1901.

Source: Etienne van de Walle, *The Female Population of France in the Nineteenth Century*, p. 345, table 5.

earliest date for which Etienne van de Walle has been able to calculate the proportion married, the departmental level is .483, substantially above even the final figure for Marlhes.[6]

The fluctuations in the departmental level of overall fertility appear, therefore, to be the result almost exclusively of the decrease in marital fertility; nuptiality played little part in the pattern of steady fertility decline. In Marlhes, on the other hand, the interaction of the two variables at different times produced different patterns in the 1851–81 period: an upswing of overall fertility, under the influence of greater proportion married at high marital fertility; and a downswing in marital fertility, along with a small downswing in proportion married, combining to produce a decline in overall fertility in the period from 1881 to 1901. In spite of the importance of the low levels of proportion married in the demographic equation for Marlhes, the level of overall fertility in that population remained substantially higher than the level in the entire department.

The comparison with the departmental figures allows more precision about the characteristics of the demographic regime in Marlhes and its development over time. Of most interest are the high absolute levels of marital and overall fertility in Marlhes and the low level of the proportion married. While levels of total fertility in 1851 were similar in both the department and the commune (.332 versus .338), the difference became more pronounced as time passed. This was the result of three characteristics of the development of the two populations. First, there is the late and weak impulse to contraception within marriage that characterized the population of Marlhes, in contrast to the departmental population that was practicing family limitation in significant proportions even in 1851. Second, there are the different patterns of development in the proportion married. In the department this variable stayed almost constant throughout the century; in Marlhes it was a strong mediator of the development of overall fertility, and its increase in the 1851–81 period, prior to any significant decline in marital fertility, led to an increase in overall fertility. Thus, finally, one may point to different relationships between contraception and proportion married in the experiences of the two populations. In the department as a whole, nuptiality patterns played little part in the decline of total fertility; central to this historical development were the contraceptive practices of the married population. In Marlhes, on the other hand, contraception and nuptiality exerted independent influences in contradictory directions and at different times during the century.

The nuptiality patterns visible in Marlhes in the aggregate estimates presented above are confirmed by more exact local sources. The mean age at first marriage for women married in Marlhes between

1841 and 1870, calculated from marriage acts, was 25.64 years. Marriages later in the century, between 1871 and 1898, took place slightly earlier, with a mean age at first marriage for women of 25.05 years. The difference between the two marriage cohorts amounts to a decrease of seven months in mean age at first marriage.

Men married later than women, and their age at first marriage was consistently higher than that of women. Between 1841 and 1870 there was a mean age of 30.56 years for men married in Marlhes. As with women's age at first marriage, this decreased slightly in the last quarter of the century: for marriages between 1871 and 1898, the mean age for men was 29.78. This decline in age at marriage was slightly greater than the decline in women's age, amounting to nine months.[7]

Age at first marriage shows a slight decrease for both men and women in the course of the second half of the century. While no data are available for an earlier period, this decrease probably was part of a longer pattern of decline in age at marriage beginning in the eighteenth century or earlier. Its level remained well above the twenty-three or twenty-four years that Hajnal used as a boundary line between western and eastern European marriage patterns.[8]

The large family sizes of the Courbon and Servie families were to some extent the result of their deviation from this pattern of family limitation through late marriage characteristic of their neighbors in Marlhes and other areas of western Europe. Catherine Riocreux was married at the age of twenty, and Catherine Cheynet even earlier, at eighteen. They both experienced five additional years of childbearing at the age of highest natural fertility. Catherine Riocreux gave birth to three of her thirteen children before she turned twenty-five, the age at which most women in nineteenth-century Marlhes married. Four of Catherine Cheynet's children were born in that period.

The other component of the western European marriage pattern, permanent celibacy, was also present in nineteenth-century Marlhes. In 1851, 15.9 percent of women aged fifty and above had never been married. In 1881 this figure was 16.8 percent, while in 1901 the percentage of women never married had declined to 6.7. Among men, 5.4 percent of those aged fifty and above in 1851 had never been married. This rose to 16.3 percent in 1881, then decreased to 6.2 percent in 1901.[9]

Because these estimates are calculated from census lists, they must be interpreted cautiously. The population of Marlhes was a volatile one, subject to high rates of migration that affected certain groups in the population more than others. This could have significantly altered the data used in these rates. The percentages above represent minimum estimates of permanent celibacy, for migration was higher among single persons than among those married or widowed. Therefore, this would reduce the numerator in these calculations and depress the percentage.

This error probably became greater as the century progressed, especially as domestic ribbonweaving declined.[10] The decline in proportion never married between 1851 and 1901 among women may be only an artifact of the source used here.

Even with these limitations it is apparent that permanent celibacy was an important characteristic of nuptiality patterns in nineteenth-century Marlhes. The proportion never married for those aged forty-five to forty-nine found by Hajnal in his initial description of the western European marriage pattern ranges from 10 to 15 percent. While the percentages found in nineteenth-century Marlhes fall in the lower range of these values, especially at the end of the century, they remain higher than the 3 or 4 percent common in eastern Europe.[11]

The western European marriage pattern formed an important buffer between the high rates of marital fertility and the total fertility rates in western Europe during the period from the sixteenth century through the popularization of family limitation in the nineteenth century. Historians have linked the pattern of late marriage and frequent permanent celibacy to a relationship between landholding and marriage, and have explained the pattern by the desire to conserve family wealth and land by limiting family size in the absence of widespread contraception.[12] Several recent studies have emphasized the importance of earlier and more universal marriage among nonlanded groups in rural society in increasing the period women were at risk to bear children and causing the population growth of western European countries in the eighteenth and nineteenth centuries.[13] The nonlanded status of rural weavers and agricultural day laborers broke the traditional association between land and marriage and removed the incentive for marriage limitation present among the western European peasantry during the Ancien Régime.

In order to examine this hypothesis in nineteenth-century Marlhes, mean ages at first marriage for men and women have been calculated for reconstituted marriages between 1841 and 1880.[14] The results are presented in table 11. These mean ages at first marriage indicate that land-ownership strongly affected the age at marriage of men but had little effect on the age at marriage of women. The difference between marriage ages for males is greatest in the earlier marriage cohort examined here, those married between 1841 and 1860. Property owners tended to marry very late, in their early thirties, whereas nonlanded men married in their late twenties. The pattern is similar in the later cohort, although the difference is reduced. Among women, in contrast, there is a difference of only about six months between landed and nonlanded groups in both marriage cohorts.

While property owning does seem to be related to a later age at marriage for men, it had little effect on women's marriage ages in nineteenth-century Marlhes. The impact of this delay on total fertility was therefore

Table 11. Mean Age at First Marriage in Marlhes

| | Marriages 1841–1860 | | Marriages 1861–1880 | | Marriages 1841–1880 | |
|---|---|---|---|---|---|---|
| | M | F | M | F | M | F |
| Property owners | 32.67 | 25.03 | 30.76 | 25.23 | 31.56 | 25.15 |
| Non–Property owners | 28.15 | 25.50 | 27.72 | 24.85 | 27.98 | 25.25 |

Source: Family Reconstitution Type MF Families; A.D.L. Série P Non-Coté, *Matrice cadastrale de la commune de Marlhes.*

muted. The later ages at marriage for men could reduce total fertility by shortening the length of the marriage, but this shortening took place at the end of the marriage, when fertility rates were very low, rather than at the beginning, when fertility rates were highest. On the whole, this evidence does not suggest conscious delay of marriage in order to preserve landed wealth.

The influence of ribbonweaving on age at first marriage also appears to be minimal. As noted in chapter 3, weaving was very common among women in all social groups in Marlhes until the last few decades of the nineteenth century. The high level of age at marriage at this time among both men and women suggests that there was no sharp reduction in age at marriage as a result of the availability of weaving work. At the end of the century, when weaving had become concentrated among those without land, the age at marriage remained high in this group. In contrast to the influence exerted on marriage patterns by weaving in rural Flanders, the Zurich highlands, and Leicestershire, weaving did not play an important role in determining marriage patterns in nineteenth-century Marlhes.[15]

The remaining characteristics of the nuptiality of the population of Marlhes in the nineteenth century to be described are the length of marriages and the frequency of remarriage. Table 12 presents data from family reconstitution forms on the length of marriages made between 1841 and 1880. It is apparent that many did not last until the wife reached her fiftieth birthday because of the death of one of the partners in the marriage. Almost half of these marriages ended after less than twenty years, and a significant proportion did not last even five years. The mean length of a marriage made in 1841–60 was 20.28 years; for the second cohort, 1861–80, it was shorter, 16.0 years. With most women marrying in their middle or late twenties, many of them would have died or been widowed by their forty-fifth birthday.

The frequency with which marriages were broken by death and the

Table 12. Length of Marriage in Marlhes

| Length | Marriages 1841–1860 | | Marriages 1861–1880 | | Marriages 1841–1880 | |
|--------|------|------|------|------|------|------|
| (Years) | N | % | N | % | N | % |
| 0–4 | 22 | 17.0 | 11 | 15.3 | 33 | 16.4 |
| 5–9 | 13 | 10.1 | 12 | 16.7 | 25 | 12.4 |
| 10–14 | 19 | 14.7 | 8 | 11.2 | 27 | 13.4 |
| 15–19 | 19 | 14.7 | 17 | 23.6 | 36 | 17.9 |
| 20–24 | 11 | 8.5 | 7 | 9.7 | 18 | 8.9 |
| 25–29 | 11 | 8.5 | 10 | 13.9 | 21 | 10.4 |
| 30–34 | 9 | 7.1 | 6 | 8.3 | 15 | 7.6 |
| 35–39 | 13 | 10.1 | 1 | 1.3 | 14 | 7.0 |
| 40+ | 12 | 9.3 | 0 | 0.0 | 12 | 6.0 |
| Total | 129 | 100.0 | 72 | 100.0 | 201 | 100.0 |

Source: Family Reconstitution Type MF Families.

relatively short duration of many marriages made possible frequent re-marriages in nineteenth-century Marlhes. There were a significant number of these, with 17.5 percent of marriages between 1841 and 1870 and 14.6 percent of marriages between 1871 and 1898 involving a survivor of a previous marriage. This was, however, a significant reduction from the experience of eighteenth-century French villages. In Crulai 22.1 percent of marriages between 1674 and 1742 were second marriages for one or both of the partners. In the Ile-de-France 25.1 percent of marriages between 1740 and 1792 were second marriages. However, remarriages in Marlhes do reflect another characteristic of these Ancien Régime villages. In Crulai and the Ile-de-France during the eighteenth century, those remarrying were more frequently men than women. In Crulai 15.4 percent of marriages involved a widower, while only 6.9 percent involved a widow. In the Ile-de-France 21.5 percent of marriages involved a widower, only 7.7 percent a widow.[16] Similarly, in nineteenth-century Marlhes, men remarried more frequently than women. Between 1841 and 1870, 14.9 percent of marriages included a widower, while only 7.7 percent involved a widow. Between 1871 and 1898, the respective figures are 11.4 percent and 6.1 percent.

Nuptiality patterns in nineteenth-century Marlhes therefore conformed closely to those found in western European rural villages during the Ancien Régime and the nineteenth century. These patterns were characterized by late marriage and frequent permanent celibacy. During the half-century we have been able to observe nuptiality in Marlhes, there are few signs of impending change in this pattern of marriage behavior. The western European marriage pattern was followed by all members of the population in Marlhes, nonlanded as well as landowners, weavers and nonweavers. While landowning men married later than nonlanded men, both groups married relatively late. Women showed no significant differences in age at first marriage between landowners and nonlandowners. The numerical differences found in Marlhes between landed and nonlanded men should not lead to the conclusion that two types of behavior were present. In contrast to rural villages in eighteenth-century Belgium, England, and Switzerland, there was no division in the marriage patterns of the population of nineteenth-century Marlhes.

The fertility patterns of landed and nonlanded members of the population of nineteenth-century Marlhes also show general conformity to a single pattern of childbearing, characterized by low illegitimacy and prenuptial conception levels and high fertility within marriage, with no evidence of contraception within marriage. As with nuptiality, the fertility of nineteenth-century Marlhes more strongly resembled rural France under the Ancien Régime than in the twentieth century.

Only an approximate measure of illegitimate fertility, the ratio of illegitimate to all births, can be calculated for Marlhes in the nineteenth century. This index can be misleading, since it will vary with a change in legitimate fertility (a rise or fall in the number of legitimate births) as well as with a change in the number of illegitimate births. The number of these was so low throughout the nineteenth century in Marlhes, however, that there can be little doubt that illegitimacy was very low in the village. Between the last years of the July Monarchy and the Third Republic, when the annual number of births ranged between seventy and one hundred, most years saw only one or two illegitimate births. While the number of births per year declined in the last twenty years of the century, the number of illegitimate births also declined slightly from its already low level. The illegitimacy ratio for the period 1841–70 was 11.3 per thousand births. By 1871–1901, in spite of a reduction in the number of births, the illegitimacy ration had declined to 8.4 per thousand births.[17]

This low level of illegitimate births in Marlhes may be the result of the proximity of Saint-Etienne and the possibility that unmarried women from Marlhes who became pregnant went to Saint-Etienne to have their child. This seems doubtful; illegitimacy in Saint-Etienne was relatively low for a city of its size. In 1851 the illegitimacy ratio in Saint-Etienne was 121.4 per thousand births, lower than Paris, Bordeaux, or Lille in the same period. In the other industrial cities of the Stephanois valley the ratio was closer to that of Marlhes than to nineteenth-century urban levels.[18] Marlhes does not seem to have exported its illegitimate births to the cities of the region.

Nor were high illegitimacy rates prevented by the marriage of pregnant women. Prenuptial conceptions were remarkably low in the entire period studied: only 4 of 207 intervals between marriage and first birth in the families reconstituted for this study were shorter than eight months. For marriages between 1841 and 1860, the percentage of prenuptial conceptions to all first conceptions was 1.7 percent; for the second cohort of reconstituted marriages, those from 1861 to 1880, the percentage was higher, 2.1 percent. This was still very low. In Crulai in the seventeenth and eighteenth centuries, Etienne Gautier and Louis Henry found that 2.8 percent of first births were the result of prenuptial conceptions; in the Ile-de-France in the second half of the eighteenth century, Jean Ganiage found a higher level, 14.0 percent. In contrast, Marcel Lachiver found that nearly a quarter (24 percent) of first births in Meulan, a small city near Paris, were the result of prenuptial conceptions in the 1790–1839 period.[19] Marlhes clearly enjoyed a very low level of both illegitimate births and prenuptial conceptions.

The low levels of illegitimacy and prenuptial conceptions in Marlhes and the similar low illegitimacy ratios in the entire Stephanois region contrast sharply with the heavy industrial development, rapid urban growth, and widespread rural industry in the region. The disorienting effects of this development seem to have been mitigated by two overriding factors. A primary reason was the restricted geographical area of recruitment of those who migrated to the growing urban areas, and this was supplemented by the continuing strong Catholicity of the entire region, both rural and urban. The first will be discussed in more detail in the next chapter, but for the present we may note that migrants to both Marlhes and Saint-Etienne were predominantly drawn from the department of the Loire and the northern cantons of the Haute-Loire, within a distance of forty kilometers of Saint-Etienne. This restricted area of migration allowed the preservation of many bonds of family, acquaintance, and community and weakened the impact of the disruptive forces of industrial and urban development on traditional social obligations.[20]

The strong Catholicity of the Stephanois throughout the nineteenth century no doubt found strength in this restricted area of migration. This Catholicity was manifested at the beginning of the twentieth century when the region became a "Second Vendée" for the Radical Republican government in its campaign for the separation of church and state in France.[21] More to the point here, however, is the strict observance in Marlhes of the restrictions of the Catholic church on marriage during Lent and Advent throughout the nineteenth century.[22] This strong Catholicism appears also to have been reflected in strict adherence to Catholic proscriptions of premarital sexual intercourse. This is particularly apparent in the low levels of prenuptial conceptions: a strong community could force men to marry their pregnant girl friends, but in the absence of widespread contraception only a strict internalized morality could prevent prenuptial conceptions. Strong Catholicism was of course no guarantee against high illegitimacy in nineteenth-century Europe, but in Marlhes it fit well with restricted migration and the maintenance of some community control of extramarital sexual relations.

The low illegitimacy ratios and minimal number of prenuptial conceptions in nineteenth-century Marlhes stand in marked contrast to the high levels of marital fertility in each age group of women. For this study, age-specific marital fertility rates have been calculated from the reconstituted family histories of 253 marriages taking place in Marlhes between 1841 and 1880.[23] These reconstituted families provide information on both the number of children born in the marriage and the length of time in which the marriage existed in each age group. The rates of marital fertility calculated from this information are presented in table 13 and indicate clearly that a natural uncontrolled pattern of childbearing was the rule for the entire population in Marlhes.

The marital fertility rates presented in table 13 show little variation between the two marriage cohorts examined, those married between 1841 and 1860 and those married in the following twenty years, 1861 to 1880. The most striking feature of these fertility rates is their strength in later age groups, when the fertility of a modern population begins to decline as families reach their target size. In Marlhes, in contrast, fertility rates remain above .300 up to age forty, and rates for the forty to forty-four and forty-five to forty-nine age groups are still strong for the reduced fecundability of women in those age groups. The entire fertility

Table 13. Age-Specific Marital Fertility Rates for Marlhes

| Age Group | Marriages 1841–1860 | | Marriages 1861–1880 | | Marriages 1841–1880 | |
|---|---|---|---|---|---|---|
| 15–19 | .375 | (16)* | .207 | (13) | .311 | (29) |
| 20–24 | .454 | (71) | .412 | (63) | .433 | (134) |
| 25–29 | .392 | (99) | .396 | (83) | .394 | (182) |
| 30–34 | .341 | (104) | .356 | (91) | .348 | (195) |
| 35–39 | .304 | (98) | .311 | (87) | .307 | (185) |
| 40–44 | .174 | (85) | .188 | (72) | .180 | (157) |
| 45–49 | .026 | (77) | .022 | (51) | .025 | (128) |
| Descendants | | | | | | |
| 20–49 | 8.46 | | 8.42 | | 8.44 | |

*The number in parentheses refers to the number of observations on which the rate has been based.

Source: Family Reconstitution Type MF Families.

schedule for nineteenth-century Marlhes resembles that of Crulai in the seventeenth and eighteenth centuries, a population in which there was no strong evidence of family limitation. The fertility rates for Marlhes in the age groups above age thirty-five exceed those for Crulai, again reinforcing the conclusion that there was little family limitation practiced in nineteenth-century Marlhes. The division into two cohorts shows no progressive movement toward family limitation, as the rates for older age groups in the second, later cohort consistently exceed those of the first cohort until the final age group, when the difference is insignificant. Their similarity is most apparent in the almost identical number of children that would be born to a woman married at age twenty and married until age fifty: 8.46 for the first cohort, 8.42 for the second.

The entire population of Marlhes appears therefore to have shared a schedule of fertility that, if it did not reach the high level of eighteenth-century Canada, was consistent with that of northern France during the seventeenth and eighteenth centuries.[24] There were, however, differences of fertility within the population of Marlhes, although these do not appear to have been the result of any conscious effort to limit family size through the practice of contraceptive measures. This can be seen in the age-specific marital fertility rates presented in table 14 for landowners and nonlandowners in Marlhes. Both schedules show the strong fertility in later age groups characteristic of uncontrolled fertility, but the land-

Table 14. Age-Specific Marital Fertility Rates by Landholding, Reconstituted Marriages in Marlhes, 1841–1880

| Age Group | Property Owners | | Non–Property Owners | |
|---|---|---|---|---|
| 15–19 | .324 | (11)* | .300 | (18) |
| 20–24 | .506 | (49) | .381 | (85) |
| 25–29 | .428 | (60) | .376 | (122) |
| 30–34 | .388 | (66) | .328 | (129) |
| 35–39 | .352 | (63) | .284 | (122) |
| 40–44 | .197 | (60) | .169 | (97) |
| 45–49 | .017 | (51) | .030 | (77) |
| Descendants | | | | |
| 20–49 | 9.44 | | 7.84 | |

*The number in parentheses refers to the number of observations on which the rate has been based.

Source: Family Reconstitution Type MF Families; A.D.L. Série P Non-Coté, *Matrice cadastrale de la commune de Marlhes*.

owners show a level of fertility consistently higher than the nonland-owners. Only in the forty-five to forty-nine age group do landowners fall below the fertility level of nonlandowners. This decline does not seem to have been the result of widespread family limitation, for the rate for property owners was still higher than that for Crulai (.017 versus .010). This does not of course eliminate the possibility of conscious limitation by several landowning families, but for the group of landowners as a whole the pattern is clearly one of high uncontrolled fertility.

Differences in levels of marital fertility have been noticed before in both historical and modern populations not practicing conscious fertility control.[25] Most relevant to our interests here, significant differences have appeared between northern and southern France in the late seventeenth and eighteenth centuries.[26] The most detailed comparison of these results has failed to arrive at a definitive explanation for the differences: Louis Henry and Jacques Houdaille suggest three possible explanations in a comparison of the northwest and southwest quadrants of France but are unable to establish the definite influence of any one. These explanations are: the role of nursing, which may have acted to postpone the return of menstruation after childbirth and hence delayed exposure to conception; the influence of intrauterine mortality that could vary from one population to another and lengthen the birth intervals of a population with higher levels of intrauterine mortality; and the place of popular attitudes, especially toward sexual relations during nursing. All three of these are possible in populations in which the differences in fertility levels arise not because of efforts late in life to end childbearing but as a result of longer intervals between births throughout life.[27]

The explanations proposed by Henry and Houdaille are more credible for geographic differences between populations than for social differences within the same population, as in Marlhes, and no definitive explanation can be given here for the differing levels of fertility between landowning and landless families in that village. But the differences in Marlhes are consistent from one age group to the next, thus seeming to result from a pattern of longer spacing of children among the landless rather than an early ending of childbearing. We may therefore consider the applicability to Marlhes of these three explanations.

Evidence on the extent and practice of nursing in Marlhes, especially from one social group to another, is virtually nonexistent. What does exist may be drawn from the practice of mercenary wet-nursing in Marlhes, and in particular from an examination of the death records of the 327 nurslings who died in Marlhes between 1841 and 1900.[28] The practice of mercenary wet-nursing was primarily carried out among the poorer, landless members of the village community: 75 percent of the families nursing infants in that period held less than one hectare of land, and 94 percent held less than five hectares. This localization of wet-nursing among the families with little land—that is, those who show low levels of marital fertility—suggests this as an explanation for those low levels of fertility. Such does not, in fact, appear to have been the case. Both social groups show similar intervals after the birth of a child who died in the first year of life—20.6 months for landowners, 19.9 months for the landless—suggesting that nurslings did not replace natural children who died soon after birth among the poor, extending birth intervals. Rather, nurslings replaced natural children when they were weaned, some five to fifteen months after their birth. This was probably too late to influence the length of postpartum amenorrhea: clinical studies have emphasized that after six months of nursing, prolonged lactation loses its effect on the length of postpartum amenorrhea.[29] Thus, in Marlhes, the practice among the poor of mercenary wet-nursing is not a likely explanation for the longer birth intervals of this social group.

However, the evidence on weaning among the poor derived from the nurslings' experience suggests a possible influence on birth intervals in the village. The point at which nurslings were brought into the family, when the preceding natural child was aged between five and fifteen months, strongly suggests that this was the normal period of weaning for children in these families in Marlhes. With a mode of 10 months, a median of 11 months, and a mean of 12.15 months, this period of nursing was quite long for this period in Europe: the extended breast-feeding characteristic of Bavaria at this time only lasted about seven months.[30] It seems apparent, therefore, that among the landless in Marlhes breastfeeding lasted for a long period of time. While no evidence is available for the landholding families who did not take in nurslings in great numbers, they may have nursed their children for a shorter period of time, perhaps only several months, and possibly sent their children to be nursed in a poorer family. This could account for the shorter intervals of landowning families in Marlhes in the nineteenth century.

Consideration of both intrauterine mortality and attitudes toward sexual relations during nursing must also remain speculative in the absence of definitive local evidence. Certainly poorer peasants in Marlhes were less well fed than landowners, and as a result of poorer nutrition their wives may have been more susceptible to early miscarriages that went unrecorded and so cannot be evaluated. If nutrition did play a part in the fertility patterns of families in Marlhes, it is more likely that it did so in this way than through an "amenorrhea of famine," which would require a severe and sudden shortage of food.[31]

Little evidence exists for Marlhes on the attitudes of different social groups toward sexual relations during nursing or other aspects of sexual behavior in the village. The existence of such taboos has been shown for France, but it is impossible to attribute them to a particular social group.[32] Published popular songs from the Stephanois region in the nineteenth century make no mention of such taboos, nor do any folklorists' accounts of the region.[33] This does not mean, of course, that these taboos did not exist; but we cannot invoke them to explain the differences in levels of marital fertility between landowners and nonlandowners in the village.

The marital fertility rates for Marlhes therefore suggest two somewhat contradictory conclusions. In the first place, there was little, if any, conscious limitation of births in Marlhes even among women married in the first years of the Third Republic. Marlhes appears unusual in a country where evidence of contraception has been found at the end of the eighteenth century and marital fertility had significantly declined by the first half of the nineteenth century. It was, in fact, unusual in the Loire, where marital fertility had declined significantly by 1891. Second, while Marlhes seems to reflect a fertility schedule that was natural in that it shows no conscious limitation of births, it does show birth spacing variation between socioeconomic groups. Landowners, a group frequently found leading the adoption of family limitation,[34] showed significantly higher rates of marital fertility, and thus shorter intervals, than did nonlandowners. No definitive explanation for these differences can be given at this time, although early weaning among landowners and higher intrauterine mortality among nonlandowners may have played roles.

The variation in marital fertility between social groups in Marlhes suggests a fact increasingly apparent to historical demographers, that a wide range of variations in fertility levels was possible in pre-Malthusian populations. It is clear that the absence of conscious family limitation in a population does not predict the level of marital fertility. Differences may in fact be very large. The high levels of marital fertility found in eighteenth-century Canada would produce 10.8 children if a woman was married for the entire period from age twenty to age fifty. In Crulai, in contrast, the total would be much lower, 8.2 children, a difference of more than 2.5 children over that thirty-year period. In a village in southern France in the eighteenth century an even lower figure, 6.52 children, is found. Yet these populations show no signs of conscious family limitation.[35] The variation in Marlhes was smaller: landowners would have a total of 9.4 children, nonlandowners 7.8. This is a difference of less than two children during thirty years of fertility experience. These differences within a natural fertility population indicate not the presence of a minority practicing family limitation, but only the variations of natural fertility possible under different nutritional, nursing, and cultural conditions.

The fertility rates presented here may be combined with mortality data from the previous chapter to calculate generational mea-

sures that provide insight into the reproductivity of the Marlhes population. A total fertility rate, expressing the influence of these marital fertility
rates as well as the role of celibacy and widowhood in determining the
married female population, has been calculated for each listing of the
marital status and age distribution of women.[36] This rate is 4.13 in
1851, implying that the average family should have 4.13 children, and a
higher 5.01 in 1901.[37]

With total fertility rates calculated it is possible to compute two further,
more exact measures of reproductivity, the Gross Reproduction Rate
(*GRR*) and the Net Reproduction Rate (*NRR*), as well as an intrinsic
growth rate. The *GRR* is a particular case of the total fertility rate,
measuring the number of daughters a cohort of women will have. It is
calculated by multiplying the total fertility rate by the proportion of
female births, here assumed to be 100 women in 205 births. The *GRR*s
for Marlhes are therefore 2.014 in 1851 and 2.445 in 1901. It should be
emphasized that these are only estimates, based on an assumed sex ratio.
For the purposes of this study, however, this method provides an adequate estimate of the *GRR*.

The Gross Reproduction Rate, while a more exact measure of reproductivity than the total fertility rate, is still a mortality-free measure. It
gauges the reproductivity of the female population, the group most important in the reproductivity of the entire population, but does not take
into account the mortality of a cohort of women during their lifetimes
and the probabilities of their reaching and living through their childbearing years. The Net Reproduction Rate adds these probabilities to the
equation.[38] Using mortality values from the life tables for Marlhes in
1851 and 1901 presented in chapter 4, we obtain an *NRR* of 1.2005 in
1851 and 1.4428 in 1901. The intrinsic growth rates (Lotka's *r*) for these
Net Reproduction Rates and a mean age at childbearing of thirty are .61
percent and 1.22 percent, respectively.

The population of Marlhes was therefore growing at the middle of the
nineteenth century, and this growth accelerated as the century wore on
and improvements were made in mortality. The *NRR* for Marlhes of
1.20 at mid-century is slightly higher than those Bourgeois-Pichat has
estimated for France since the eighteenth century. He calculated an *NRR*
of between 1.08 and 1.15 in the late eighteenth century; this declined
slightly in the first half of the nineteenth century, with a maximum of
1.12 between 1806 and 1815 and a minimum of 1.00 in 1851–55. The
decline continued during the second half of the century, falling below
unity in 1856–60 and again after 1891. Only in the 1950s, during the
population boom after World War II, did the *NRR* for France rise again,
reaching 1.32.[39] During the entire period under study, therefore, the
population of Marlhes was growing faster than that of eighteenth- or

nineteenth-century France. At the end of the nineteenth century the difference was increasing as the growth of the French population decreased and that of Marlhes increased.

France is of course a country known for its low rate of growth. Thus it is interesting to compare Marlhes with the experience of Great Britain, a country known for its rapid population growth and one that has served as a model for most theories of population development during industrialization. The best data on the English experience may be found in a recent article by David Levine on Shepshed, a parish in Leicestershire. Levine estimates that during the seventeenth century Shepshed had an NRR of 1.10, below that of Marlhes in the nineteenth century, and an intrinsic growth rate of 0.28 percent, again below that of Marlhes. The eighteenth century, however, was a period of industrial development in Shepshed, and its reproductivity rates increased greatly. In 1700–1749 the NRR was 1.12 and the annual growth rate 0.39 percent; in 1750–1824 it peaked at an NRR of 1.74 and a growth rate of 1.74 percent before declining slightly to an NRR of 1.57 and a growth rate of 1.61 percent in 1825–51.[40] Clearly the mid-nineteenth-century growth of Marlhes more closely resembled that of Shepshed during the late eighteenth and nineteenth centuries, when industrial development came to Shepshed in the form of domestic weaving, than the earlier period. The population of Marlhes was growing at a rate similar to an English village during the industrial revolution, in sharp contrast to the slow growth typical of eighteenth- and nineteenth-century France.

A model of reproductive behavior frequently employed by students of peasant societies assumes that the reproductive goal of the population is replacement from generation to generation without significant population growth. Mortality and total fertility are assumed to be in a homeostatic relationship, with variations in mortality being matched by changes in total fertility. Marriage plays an important part in this adjustment process, as high mortality leads to younger marriage and declines in mortality are compensated by later marriage and lower total fertility. The high fertility of predemographic transition marriages was therefore only a compensation for equally high rates of mortality: it was necessary for a family to have many children in order to replace itself in the next generation. The spread of family limitation is also seen as an adjustment to the lower rates of mortality characteristic of demographic transition. The preservation of the homeostatic relationship between mortality and total fertility through either delayed marriage or family limitation was encouraged by the desire among peasants to preserve the integrity of their holdings into the next generation, possible only in the absence of multiple heirs.[41]

The replacement hypothesis suggests a part of the explanation for the fertility and nuptiality patterns in Marlhes, but only a part. Marlhes was far above this level, growing at a rate close to that of eighteenth-century England and with its rate of growth increasing as the nineteenth century came to a close. This fits poorly with a replacement hypothesis of reproductive behavior by the peasants in Marlhes. If, for example, Jacques Courbon and Catherine Riocreux had wished to conserve their land into the next generation, they would certainly have wished to have fewer than the thirteen children they did have. And, most certainly, they would have attempted to prevent births in their later years, after they had already had six or seven children and the reproduction of their family was assured. Instead, their high fertility continued until almost the end of their marriage. Three of their children were born after Catherine passed her fortieth birthday, suggesting that there was no attempt at family limitation. Indeed, as we have seen in this chapter, those with the most to gain by family limitation—landowners—showed even higher fertility levels in marriage than those without land. The reproductive experience of Marlhes bears little relation to that expected from the replacement model.

The experience of Marlhes also differs from that of other rural populations feeling the impact of rural industrialization. The populations studied by David Levine and Franklin Mendels in England and Belgium increased their growth rates primarily through changes in nuptiality, as the availability of industrial work as an alternative to agriculture lowered ages at marriage and increased the length of wives' childbearing. In contrast, in Marlhes the ages at marriage of both men and women remained elevated, and there were no significant differences in age at first marriage between women in landowning families and those in poorer, landless families. The growth of the population of Marlhes was due, rather, to the mortality levels in the population, and the increased rate of growth in the second half of the nineteenth century was the result not of lowered age at marriage or more frequent marriage, but of a slight mortality decline, allowing more children to reach adulthood and marry. This decreased mortality did not find a counteracting response in either nuptiality or marital fertility, and the result was population growth entirely untypical of nineteenth-century France.

How then are we to explain the high reproductivity of the population of Marlhes? One solution is that the peasants of Marlhes simply did not know about contraception. This is hard to credit, in spite of the strong Catholicism of the region. The peasantry of Marlhes was highly literate even in the 1840s.[42] The economy of the region encouraged not only the flow of goods but also of people and information. Further, the traditional method of restricted marriage remained available as a last resort to discourage population growth. It is difficult to believe that this population, in the second half of the nineteenth century, was not aware of the means of limiting the size of their families.

It is then a question of explaining their failure to use this knowledge to limit family size. The strong Catholicism of the Stephanois region may have discouraged its use, just as it seems to have discouraged illegitimacy and prenuptial conceptions, and this certainly must be a part of the explanation. Far better, however, is an explanation that focuses on a strategic family size, just as most explanations of the use of family limitation by peasants do. The replacement hypothesis is one aspect of this logic of strategic family sizes, but it usually considers only the interaction of mortality and fertility, assuming a closed peasant community and a stagnant rural economy that cannot employ the additional members in each generation of a growing population. Obviously, using such assumptions we must assume that the goal of each family was only replacement and no growth. Yet in the Stephanois region during the nineteenth century these assumptions were far from true. It is important to consider the peasants of Marlhes in the context of a regional economy rather than the economies of individual peasant farms. The Stephanois economy was not stagnant; it was growing under the impetus of the industrial expansion of Saint-Etienne and the other cities of the industrial valley. While this stood in sharp contrast to the lessening opportunities for industrial work in the countryside during the second half of the nineteenth century, these expanding industries in the valley provided ample opportunity for children of the rural villages in the region around the industrial area. There was no reason in nineteenth-century Marlhes for a family strategy aimed only at replacement. Even within the logic of the replacement argument, we should not expect the peasants of Marlhes to be attempting to limit the sizes of their families.

The failure of nineteenth-century peasants in Marlhes to limit their family size therefore draws attention to the importance of the regional economy in explaining the reproductive behavior of peasants. In Marlhes the rapid expansion of the nearby urban economy provided opportunities for many children, even if they could not all be established on the family farm as adults. This expansion of opportunity is one of the central features of a developing economy, and must be appreciated not only for its impact on the urban population but also for the way it influences the behavior of nearby rural populations. The slow growth of the economy in other regions of France may have encouraged the adoption of family limitation in some peasant families by restricting nonagricultural opportunities. In Marlhes, however, the developing Stephanois economy complemented the traditional reproductive behavior of the population within marriage. The two supported each other, with the developing economy providing oppportunities for the growing rural population and the high fertility of the rural villages providing the labor force for the expanding industrial economy. The high marital fertility of nineteenth-century Marlhes and the absence of family limitation was not an atavism; rather, it was an adaptation of traditional reproductive behavior to the new opportunities provided by the developing Stephanois economy.

# Chapter 6
# The Framework of Family Life: Migration

The final demographic factor important to family behavior in Marlhes was migration into and out of the commune. This was very heavy throughout the nineteenth century: Saint-Etienne and the other cities of the industrial valley grew with the help of substantial migration, and these migrants were largely recruited from the arrondissement of Saint-Etienne and the border cantons of the Haute-Loire to the south.[1] Marlhes served two functions in this migration process. First, it was a temporary stopping point for those working their way towards the cities; second, it supplied a large contingent of native sons and daughters to the growing industrial population in the valley below.[2]

For this study of the family system in nineteenth-century Marlhes, the heavy migration into and out of the rural community suggests two problems for examination. First, this movement took place at definable moments in the individual's life cycle and to some extent determined the relationship of the individual to his or her families of origin or procreation. This question considers the impact of migration on the family system. The second approach reverses the roles of migration and family behavior and considers the ways family patterns determined the patterns of migration that existed in the Stephanois region.

Migration into Marlhes during the nineteenth century was an important source of the rural population, although the area of recruitment was limited. These conclusions are apparent from two independent sources, the 1881 census listing and acts of marriages celebrated in Marlhes, each of which provides the place of birth of the individual. Tabulations of these data are presented in tables 15 and 16. The census list indicates that almost 30 percent of the population in 1881 was not born in Marlhes. The marriage acts show higher percentages of non-natives, with about two-fifths of those married not being born in the commune. The two marriage cohorts in table 16 do not show significant variation during the entire period, suggesting a relatively consistent pattern of migration at marriage throughout the entire period under consideration. This movement was as important for women as for men. Moreover, marriage was probably an important cause of migration

**Table 15.** Place of Birth of Population of Marlhes
in 1881

|  | N | % |
|---|---|---|
| Marlhes | 1,405 | 70.4 |
| Canton of Saint-Genest | | |
|    Saint-Genest-Malifaux | 71 | 3.6 |
|    Jonzieux | 69 | 3.5 |
|    Planfoy | 1 | 0.1 |
|    Saint-Romain | 5 | 0.3 |
|    Saint-Regis | 10 | 0.5 |
|    Tarantaize | 9 | 0.5 |
|    Total | 165 | 8.5 |
| Other Department of Loire | 87 | 4.6 |
| Haute-Loire | 323 | 16.1 |
| Rhône | 1 | 0.1 |
| Puy-de-Dôme | 2 | 0.1 |
| Ardèche | 9 | 0.5 |
| Paris | 1 | 0.1 |
| Foreign (Switzerland) | 3 | 0.2 |
| Total | 1,996 | 100.0 |

Source: A.D.L. 49 M 260, *Liste nominative de recensement de
la commune de Marlhes*, 1881.

into the commune: out of 852 marriages in the commune between 1841
and 1898, 393 (46.1 percent) involved a bride or groom not living in
Marlhes.[3] The proportion of permanent migrants was probably not this
high, since some would return to their native commune with their spouse
after the ceremony, but the formation of a new family appears to have
been an important part of the migratory process in the mountain region.

Marlhes was therefore far from being a self-contained unit. An important part of its population came from beyond its borders. The area of
recruitment for this immigrant population was not large, however. Many
of the non-natives were born in surrounding communes of the same
canton: 8.5 percent of the residents in 1881 were born in one of the other
six communes of the canton of Saint-Genest-Malifaux (see table 15). A
large part of the mobility in the region was therefore localized, with
individuals moving across administrative borders but not moving great
distances. The two communes that bordered on Marlhes, Saint-Genest-
Malifaux and Jonzieux, provided most of this contingent; 140 out of
165 persons. The ties of kinship and intermarriage existing in the can-

**Table 16.** Place of Birth of Men and Women Married in Marlhes

| | 1841–1870 | | | | 1871–1898 | | | |
| | Males | | Females | | Males | | Females | |
| | N | % | N | % | N | % | N | % |
|---|---|---|---|---|---|---|---|---|
| Marlhes | 300 | 59.5 | 298 | 59.7 | 216 | 63.7 | 203 | 59.3 |
| Canton of Saint-Genest | | | | | | | | |
| Saint-Genest | 24 | 4.8 | 33 | 6.6 | 9 | 2.6 | 12 | 3.5 |
| Jonzieux | 10 | 2.0 | 21 | 4.2 | 9 | 2.6 | 18 | 5.3 |
| Planfoy | 0 | 0.0 | 0 | 0.0 | 0 | 0.0 | 0 | 0.0 |
| Saint-Romain | 2 | 0.4 | 4 | 1.0 | 0 | 0.0 | 0 | 0.0 |
| Saint-Regis | 0 | 0.0 | 0 | 0.0 | 3 | 1.0 | 7 | 2.0 |
| Tarantaize | 2 | 0.4 | 2 | 0.5 | 0 | 0.0 | 3 | 1.0 |
| Total | 38 | 7.5 | 60 | 12.0 | 21 | 6.2 | 40 | 11.8 |
| Other Loire | 26 | 5.2 | 31 | 6.2 | 20 | 5.9 | 17 | 5.0 |
| Haute-Loire | 135 | 26.7 | 107 | 21.4 | 76 | 22.4 | 77 | 22.5 |
| Puy-de-Dôme | 2 | 0.4 | 0 | 0.0 | 0 | 0.0 | 0 | 0.0 |
| Ardèche | 1 | 0.2 | 2 | 0.5 | 3 | 1.0 | 3 | 1.0 |
| Cantal | 1 | 0.2 | 0 | 0.0 | 1 | 0.3 | 0 | 0.0 |
| Rhône | 0 | 0.0 | 1 | 0.2 | 1 | 0.3 | 1 | 0.3 |
| Creuse | 0 | 0.0 | 0 | 0.0 | 1 | 0.3 | 1 | 0.3 |
| Foreign (Italy) | 1 | 0.2 | 0 | 0.0 | 0 | 0.0 | 0 | 0.0 |
| Total | 504 | 100.0 | 499 | 100.0 | 339 | 100.0 | 342 | 100.0 |

Source: A.C. de Marlhes, *Registres des actes de mariages*, 1841–98.

ton encouraged this, and much of this migration was due to marriages crossing borders of the commune but not those of the canton.

A smaller group was also drawn from the other communes of the arrondissement of Saint-Etienne, totalling 3.4 percent of the population in 1881. Two cantons provided much of this group: Bourg-Argental, a canton east of Marlhes, with similar economic and social structure; and Saint-Etienne itself. This last pattern is important to note because it suggests a small flow (35 people, 1.8 percent of the population) running against the main stream of rural-urban migration. As with other types of migration, marriage was the principal event causing this movement of population, and it was encouraged by the numerous contacts between rural and urban populations that the Stephanois region and its urban-oriented economy afforded.

But the principal direction of the migration revealed in the census list was toward Saint-Etienne and the industrial-urban valley. This is indicated by the high number of individuals born in the Haute-Loire. More than half of the non-native population (16.1 percent of the total population) came from the Haute-Loire, most of them from the arrondissement of Yssingeaux directly across the southern border of Marlhes in the Haute-Loire. The important contribution of the Haute-Loire in the formation of the population of Saint-Etienne that Jean Merley has noted appears to have been more complex than a long walk from the mountainous area south of the Loire border to the industrial center.[4] Raw totals from marriage records in Saint-Etienne and net migration rates for communes in the Haute-Loire mask the stages of the process: it was a slow movement involving several moves from communes forty kilometers away from the city to closer rural communes, such as Marlhes, and finally down the slope to the industrial city. The communes on the periphery of the industrial valley served as temporary stopping points in this multistage migration. The stopover may have lasted for several years or for a lifetime, with the migration being taken up again by the next generation.

The patterns visible in the census data are generally confirmed by the information contained in acts of marriage, displayed in table 16 in two cohorts, those married between 1841 and 1870 and those married between 1871 and 1898. Migration from other communes in the canton of Saint-Genest is virtually identical in the two sets of records, with 8 to 10 percent of the census list and those married drawn from these other communes. In the marriage acts, as in the census, Saint-Genest and Jonzieux provide the bulk of these immigrants. One aspect that should be noted is the significant difference between men and women in this line of table 16. Women in both cohorts were more likely than men to come from a neighboring commune. Other cantons in the arrondissement of Saint-Etienne contributed about 5 percent of the census populations as well as of the total married.

Nevertheless, the evidence from the marriage acts suggests an evolution over time in this flow of immigrants. In the earlier cohort, as in the census data, the most important contributor outside of the canton of Saint-Genest was the neighboring rural, mountainous canton of Bourg-Argental (78 percent of those from the arrondissement). By the last quarter of the century this had declined sharply, to 40 percent of those from the arrondissement. At the same time the importance of urban-rural migration, especially from the two cantons of Saint-Etienne, the heart of the industrial region, sharply increased. In the first cohort of marriages, Saint-Etienne contributed 11 percent of those from the arrondissement; in the second, this had risen to 47 percent and was the most important point of origin for those from the arrondissement. Thus the movement out of the urban area into the countryside seems to have grown in importance as the century progressed. It was a minor pattern throughout the period, however, and the increase must be seen in the context of the very small number of individuals—less than twenty over a period of twenty-eight years—that this counterflow of migrants included.

In the marriage acts as in the census, the single most important source of migrants to Marlhes was the nearby department of the Haute-Loire. More than one-fifth of those married were born in that department. This is slightly greater than in the census list, but the two sources are not contradictory: the census figures for nonnatives were probably diluted by the presence of children born in Marlhes to non-native parents. There does not seem to have been any significant alteration in this pattern over time, as the proportions from the first marriage cohort are closely matched by the second.

Finally, each source indicates a small number of individuals from other departments of France. The Ardèche, southeast of Marlhes, was the most important. With the exception of migrants from Paris and a few foreign born, the remainder of the population came from other departments bordering on the Loire, reflecting the geographical position of Marlhes between the Auvergne and the Lyonnais.

The area of recruitment for the population of Marlhes therefore suggests a limited but not closed rural community. If a significant proportion of the population was not native born, the origins of these newcomers argues that their movement was the result of traditional regional patterns of migration whose limits were defined by means of transport, lines of communication, and the regional economy in which Marlhes participated. The passage of travelers, carters, and those in search of work provided the peasant with contact with the cities of the valley as well as the rural hinterland to the south, as far as Yssingeaux to the southwest and Annonay in the southeast. His contact with these regions was strengthened by ties of family to other communes within this region. This large area, extending some forty kilometers from the urban valley, was the community in which the peasants of Marlhes lived, worked, and traded their goods.

In spite of the substantial proportion of the population not born in Marlhes and the high fertility rates in the commune, the population of the commune declined during the second half of the nineteenth century. The population in 1861, the year of the first census after the division of the commune, was 2,246; by 1901 that figure had declined to 1,848.[5] The reason for this decline was the substantial migration of residents from Marlhes. Between 1841 and 1851, the commune showed a net outmigration rate of 16.3 persons per year; later in the century, between 1881 and 1891, this rose to 25 per year.[6]

The extent of this migration is less important for the purposes of this study than its incidence among different groups in the rural population. We need to know at what ages individuals migrated, what occupational groups contributed most to the migration, and what the relationship of different types of family structure to out-migration was. In order to answer these questions, all individuals listed in the 1851 and 1901 census lists for Marlhes have been traced to the next available census, 1856 and 1911 respectively. The results of this tracing have been used to calculate annual rates of emigration per thousand by age, occupation, and family structure.[7]

Examination of emigration rates by age group (table 17) suggests two initial judgments on the migration process in Marlhes. In both parts of the table it is evident that rates of out-migration tended to decrease with increased age. The only exceptions to the steady decline are slight increases between the forty-five to fifty-four and the fifty-five to sixty-four age groups in both 1851–56 and 1901–11. The decreases with age in both rows of the table are not steady but become particularly sharp after the twenty-five to thirty-four age group.

At the same time there is a contrast visible between the two rows of the table: the population was less mobile at the end of the period than at its beginning. The initial level of the 1901–11 rates is lower than in the earlier period, and the decline with age sharper. The patterns of out-migration in 1901–11, while conforming to the same general pattern of decline with increased age as in 1851–56, suggest a less volatile population. The increased stability was linked to a particular section of the population, however. Young adults and children remained very mobile even at the end of the nineteenth century, and it is only in the middle and upper age groups, over the age of thirty-five, that the decrease is clearly visible. The higher rate in 1901–11 for those over sixty-five slightly alters this pattern, but is still very low.

Both characteristics of migration patterns in Marlhes seem closely related to the life cycle of individuals. Youth was a period of high mobility, probably resulting from the combination of the high fertility of the rural population creating competition among children for the scarce economic resources of their families, and the opportunities for employment outside

Table 17. Estimated Rates of Out-Migration per Thousand, Population of Marlhes

| | Age Group | | | | | |
|---|---|---|---|---|---|---|
| | 0–24 | 25–34 | 35–44 | 45–54 | 55–64 | 65+ |
| 1851–56 | 74.7 | 57.0 | 32.9 | 23.3 | 32.9 | 0.0 |
| 1901–11 | 48.1 | 47.5 | 30.1 | 22.6 | 24.9 | 6.5 |

Source: A.D.L. 49 M 85, 49 M 113, 49 M 353, 49 M 387, *Listes nominatives de recensement de la commune de Marlhes*, 1851, 1856, 1901, 1911.

Marlhes, especially in the industrializing valley. Increased age brought greater stability throughout the period under examination. In both periods, however, even the older age groups showed significant rates of emigration, suggesting that this was a way of life, not an unusual event limited to youth. The vitality of the developing economy of the industrial valley in this period as well as the numerous contacts between Marlhes and other rural communities of the Stephanois region stimulated the continuous mobility of the population.

The events of marriage and widowhood were important in determining migration rates at both the middle and the end of the nineteenth century (see table 18). Both periods exhibit a pattern of heavy out-migration among single men and women, especially in the young age groups, which contrasts sharply with the reduced mobility of married men and women. With the exception of the thirty-five to forty-four age group in 1851–56, in which there were few widowers, and older groups with few single men, the rates for both single men and women always exceed those for married men and women. At times the differences are very great; this is particularly true in older age groups, for the rates for married men and women tend to decline sooner and more sharply than those for single

**Table 18.** Estimated Rates of Out-Migration per Thousand by Sex and Marital Status in Marlhes

| | Age Group | | | | | |
|---|---|---|---|---|---|---|
| | 0–24 | 25–34 | 35–44 | 45–54 | 55–64 | 65+ |
| **1851–1856** | | | | | | |
| Single males | 83.5 | 72.9 | 51.7 | 75.1 | 9.0* | 0.0* |
| Married males | 60.5* | 57.9 | 33.4 | 5.0 | 14.4 | 0.0 |
| Widowers | 93.8* | 88.4* | 25.0* | 44.2 | 20.5 | 46.4 |
| Single females | 67.7 | 65.7 | 43.5 | 53.8 | 49.9 | 33.0 |
| Married females | 63.4 | 38.9 | 26.2 | 15.7 | 37.4 | 0.0 |
| Widows | 93.8* | 38.4* | 45.0 | 46.1 | 69.3 | 1.8 |
| **1901–1911** | | | | | | |
| Single males | 45.7 | 48.3 | 50.5 | 66.8* | 41.0* | 21.8* |
| Married males | 92.1* | 39.1 | 26.0 | 9.4 | 11.0 | 0.0 |
| Widowers | — | — | — | 56.1* | 16.0* | 7.5* |
| Single females | 53.4 | 67.2 | 76.2* | 14.4* | 41.0* | 21.8* |
| Married females | 52.1 | 39.7 | 12.0 | 12.9 | 11.7 | 11.4 |
| Widows | — | 91.0* | 57.2* | 6.1* | 47.8 | 15.9 |

*Rate based on fewer than ten cases.

Source: See table 17.

men and women. The decline in mobility with increased age was reinforced by the stabilizing effects of marriage and the increased proportions of the male and female populations that were married in older age
groups. Both in the middle of the nineteenth century and at its end, the
declining mobility of older persons was to a large extent the result of
their movement from single to married civil status.

The death of a spouse, in contrast, meant less stability and the effect of
marriage as a factor reducing migration rates was partially counteracted
by higher rates among widowed persons in most age groups. The effect
of the loss of a spouse seems clear from both parts of table 18 in spite of
its haphazard impact on the age structure of migration. Especially in the
middle age groups, between the ages of thirty-five and fifty-four, the loss
of a spouse meant a sharp increase in mobility. This is true for both men
and women but is especially strong among women. In 1851–56, beginning at age thirty-five, migration rates for widows are double or quin-
tuple the rates for married women. The patterns are more erratic at the
end of the century but follow the same trend. The decline of migration
rates with age apparent in the total rates for 1851–56 and 1901–11
(table 17) seems at least partially due to differential rates for sex and civil
status and the changing proportions of the population in different civil
statuses.

The overall reduction in mobility between the middle and the end
of the century was to a large extent influenced by lower rates among
two groups, single and widowed women. The reductions at the end of
the century were particularly noticeable at older ages when single and
widowed women were far less mobile than they had been fifty years
before. Among single women the rate for the forty-five to fifty-four age
group in 1851–56 was 53.8; fifty years later it had fallen to 14.4. The
reductions in the groups over age forty-five also occurred among widows.
The forty-five to fifty-four age group is particularly notable, declining
from 46.1 to 6.1 in fifty years.

In contrast to this sharp descent of migration rates among single and
widowed women, rates for men either increased or declined only slightly
in the fifty-year period. The group showing the most noticeable increase
was that of single men over the age of fifty-five, an age group in which
most men were either married or widowed. The rates for older widowers
were erratic from one age group to the next in both parts of the table,
probably because of the small numerical bases of these rates. While there
is some diminution visible in these rates between the middle and the end
of the century, there is also an increase (from 44.2 to 56.1 in the forty-
five to fifty-four age group) that begins to balance the decline. If there
was a decline in the mobility of older widowers, it was not of the same
magnitude as the change in mobility of widows. The stabilization of the
population in Marlhes noticeable at the end of the period was therefore

the result of a sharp decrease in the emigration rates of single and widowed women in older age groups, declines so sharp that in most age groups they more than counterbalanced the increased emigration rates among men.

The foregoing analysis has established the importance of viewing the decision to migrate in the context of the individual life cycle. Increasing age, marriage, and the death of a spouse exerted great influence on this decision. The decision was also influenced by the structure of the rural economy and the intersection of the individual life cycle with the opportunities afforded by this economy. In Marlhes the economic context of the decision to migrate changed in important ways between the middle and the end of the nineteenth century. These changes affected both the absolute level of migration rates and the pattern of migration during the individual life cycle.

Migration rates by occupational group are presented in table 19. There is a consistent decrease in the mobility of agricultural workers in Marlhes between the middle and the end of the nineteenth century. With the exception of those over sixty-five, each age group shows a lower rate in 1901–11 than in 1851–56, with rates five to thirty per thousand lower in the later period. The overriding explanation for this decline must be the increased viability of agriculture in the region in the second half of

Table 19. Estimated Rates of Out-Migration per Thousand by Occupational Group in Marlhes

| | Age Group | | | | | |
|---|---|---|---|---|---|---|
| | 0–24 | 25–34 | 35–44 | 45–54 | 55–64 | 65+ |
| **1851–1856** | | | | | | |
| Agriculture | 87.3 | 55.8 | 28.7 | 26.5 | 30.1 | 0.0 |
| Forestry | 0.0* | 55.0* | 45.0 | 0.0* | 0.0* | 0.0* |
| Ribbonweaving | 75.6 | 46.8 | 30.8 | 8.5 | 25.6 | 0.0* |
| Liberal professions and artisans | 112.3 | 84.5 | 53.1 | 31.7 | 32.7 | 13.3 |
| **1901–1911** | | | | | | |
| Agriculture | 57.4 | 39.2 | 21.3 | 17.8 | 23.0 | 5.5 |
| Forestry | 42.1* | 28.5* | 40.5* | 0.0* | 0.0* | 21.8* |
| Ribbonweaving | 65.8 | 66.0 | 68.3* | 58.0 | 43.8* | 9.3* |
| Liberal professions and artisans | 58.8 | 68.5 | 49.5 | 27.2 | 13.1 | 0.0 |

*Rate based on fewer than ten cases.

Source: See table 17.

the nineteenth century as the urban market for dairy products developed and became accessible to rural agricultural products.

Both forestry and the artisanal and shopkeeping professions show similar patterns in 1851–56 and 1901–11. The rates given for these occupational groups must be considered only very rough approximations because they are based on very small numbers of individuals.[8] The only difference in rates between the two periods that may be accepted with confidence is the decline in the two oldest age groups of emigration rates for those in shopkeeping and artisanal professions. These lower rates are a part of the long-term decline in mobility among older individuals in the more market-oriented economy of late nineteenth-century Marlhes.

The remaining occupational group, ribbonweaving, exhibits significant changes between 1851–56 and 1901–11 in its members' migration patterns. While rates for the first age group, below age twenty-five, are very similar, over the fifty-year period the older age groups in ribbonweaving show more clearly the changing role of ribbonweaving in migration. Rates for those aged between thirty-five and fifty-four more than doubled between mid-century and the end of the period. Further, while in 1851–56 ribbonweaving was clearly a strong factor reducing migration among the three oldest age groups, in 1901–11 those aged forty-five to fifty-four showed a very high out-migration rate (58.0 per thousand) and those aged fifty-five to sixty-four also showed substantial out-migration (43.8 per thousand). Only in the oldest age group, of those over sixty-five, did the rate drop close to the low level characteristic of 1851–56. This high mobility of older people suggests the inability of the declining trade to support either the female population that depended on it at mid-century or the growing number of skilled *passementiers* who came to Marlhes at the end of the nineteenth century.

A contradiction appears when these figures showing increased mobility among ribbonweavers in late nineteenth-century Marlhes are compared with those presented above indicating that one of the most significant parts of the overall decline in mobility in Marlhes by the end of the nineteenth century was the very sharp reduction of migration rates among single and widowed women, especially in older age groups. At mid-century the principal support for these groups was the domestic industry of ribbonweaving. The changes in recruitment to weaving that accompanied its transformation from domestic to factory organization made it difficult for older women to participate in the trade. Indeed, it is precisely in these groups that the increase in migration among weavers is most noticeable. How can we explain the decline in migration among those most likely to seek support through work in the weaving trade?

The solution lies in the changing structure of women's work in nineteenth-century Marlhes. Between 1851 and 1901 the importance of weaving declined dramatically, while at the same time agriculture improved and dairy farming became more important. This type of agriculture drew more heavily on women for its work force than did the mixed agriculture of the middle of the century. The result was a shift in the weight of women in the work force from their preponderant and near-universal participation in domestic weaving at mid-century to the agricultural sector, preparing dairy products for the market. Thus in 1901–11 most women appear not in the ribbonweaving line of the lower half of table 19, but in the agricultural occupational group, where out-migration rates were significantly lower in 1901–11 than in 1851–56.

The significant changes that occurred in the migration rates of different occupational groups in Marlhes during the second half of the nineteenth century were therefore largely limited to the two major sectors of the traditional economy, agriculture and ribbonweaving. The increased viability of the former, the result of a half-century of development of dairy agriculture for the urban market, resulted in much lower rates for that group at the end of the century. The impact of this on overall migration patterns was increased by the growing specialization of the rural economy in agricultural production. The decline of ribbonweaving as well as its change from a domestic to a factory trade led to much higher migration rates for the reduced number of individuals who worked in the trade in 1901.

To this point migration has been considered as an individual decision, with the line of causation running directly from the economic situation of the individual to the decision to remain in Marlhes or to emigrate. Such a model oversimplifies the relationship between economic status and migration by ignoring the tissue of social relations whose presence or absence may mediate the effects of economic status on migration. In a rural society such as Marlhes it seems especially important to consider the possible mediating influences of family relations and structure on the decision to migrate.

Age-specific out-migration rates for each type of family structure have been calculated for 1851–56 and 1901–11 and are presented in table 20. These data suggest that family structure was an important determinant of migration levels during the life cycle.[9] The rates for members of nuclear families in both 1851 and 1901 adhere closely to the general pattern apparent in table 17. The overwhelming majority of families in Marlhes in both 1851 and 1901 were nuclear in structure, and it is not surprising to find such similarity between these rates and those for the population as a whole. The rates for nuclear family members show the same general characteristics as those mentioned above for the total population: a steady decline with age in rates of migration, with a particularly sharp decrease above the age of thirty-five; and the decrease over time, between the middle and the end of the century, in the level of migration rates.

**Table 20.** Estimated Rates of Out-Migration per Thousand by Family Structure in Marlhes

| Family Type | Age Group | | | | | |
|---|---|---|---|---|---|---|
| | 0–24 | 25–34 | 35–44 | 45–54 | 55–64 | 65+ |
| **1851–1856** | | | | | | |
| Nuclear | 75.4 | 59.3 | 32.2 | 25.1 | 32.8 | 0.0 |
| Extended— parent, sibling | 62.4 | 38.4 | 27.8 | 0.0 | 59.0 | 38.9 |
| Extended— married child | 67.6 | 76.0 | 35.0* | 26.3* | 13.5 | 0.0 |
| Extended— other kin | 120.1 | 13.4* | 61.9 | 69.2* | 0.0* | 23.5* |
| **1901–1911** | | | | | | |
| Nuclear | 47.6 | 49.2 | 30.4 | 25.4 | 24.2 | 6.5 |
| Extended— parent, sibling | 43.9 | 42.3 | 21.3 | 16.4 | 43.3 | 10.0 |
| Extended— married child | 39.7 | 33.9* | 50.5* | 0.0* | 0.0* | 0.0* |
| Extended— other kin | 59.6 | 46.0 | 34.9 | 3.3* | 0.0* | 0.4* |

*Rate based on fewer than ten cases.

Source: See table 17.

This pattern of migration during the life cycle suggests that mobility was related to the development of the nuclear family group and was closely linked to roles in the family. Rates are high in young adult age groups, when the young couple would be seeking to establish itself and might be willing to move in order to do so. In older age groups the rates of migration decline, suggesting the increased stability of the conjugal pair who have established an economic basis for their family and are reluctant to leave it. At the same time, however, their children reach young adulthood and themselves begin to move, raising the rates in the youngest age groups. The nuclear family seems to provide a social situation conducive to high mobility that fits well in an economy demanding high mobility of the population, such as that of the Stephanois region.

Members of extended families in both years exhibit different age patterns of migration, but also conform to the developmental dynamics of the family structure. In general these patterns suggest the high propensity to migrate of additional family members. Those families extended by a parent or sibling of the household head, for example, show an unusual age pattern of out-migration: rates are high in younger age groups but decline to their lowest points in the middle age groups before increasing again with higher age. This pattern is particularly apparent in 1851–56; in 1901–11 it is less emphatic but still clearly visible.

This age pattern suggests that the principal source of migrants in these families was the additional member of the extended household. Rates were very high in the youngest age groups, those including the householder's younger brothers and sisters who had not yet established themselves in a separate household at the time of the first census but were able to do so by the second. In the middle years, encompassing the head of the household and his wife, rates of migration were very low. There was little reason for anyone in these age groups to migrate; the household had already been turned over to the new head and he had established himself and his family on a farm. But rates rose again in the older age groups comprising the retired parents of the head of the household. The import of these rates seems apparent: the most stable members of the household were the central conjugal pair, the head of the household and his wife, who in this type of family structure would be aged between thirty-five and fifty-five. The least stable members were the peripheral members of the family—the parents who had retired and relinquished their control over the farm, and the younger brothers and sisters of the householder, waiting until they were able to establish themselves in their own households. Patterns of migration seem closely linked to the developmental process of the extended family.

Extended families in which the parents did not relinquish control of the household but allowed a child to marry and live in their household— the classic stem family—exhibit different age patterns of emigration. Again there is a similar pattern at both mid-century and the beginning of the new century. Migration rates are highest among youths, approaching the rates of the general population. These rates remain relatively high until age forty-four, when they decline sharply and become very low, especially in 1901–11. This age pattern also is explicable in terms of the developmental cycle of the stem family. Most important is the very low mobility of older age groups in this type of family. Frédéric Le Play's insistence that the stem family provided for the old age of parents seems remarkably well borne out by these data.[10] This conclusion can be accepted, however, only with the clear understanding that the reason for the stability of parents was that they themselves retained control of the household and did not cede this authority to a child. The high migration rates of older age groups in families extended by parents of the head suggest the consequences of retirement.

The last type of complex family structure, extended by the presence of a cousin, niece, nephew, aunt, or uncle of the head of the household, shows a very erratic pattern of migration throughout the life cycle, a pattern no doubt due to both the small number of individuals who lived in this type of family and the haphazard distribution of the additional members in different age groups. This erratic pattern, however, does show high peaks in younger age groups with declining mobility in older age groups. The dominant pattern in these families was probably that of the nuclear family, supplemented by the departure of the additional kin present in them.

Thus family structure appears to be an important variable in explaining the decision to migrate or remain in Marlhes. The out-migration rates among members of nuclear families to a large extent resemble those of the overall population, suggesting that this type of family, to which the majority of the population belonged, provided migrants in younger age groups and a more stable population with increased age. The developmental cycles of other types of family structure, however, strongly altered the rates of migration of different age groups. The unifying theme emerging from migration rates for all types of extended families was that the most stable members of the family were the conjugal pair and their children, and the least stable members were those whose addition formed the extended family. While the extended family served as a means of support for kin outside the conjugal family, the stability of the family group clearly lay with the household head and his immediate family, with other family members forming a distinct, less stable part of the family group.

The patterns of migration into and out of Marlhes during the nineteenth century suggest several conclusions about the family system in the village as well as the more general problem of economic development. There is little reason to dispute an essentially economic explanation of the migration from Marlhes to the cities of the valley.[11] Wages were consistently higher in Saint-Etienne and the other industrial cities than in the countryside. The contrast was sharp between rural agricultural wages and the wages earned by a miner, the trade most migrants entered in the city. At mid-century an agricultural day laborer in the rural cantons of the arrondissement of Saint-Etienne could not hope to earn much more than two francs per day; in the coal industry in the same period the average daily wage, calculated on the amount of coal actually mined by the worker, was close to three francs. The differences in favor of the city even extended to the crafts and trades that were only indirectly affected by industrialization: in 1858 a mason in Saint-Etienne could earn three and a half francs per day; in the rural cantons of the arrondissement the daily wage was usually three francs or less. A cabinet-maker in Saint-Etienne or Le Chambon earned three and a half francs or more; in the other cantons the daily wage was three francs. The late nineteenth century was generally a period of rising wages in urban industry and stabilizing costs of living, and the differences in favor of the city probably remained strong until the end of the century.[12] The urban valley appears to have been a place of economic opportunity for the peasants living in the Stephanois countryside.

Alongside the pull of this economic framework, however, local social forces were at work pushing migrants out of the countryside. Family sociologists have long argued that the nuclear family structure characteristic of twentieth-century America provided a better "fit" with the demands of a modern industrial economy than the more complex family structures characteristic of traditional societies,[13] and economists frequently point to the need for a mobile population in a developing economy.[14] The experience of nineteenth-century Marlhes suggests that while the family was certainly an important actor in the migration process, any linkage between these two statements should be accepted with qualification if it is to be accepted at all. Migration was intimately linked to both individual and family developmental cycles. The individual milestone of marriage proved crucial in two respects: it served as a focal point for migration into Marlhes and, once achieved, it was a stabilizing force in the population, deterring migration from the commune. A related phenomenon was the way another landmark in individual lives, the death of a spouse, raised migration rates. Both of these events, marriage and the loss of a spouse, were important to individuals; their significance is magnified by their central position in family organization.

Family patterns were important in another way as well. The age pattern of migration was related to the structure of the migrant's family, following closely the developmental rhythms of different family structures. In each type of family structure the conjugal pair of the head of the family and his wife was most stable; additional members, whether children, parents, siblings, or more distant kin, were less stable. The different types of family structure found in nineteenth-century Marlhes all provided migrants for the growing industrial economy of the Stephanois valley during the nineteenth century. All types of family structure, complex as well as nuclear, produced high migration rates among youths and young adults, those age groups most in demand for an industrial labor force. In older age groups, the differences between types of family structure and their related migration patterns were primarily in the timing of migration during the individual life cycle. If nuclear families "fit" the requirements of modern industrial economies, therefore, they were not the only form of family structure that could fulfill those requirements. As Eugene Litwack has argued for twentieth-century America, there is no inherent contradiction between extended family structure and the labor demands of an industrial economy.[15]

The peasant family was more, however, than a provider of strong arms for the industrialization process. It formed a bulwark against the fluidity of family life caused by the industrialization and urbanization of the Stephanois valley. The flood of migrants from the countryside to the urban valley did not destroy the peasant family; rather, the constancy of the conjugal couple provided the family system in Marlhes and in the Stephanois region with a firm anchor around which the less stable members of the family could float.

# Chapter 7
# The Structure of the
# Peasant Family

The demographic patterns of nineteenth-century Mar-
lhes describe a process of growth and dispersal of the family unit during
the life cycle of the family. Births of children increased the size of the
family; deaths, marriages, and migration reduced its size and changed its
structure. The rates of mortality, fertility, and migration presented in the
previous three chapters are the expression of these different processes
and the ways in which they affected the families living in nineteenth-
century Marlhes. The configuration of these demographic events, remarkably resilient in the changing circumstances of the region during the
nineteenth century, provides the beginnings of an understanding of the
peasant family, a series of basic facts that circumscribed family behavior.

Demographic events by their nature occur at points in time, not over a
period of time. They mark the outlines of the peasant family, the framework within which the families of Marlhes lived. A full view of these
families requires that we fill in the demographic framework. Our interest
now must be to discover the meaning of the family for these peasants.
What did families mean as the residential groups in which peasants spent
their childhoods, adult years, and old age? What kinds of property relations existed between the members of families? How was work allocated
in the peasant family and what happened to the earnings of individual
members? How important was the family as a reference group for individuals during their life cycles? And, most importantly, do the answers
to these questions change from one social group to another, from one set
of economic circumstances to another within the rural community? That
is, did the changing relationship of Marlhes to the urban valley alter
these aspects of family life?

The following four chapters attempt to answer these questions. The
concern of the present chapter is the residential structure of the peasant
family. The kin who chose to live together under the same roof formed
the most visible sign of the family. This structure determined many aspects of family life: the persons available for daily social relations, the
available labor for the needs of the family farm and other economic
activities. In the following chapter, the property relations between family
members and the ways these relations defined the family group are dis-

cussed. The organization of work in the family and the disposition of earnings are then taken up, and finally the changing relationship of the individual to his family is described. By determining the rules under which these different aspects of family relations operated, the outline provided by the demographic events already described will take on color and substance.

The majority of peasant families in Marlhes in the nineteenth century were nuclear in structure, consisting only of husband and wife and their children, emphasizing the central role of the conjugal couple that we have already noted. In both 1851 and 1901 over 80 percent of families were similar to the family of Denis Olagnon and his wife, Marie Fournel, who lived in 1851 at Peybert with their five young children. Other types of family structure could also be found, however. Slightly more than one-tenth of the families included not only the married couple and their children but also either parents or siblings of the head of household or his wife. François Convert and his wife Jeanne Liogier, for example, lived with their four children, aged from two to six years. But their household also included the widowed mother of François, Claudine Padel, eighty-six, as well as his sister, Marie Convert, forty-eight, who had never married and worked as a ribbonweaver. A very small percentage were "classic" stem families of parents and their married child. The family of Jean-Baptiste Barralon may be typical of these families: besides Jean-Baptiste and his wife Marguerite Tardy, in their late sixties, the household included their son, Jean-François; his wife, Jeanne Marie Massardier; their six young children; a daughter of Jean-Baptiste and Marguerite, Françoise, twenty-one; and three farm workers.[1] Finally, other kin, such as aunts, uncles, cousins, nieces, or nephews, made the few remaining families in the village extended in structure (see tables 21 and 22).

The knowledge that a large majority of families were nuclear in structure at the time of a census tells little about the family system of the region. The household has its own developmental cycle and ideally should be viewed as a process going on over time rather than as a static group visible in a census list.[2] The data presented in tables 21 and 22 approximate this developmental cycle and indicate that not only does nuclear family structure predominate in the total figures for family structure, it also predominates in every stage of the family developmental cycle. There seems to be little doubt that during the nineteenth century the family system in Marlhes was overwhelmingly nuclear in structure: most individuals were born, raised, and lived their adult lives in a family consisting only of parents and their immediate children.

This does not mean that extended families were insignificant in Marlhes. While nuclear family structure predominates throughout the life

**Table 21.** Family Structure by Age of Head of Household in Marlhes, 1851

| Family Type | 15–24 | 25–34 | 35–44 | 45–54 | 55–64 | 65+ | Total |
|---|---|---|---|---|---|---|---|
| Nuclear | 11 | 67 | 125 | 135 | 93 | 70 | 501 |
| | 78.6% | 79.8% | 81.4% | 83.2% | 89.4% | 81.4% | 83.2% |
| Extended— | 3 | 16 | 20 | 19 | 6 | 3 | 67 |
| parent or sibling | 21.4% | 19.0% | 13.1% | 11.8% | 5.8% | 3.5% | 11.1% |
| Extended— | 0 | 0 | 1 | 2 | 5 | 10 | 18 |
| married child | 0.0% | 0.0% | 0.6% | 1.3% | 4.8% | 11.6% | 3.0% |
| Extended— | 0 | 1 | 6 | 6 | 0 | 3 | 16 |
| other kin | 0.0% | 1.2% | 3.9% | 3.7% | 0.0% | 3.5% | 2.7% |
| Total | 14 | 84 | 152 | 162 | 104 | 86 | 602 |
| | 2.3% | 13.9% | 24.2% | 26.9% | 17.3% | 14.4% | 100.0% |

Source: A.D.L. 49 M 85, *Liste nominative de recensement de la commune de Marlhes*, 1851.

**Table 22.** Family Structure by Age of Head of Household in Marlhes, 1901

| Family Type | 15–24 | 25–34 | 35–44 | 45–54 | 55–64 | 65+ | Total |
|---|---|---|---|---|---|---|---|
| Nuclear | 2 | 48 | 78 | 64 | 83 | 67 | 342 |
| | 40% | 73.8% | 73.6% | 81% | 88.3% | 88.1% | 80.4% |
| Extended— | 1 | 13 | 15 | 8 | 8 | 3 | 48 |
| parent or sibling | 20% | 20% | 14.2% | 10.1% | 8.5% | 3.9% | 11.3% |
| Extended— | 0 | 0 | 2 | 1 | 1 | 3 | 7 |
| married child | 0.0% | 0.0% | 1.9% | 1.3% | 1.1% | 3.9% | 1.7% |
| Extended— | 2 | 4 | 11 | 6 | 2 | 3 | 28 |
| other kin | 40% | 6.2% | 10.3% | 7.6% | 2.1% | 3.9% | 6.6% |
| Total | 5 | 65 | 106 | 79 | 94 | 76 | 425 |
| | 1.2% | 15.3% | 24.9% | 18.6% | 22.1% | 17.9% | 100.0% |

Source: A.D.L. 49 M 353, *Liste nominative de recensement de la commune de Marlhes*, 1901.

cycle, there are clearly age groups in which extended families include a large proportion of the population. Extended family structure is most important in the younger age groups. This is the period in a householder's life when he has just taken over control of the family: his parents have retired but one of them may remain alive, and his younger brothers and sisters are not yet old enough to leave home and establish their own households. This accounts for the high percentage of families extended through the presence of parents or siblings in the twenty-five to thirty-four age group, a phase in which the extended families reach almost twice their normal distribution in the total population (19 percent versus 11.1 percent in 1851; 20 percent versus 11.3 percent in 1901). The percentage of families extended upward or laterally declines continually throughout the life cycle, with a particularly sharp decline after the thirty-five to forty-four age group. By this time the parents of the householder have died and younger brothers and sisters themselves have married or migrated away from their family of origin. While these types of extension are losing ground, however, extension through the presence of a married child gains ground and is particularly important when the head of the family is aged fifty-five or above. At different phases of the life cycle of the family, therefore, extended families represented as much as one-fifth of the population in that age group. There is a group within the population for whom extended family structure represents an important part of the life cycle. Not one but two family systems may be present: one characterized by nuclear structure throughout the life cycle, the other extended at certain points in the life of the individual.

Of course not every family in a population can be extended; for many individuals there are no kin available with whom they can form an extended household. In order to appreciate fully the significance of extended family structure in Marlhes, the influence of demographic conditions on extended family formation must be considered. The demographic variables intervening to reduce the possibility of formation of extended families are mortality and fertility. These two variables affect above all the possibility of forming three-generation households: in order for parents to have a married child with whom they could form an extended family, it is necessary that they have a child who lives to adulthood and that they themselves (or one of them) live to see their child reach adulthood. The probability of the first is dependent on both fertility (the number of children born, and therefore the number of chances a couple would have to form an extended household) and mortality (the probabilities of the child living to adulthood and the parents living to see him reach that age). Using data on mortality and fertility in Marlhes in the nineteenth century, it is possible to calculate that only 33.5 percent of households could be extended in this way in 1851 and 39.1 percent in 1901 (see appendix 3). In both 1851 and 1901 in Marlhes 9 percent of families were extended in this way. Thus the commune had 26.9 percent and 23.0 percent of the extended families it could possibly have had in the two censuses. The relatively low raw figure of 9 percent clearly does not express the true importance of three-generation families in nineteenth-century Marlhes. Although limited to a specific phase of the life cycle of the family, when the householder was in his twenties and thirties, and constrained by the high mortality rates of the population which reduced the possibility of a grandparent surviving to be a member of a three-generation household, this type of family pattern was frequent for some members of the rural population during a part of their family cycle.

The possibilities of formation of other types of extended family are also dependent on fertility and mortality, but are much greater than for vertical extension. It was possible for 78.4 percent of the families in 1851 to be extended by a sibling of the householder and 70.2 percent in 1901 (see appendix 3). The empirical figures of 5 percent in 1851 and 6 percent in 1901 appear relatively low in comparison, forming only 6.3 percent and 8.5 percent respectively of the possible combinations. This is a much less significant form of family extension than that involving a parent or married child. Finally, it should be possible for all families to be extended through the presence of more distant kin than parents or siblings, since virtually every household should have at least one uncle, cousin, or other relative surviving to form an extended family. Again, this type of extension is relatively unimportant in Marlhes, with less than 5 percent of families in either census extended in this way.

With these estimates in mind the raw percentages in tables 21 and 22 take on different meanings. Extended family structure clearly was more important than the data initially suggested. For a significant part of the population of Marlhes a complex family group was a part of the life cycle. These patterns of family extension in 1851 and 1901 were however relatively limited, and were largely defined by the immediate family of the householder. Few households included kin other than parents or siblings of the head of the household. The extended family in Marlhes was important not as a large social group bringing together numerous kin in the same residential unit. It most often consisted only of remnants of a family of origin—the retired parents or unmarried siblings of the householder.

The presence of two patterns of family development in nineteenth-century Marlhes seems confirmed. The overwhelming majority of people grew up and lived in nuclear families, consisting only of husband, wife, and their young children. When children married they established their own household, and to a large extent marrying must have depended on the acquisition of the means to establish a separate household. A much smaller part of the rural population experienced a different type of family, made larger and more complex by the presence of additional kin of the head of the family during a few years of the family cycle. Most often this occurred when the head of the household was in his late twenties and thirties, and the additional kin was a parent or sibling of the householder. The complex structure disappeared with the death of the parent or the marriage of the brother or sister, usually before the house-holder passed his forty-fifth birthday.

The two forms of family structure in nineteenth-century Marlhes may be related to distinguishable groups within the rural community. The evidence presented in table 23 suggests that extended family structure was related to landownership by the family. The age of the householder was very important in determining the structure of the household, and therefore it is not surprising to find that a majority of the families of those owning more than five hectares in both 1851 and 1901 were nuclear rather than extended in structure. The import of these data, however, is clear. Jean-Baptiste Barralon, who lived with his married son and his family and owned twenty-eight hectares of land in 1851, represents well the tendency of landowning families to have complex structures.[3] Whereas in 1851 only 16.8 percent of all families were extended, almost twice that proportion, 29.5 percent, of those owning five hectares or more were extended in structure. In 1901 a similar disproportion of landholding families were extended: 19.5 percent of all families were extended, but 36.4 percent of those owning five or more hectares of land were complex in structure. In spite of the uncontrolled influence of the age of the head of household in these tables, both censuses show a significant relationship between landholding and family structure.

The tendency for small landholding families to be nuclear is less clear

Table 23. Family Structure by Landholding in Marlhes

| Family Type | 0–4 Hectares | | 5+ Hectares | | Total | |
|---|---|---|---|---|---|---|
| **1851*** | | | | | | |
| Nuclear | 458 | 84.6% | 43 | 70.5% | 501 | 83.2% |
| Extended | 83 | 15.4% | 18 | 29.5% | 101 | 16.8% |
| Total | 541 | 89.9% | 61 | 10.1% | 602 | 100.0% |
| **1901†** | | | | | | |
| Nuclear | 321 | 81.8% | 21 | 63.6% | 342 | 80.5% |
| Extended | 71 | 18.2% | 12 | 36.4% | 83 | 19.5% |
| Total | 392 | 92.2% | 33 | 7.8% | 425 | 100.0% |

*Chi squared with Yates' correction = 6.978; significance = .01; contingency coefficient = .110

†Chi squared with Yates' correction = 5.195; significance = .05; contingency coefficient = .110.

Source: A.D.L. 49 M 85, 49 M 353, *Listes nominatives de recensement de la commune de Marlhes*, 1851, 1901.

from these tables. In both censuses the distribution of small landholders between nuclear and extended family structures is very close to the distribution of all families. In 1851, 84.6 percent of smallholder families were nuclear, while 83.2 percent of all families were nuclear in structure. In 1901, 81.8 percent of smallholder families were nuclear, again very close to the 80.5 percent of all families that fell into the nuclear category. There does, however, seem to be a strong tendency for agricultural day laborers, called *journaliers* in the census lists, to live in nuclear families. In 1851, eighty-five out of ninety-one families of *journaliers* (93.4 percent) were nuclear, while only six were extended in any way. In 1901, of twenty *journalier* families, eighteen were nuclear, only two extended.[4] These proportions are far below what would be expected in a normal distribution of these types of family structure. The group in rural society that had the least connection with the land—those reduced to agricultural wage labor—shows a strong tendency away from extended family structure and toward nuclear family structure.

Analysis of family structure in terms of landholding therefore seems to confirm the relationship of landownership to family structure. The ownership of a farm of at least five hectares encouraged the peasant family to grow beyond the conjugal pair and their children, bringing retired parents or other kin into the residential group. The agricultural occupation indicating the least landownership and the most dependence on wage labor, *journaliers*, tended to have nuclear family structure in excess of the distribution of this family type in the population.

The relationship between the ownership of land and complex family structure is usually associated by family historians with the transmission of the land from one generation to the next, through a patriarchal or stem family structure and impartible inheritance practices.[5] As will be seen in the next chapter, the inheritance practices of families in nineteenth-century Marlhes did play an important part in providing a locus for the family group, especially for the siblings of young householders. This is not, however, the entire explanation for the relationship between land and complex structure, and other evidence from Marlhes suggests that a direct correspondence between these variables may not have been present in the village. In Marlhes land was a form of wealth, but it represented primarily a means to earn a living, the economic basis of a family economy. Complex family structure required above all the economic resources to support the larger family economy of the complex household. It was usually among larger landholders that such resources existed in nineteenth-century Marlhes. The type of cultivation, whether subsistence cereal agriculture or market animal husbandry, does not seem to have made a difference, for even with the increased emphasis among larger landholders on husbandry and dairy production in the late nineteenth century the relationship of land to complex family structure remained constant.

The industrial work available in the countryside, however, also provided additional resources for the family, and it is important to qualify the relationship of land to complex family structure by examining the relationship of domestic and factory weaving to the structure of the family group. The ribbonweaving industry was most important for the female members of the family, as a type of employment that allowed them to remain in the household and earn income. As is evident from table 24, more families with ribbonweavers as members were extended than would be expected given the distribution of the trade in the population. The case of Marie Convert, who worked as a ribbonweaver and lived in the household of her brother François, seems representative of the use of industrial work to support extended family structure. While 49 percent of the families in the commune had members working as *rubannières* in 1851, 55 percent of the families extended by the presence of a parent or sibling, 61 percent of those extended by a married child, and 68 percent of those extended by other kin had *rubannières* as members. In spite of the low number of cases involved, there does seem to be some influence of domestic weaving toward family extension.

The importance of domestic weaving in hindering the out-migration of women from Marlhes during the middle years of the nineteenth century is of great importance in explaining this relationship. As noted in chapter

**Table 24.** Family Structure by Presence of *Rubannière* in Household in Marlhes, 1851

| Family Type | *Rubannière* Present | | *Rubannière* Not Present | | Total | |
|---|---|---|---|---|---|---|
| Nuclear | 236 | 47% | 265 | 53% | 501 | 83.2% |
| Extended— parent or sibling | 37 | 55.2% | 30 | 44.8% | 67 | 11.1% |
| Extended— married child | 11 | 61.1% | 7 | 38.9% | 18 | 3.0% |
| Extended— other kin | 11 | 68.8% | 5 | 31.2% | 16 | 2.7% |
| Total | 295 | 49% | 307 | 51% | 602 | 100.0% |

Chi squared = 5.37 with three degrees of freedom; significance = .155; contingency coefficient = .094.

Source: A.D.L. 49 M 85, *Liste nominative de recensement de la commune de Marlhes*, 1851.

6, ribbonweavers had the lowest migration rates of any occupational group in Marlhes between 1851 and 1856. The great majority of the members of this occupational group were women. It is probable that domestic weaving hindered the migration of women who were single or widowed and kept them in the countryside by providing them with chances to earn income and contribute to the family economy. These women joined the families of their brothers or married sisters, as did Marie Convert, or if they were widowed they stayed with their married children. The influence of domestic weaving in discouraging out-migration by individuals who were not part of a nuclear family explains its influence in encouraging extended family structure.

The situation was different in 1901, when ribbonweaving had changed from a domestic putting-out industry into one based on factory organization of production. Again the weaving trade employed primarily women, but only seven of the eighty-three cases (8.4 percent) of extended family structure in the commune had a factory operative present in the family, whereas almost 13 percent of the families as a whole contained an operative (see table 25). This is not strong proof in either direction, and while there seems to be a slight relationship between nuclear family structure and the presence of a factory operative, it is not significant. It seems more likely that ribbonweaving became a negligible factor with the advent of factory organization rather than that it exerted a strong push in the direction of nuclear structure.

The differences in the impact of domestic and factory weaving reflect

Table 25. Family Structure by Presence of *Ouvrière en Soie* in Household in Marlhes, 1901

| Family Type | *Ouvrière en Soie* Present | | *Ouvrière en Soie* Not Present | | Total | |
|---|---|---|---|---|---|---|
| Nuclear | 48 | 14.0% | 294 | 86% | 342 | 80.5% |
| Extended— parent or sibling | 4 | 8.3% | 44 | 91.7% | 48 | 11.3% |
| Extended— married child | 0 | 0.0% | 7 | 100.0% | 7 | 1.6% |
| Extended— other kin | 3 | 10.7% | 25 | 89.3% | 28 | 6.6% |
| Total | 55 | 12.9% | 370 | 87.1% | 425 | 100.0% |

Chi squared = 2.40 with three degrees of freedom; significance = .45; contingency coefficient = .075.

Source: A.D.L. 49 M 353, *Liste nominative de recensement de la commune de Marlhes,* 1901.

the different ways that these types of labor related to the family economy of the Stephanois peasantry. In 1851, when ribbonweaving was solely a domestic industry and was available to all women throughout their life cycles, it was possible for adult women to gain nonagricultural income and earn their keep. In a domestic economy in which each individual was expected to provide the resources that would support himself, domestic weaving was ideally suited to the needs of the sisters or widowed mother of the householder. The agricultural holding may have been adequate to support only a small nuclear family; with income from domestic weaving, however, the additional women living in extended families could support themselves.

As we know, two elements separated the factory operative of 1901 from the domestic weaver of mid-century Marlhes. In the first place, factory labor was less a life's work for women than temporary employment lasting from youth to marriage. This lessened the impact of factory work on the life of the family. Whereas domestic weaving was a lifelong occupation for the weaver, factory work affected the weaver and her family only during the phase when there was a daughter in her late teens and early twenties. The ability of such a temporary occupation to influence family structure was not great. Certainly it would not work toward family extension; yet it was not central enough to the domestic economy to exert a very powerful influence toward nuclear family structure. Its primary effect was to end the ability of older women to remain in the mountains, and by the beginning of the twentieth century factory work was encouraging migration.

The second difference was in the social group from which the two types of industrial workers were recruited. The women who were domestic weavers came from the entire spectrum of the rural social structure. Factory operatives, on the other hand, were drawn primarily from the lower agricultural classes, those unable to benefit from the increasing market for agricultural goods in the Stephanois region during the second half of the nineteenth century. Factory operatives were therefore recruited from the same groups that even in 1851 had shown a propensity toward nuclear family structure. In 1901 the presence of a factory operative may simply have overlapped with a family headed by an agricultural wage laborer. Even with rural industrialization and factory organization, the ownership of land or the lack of it seems to have been the dominant independent variable determining family structure.

Nuclear family structure was overwhelmingly the most important form of family structure in Marlhes in both 1851 and 1901. A significant number of families did, however, exhibit extended family structure, and the presence of these families allows conclusions about factors encouraging both extended and nuclear family structure. In 1851 two factors were important in extending the family: the ownership of land and the participation of a family member in the domestic weaving of ribbons. Landownership probably was the more important of these factors, but the principal conclusion must be the compatibility of extended family structures with both substantial landownership and domestic industrial work. There were not strong lines of separation drawn through the rural community by the domestic weaving industry. On the contrary, weaving and landownership complemented each other in the domestic economy and encouraged family extension. In a region of impoverished agriculture such as the Stephanois area in the mid-nineteenth century, the complementary relationship of landownership and weaving provided the economic foundation for the continuation of extended forms of family structure. The system of family structure is marked above all by the flexibility of its economic base.

The changes experienced by both agriculture and weaving in the second half of the nineteenth century upset this complementary relationship. While the ability of agriculture to support extended families was increasing, the viability of an extended family partially supported through weaving was reduced. By the end of the nineteenth century the only factor that supported family extension was landownership. That the total proportion of extended families in the population did not change between 1851 and 1901 may be attributed to the greater number of landowners able to support an extended family. The conversion of the weaving industry into factory organization and its numerical decline reduced the influence of that factor on family organization, ending the tendency of domestic industrial work to discourage the migration of single and widowed women who had become additional members of complex families.

It was therefore among the landed peasantry that extended family structure was most likely to be found in nineteenth-century Marlhes. An important proportion of the extended families in the commune showed commitment to the land in the form of ownership of a substantial farm. The commercialization of agriculture in the second half of the nineteenth century did not work against this pattern; by making more economic resources available to those able to take advantage of the growing urban market for dairy products, it increased the influence of landownership on family extension.

The relationship, however, was not direct. An important component of the link between landholding and complex family structure was the resource provided by the land to support the larger, complex family economy. The more land owned by a family, the more members of the family it could support and employ on the land. This economic function in traditional peasant societies that depended solely on agriculture to support the family economy was filled only by land. In Marlhes, however, the economy was more differentiated, and ribbonweaving presented an alternative form of employment and income for the family group. In its domestic phase, ribbonweaving in the Stephanois region supported extended family structure by making it possible for more people, especially women, to be supported on the same size holding. This pattern worked as a complement to landownership. Because of the way it recruited throughout the rural population, the proto-industrial work of domestic ribbonweaving did not create a rural proletariat differentiated from the landed peasantry. More important in this process of differentiation was the break with the land symbolized by the occupational title of *journalier*: dependence on wage labor within the agricultural sector led to nuclear family structure.

With the change from domestic to factory organization and improvements in agriculture in the second half of the nineteenth century, the social groups in the rural community became increasingly differentiated into two distinct groups: a landed peasantry that took advantage of agricultural commercialization to increase its income and that continued to show a tendency toward extended family structure; and a landless group dependent on wage labor from both agriculture and the weaving industry, exhibiting nuclear family structure. In both 1851 and 1901, therefore, the society was differentiated on the basis of landownership; only with the coming of factory organization did industrial work require a choice between agricultural work and industrial work. Larger landowning families left the weaving industry, while poorer agricultural families patched together a living from whatever means were available.

While the residential organization of the peasant family in Marlhes is readily apparent from the census lists and other records used in this chapter, the import of these residential patterns is not. I have employed a narrow definition of the family: those persons who live together in the same household under the same roof. Household structure, defined in this way, has long held a primary position in family studies, but this has been more for what historians and sociologists have taken residential structure to mean than for the inherent interest of living arrangements. The complex family has been assumed to favor the authority of the patriarch, the obedience of children to their elders, the stability of the family group, and the absence of strong emotional bonds between family members. The modern nuclear family, in contrast, is associated with reduced parental authority, increased instability, and an intensified emotional atmosphere.[6]

It should go without saying that the mere patterns of residence among kin that are reflected in household structure are not good proxies for a whole range of emotional and psychological characteristics of the peasant family. The prevalence of nuclear households in Marlhes furthers our argument that the conjugal pair, the basis of the nuclear household, was central to the stability of the peasant family in a period of economic and social development. But we cannot therefore conclude that these nuclear households were "modern" in some emotional sense. Above all, the nuclearity of most households in Marlhes should not be taken to mean that these families were in any way a "privileged emotional climate" that was protected "from outside intrusion through privacy and isolation."[7] The nuclear family in Marlhes was most common among the poorer members of the community, and it would be incorrect to argue that these peasants were able to isolate their families from outside influences. Living on the edge of subsistence did not make for privacy and isolation. It led to frequent disruption of the household by poverty, temporary migration, and death. The strong relationship we have found between economic resources and family complexity argues that these were not households that functioned on the basis of sentimental bonds between family members. The basis of the family in Marlhes was economics, in the long term represented by access to property, in the short term by the day-to-day functioning of the domestic economy. To these economic arrangements we now turn.

# Chapter 8
# Property and the Family: Inheritance under the Napoleonic Code

The preceding chapter has underscored the importance of landholding as a variable determining whether family structure would be nuclear or extended in nineteenth-century Marlhes. This and the following chapter examine more closely the relationships between the rural economy and the family system in the village. This chapter surveys the inheritance patterns of the Stephanois peasantry; the following one considers the family as a unit of production and consumption, under the rubric of the domestic economy.

Scholars have long emphasized the importance of partible or impartible inheritance systems in determining the structure of the family. This notion was initially associated with the work of the nineteenth-century French sociologist Frédéric Le Play, who argued that the stem and patriarchal, or stable, families of traditional rural France were being destroyed by the imposition of partible inheritance by the Napoleonic Code. Marc Bloch contested the importance of revolutionary legislation in leading to partible inheritance, but concurred that these practices influenced family structure. Walter Goldschmidt and Evalyn Kunkel have analyzed forty-six rural communities around the world and have argued that patrilineal partible inheritance leads to patrilocal joint families, impartible inheritance is associated with stem families, and nuclear families are highly associated with bilateral partible inheritance. Lutz Berkner has recently provided several examples of the influence of inheritance practices on family structure.[1]

The discussion of family structure in this literature has also alluded to a less concrete issue in family history, the relations between members of the family. Le Play was interested above all in the maintenance of parental authority over children and sharply criticized the loss of this authority that he associated with the revolutionary restriction of testamentary freedom in France. An economic historian, H. J. Habakkuk, directly relates inheritance practices and family relations in western Europe, calling attention to the role of inheritance practices in resolving peasant efforts to maintain a family patrimony while providing for younger children. Inheritance practices therefore are related not only to family size but also to the relations of parents and children and to conflicts among children.[2]

Thus the study of inheritance practices provides a lens on two issues in the history of the peasant family. On one level inheritance is important to a full understanding of the relationship between land and the residential structure of the family. On a different level inheritance practices suggest the outlines of the emotional structure of the family: who is considered a member and what the implications of that membership are.

Inheritance practices do not take place in a historical vacuum; their relationship to family structure and to relations of family members suggests that they may link these variables to broader changes occurring in nineteenth-century France and western Europe. At this juncture two general structural changes may be briefly mentioned. One has already been invoked in this study: the separation of the European peasantry from the land by the incursion of industrial and commercial activity into the countryside and by the alternatives to agricultural employment offered by the development of a modern industrial economic sector. This separation was accompanied by an increase in the importance of liquid capital in personal wealth and decreased importance in landed wealth. Both of these developments may have reduced the influence of inheritance practices on family behavior.[3]

The second structural change affected the political context of inheritance and family life: the increasing centralization of the state. This advanced on several fronts during the late eighteenth and nineteenth centuries, including the development of national tax systems, increased bureaucratic control over provinces, and the imposition of unified national legal systems over the regional systems of customary and written law characteristic of Ancien Régime Europe. In France the inheritance provisions of the Convention and the Empire form an important aspect of this centralization process, as important for the peasant as the increased interest of the state in food supply. The nineteenth century witnessed a continuous skirmishing between peasants and the requirements of the Civil Code. Understanding this conflict requires regard for the inheritance practices of the Ancien Régime and the attempts, expressed in numerous notarial acts of nineteenth-century French peasants, to balance their traditional practices and goals with the requirements of revolutionary and Napoleonic legislation.[4]

        The Stephanois region is located on the northern border of the French Midi; from the perspective of Ancien Régime successoral practices this placed it on the border of the area under the jurisdiction of written law, in contrast to the customary law of northern France.[5] The written law of the Midi allowed complete testamentary freedom to the parent. In customary France, in contrast, two restrictions were common: limits on the amount of his estate that a parent could will to one child and the customary rule "nul ne peut être héritier et légataire," which excluded children who had received donations from their parents from inheritance at death.[6] The absence of customary or legal restrictions on testamentary freedom in southern France allowed the testator to employ a wide variety of practices. This freedom and the absence of scholarly study of the actual practices in the Velay and Forez obscure the Ancien Régime heritage of the nineteenth-century Stephanois peasant. Two pieces of evidence may be offered that suggest that the actual practice of inheritance in the region was far from favoring one heir to the exclusion of others. The first is the proximity of the Velay to the Auvergne, a region in which customary law allowed the donation to a favored heir of a portion up to the limit of one-quarter of the succession.[7] This is consistent with Jean Merley's suggestion, based on a study of a village in the diocese of Brioude, that in the Velay both bourgeois and peasants tended to institute as heir the child, either daughter or son, who appeared most likely to maintain the family homestead, or *houstau*, intact. Merley attributes this to the desire of the father that the family home should become the legal property of one of the children but remain a shelter for the entire family and that all of the children would have the right to remain there until they were able to establish their own households.[8]

Neither of these suggestions is strong, and they are a poor substitute for detailed study in notarial minutes of the actual practices of the Stephanois peasantry under the Ancien Régime. They do suggest, however, that these inheritance practices struck a balance between the demands of maintenance of family property and the needs of many children. They provide a further focus for the inheritance strategy: not the arable land but the *houstau* is the object of preservation attempts. A similar strategy appears, as will be seen, in the inheritance records of the nineteenth century.

The revolutionary attack on local inheritance practices began in the National Convention with a decree stating that "the faculty to dispose of his goods, be it because of death or between living persons, be it by contractual donation, in direct line, is abolished. In consequence, descendants have an equal right to the goods of their parents."[9] The measure was less an attempt to alter dramatically the social structure of France than an attempt to keep parents from punishing their patriotic children by excluding them from their succession. Cambon indicated his approval for Prieur's proposal for retroactivity to 14 July 1789 with the words: "It will be approved by all those who know the region of written law. In that region, people have made arrangements, above all since our law on emigrés, all to the prejudice of patriotic children."[10] The strict equality of inheritance imposed by the Convention was moderated during the Consulate in the law of 4 Germinal An VIII (25 March 1800) which allowed a parent to dispose freely of a portion of his estate with all heirs enjoying equal rights to the remainder. The disposable portion was usually a quarter; in any case it was not less than a quarter nor more than a half. This was the provision for inheritance that was incorporated into the Civil Code in 1804.[11]

The relative simplicity of the specific provisions of the Code masks their complexity in practice. Exercise of the restricted testamentary freedom of the Napoleonic Code could take place at a number of moments in the life cycle of the individual. A portion of his estate could be set aside in his own marriage contract for a surviving spouse. In this case the exercise of the right of testament was in the hands of the individual's parent rather than himself. Later, when his own children came to marry, it was possible for the individual to provide the disposable portion as a dowry for a child. The marriage of a child could also be the occasion for an advance donation of the normal share of a child. In either case the property could be actually transferred at the time of marriage or the child could be given only the right to use the property at marriage with full ownership coming at the death of the parent. A third means of transferring the property and exercising testamentary rights was through a *donation entre vifs*, in which the parent transferred all or part of his property to his children while he was still alive, making whatever provision for the disposal of the free portion that he wished. This could take place at any time the individual chose, but probably occurred late in life and usually provided for an annual pension to be paid by his heirs to the donor until his death. This type of disposition allowed retirement from the duties of managing the family property and transfer of authority from the older to the younger generation within the household. Finally, an individual could make a will which would allocate the disposable portion to a particular heir or to the surviving spouse of the individual.[12]

These four means of disposition of an estate were not mutually exclusive, further complicating possible successions. An individual's marriage contract might provide that his surviving widow would receive the right to the use of one-quarter of his estate. It would still be possible for him to allocate the eventual ownership of this quarter to a son in that child's marriage contract. He also might decide to retire and donate the remaining three-quarters of his property to his children prior to his death. The implications of this legal tangle are that while the parent was limited in the amount of his estate that he could control, he still retained control over the timing of the transfer and his own resignation as head of the family.

Once this transfer had taken place, the ultimate disposition of the succession was far from complete, for the inheritance laws of nineteenth-century France allowed the heirs an equal number of alternatives. These gave equal rights to all children to the ownership of their parents' property but placed no requirements on the disposition of that property after the succession. The heirs could divide the property into equal shares; this required agreement among the heirs on the equality of different types of land, farm buildings, and equipment. The result was a genuine partition of the succession, with each child becoming owner of a part of the succession instead of remaining part-owner of the entire succession. Another alternative was for one child to buy out the shares of his brothers or sisters in return for an amount of money or a mortgage. This preserved the integrity of the inheritance at the expense of burdening one child with the necessity of paying his brothers and sisters the equivalent in cash of their shares in the succession. It was also possible to liquidate the succession, converting all property into cash and dividing that among the heirs according to their shares in the succession. Lastly, no further action needed to be taken by the heirs, and they would all remain partial owners of the entire succession.

The interaction of parental control over the timing of the succession and children's ultimate decision over the disposition of the property transferred may be illustrated by following the succession of Claude Terrat, a farmer living in Marlhes in the third quarter of the nineteenth century. Terrat was born in 1801 in Riotord, in the Haute-Loire bordering on Marlhes, and lived in Marlhes in the hamlet of Espinasse during the 1860s and 1870s. Prior to moving to Marlhes he lived in the commune of Saint-Romain-la-Chalm next to Riotord in the Haute-Loire, and it was there that his children were born in the 1840s.[13] His first wife, Catherine Freyssinet, died on 15 October 1846, probably in Saint-Romain-la-Chalm.[14] He remarried, again probably in Saint-Romain.[15] He does not seem to have had any children by this second wife, and outlived her as he had his first wife. While he did not own land in Marlhes, Claude Terrat was a wealthy man, leaving personal property inventoried at more than five thousand francs in 1873.[16] This amount places him in the upper 10 percent of personal property successions in Marlhes in this period.

Claude Terrat's disposal of his property covered more than six years and made use of many of the legal avenues available to nineteenth-century Frenchmen. When his older son Pierre married Françoise Poule of Saint-Julien-Molin-Molette in the Haute-Loire in the fall of 1867, he received a donation from his father of 600 francs in cash, payable one year from the date of the marriage contract.[17] With this stake Pierre moved to Monistrol in the Haute-Loire and established himself as a *cafetier*.[18] Three years later, in April 1870, Claude's daughter Marie Claudine married Jean-Marie Play, a farmer living in the hamlet of Peybert in Marlhes. Claudine received a donation of 300 francs from her father to add to her trousseau valued at 300 francs and her portion of the succession of her mother, Catherine Freyssinet.[19] Another daughter, Marie, married Jean-Marie Pacalon, a cultivator from Saint-Romain-la-Chalm, sometime in this period and also probably received a donation from her father.[20] The remaining child, Claude's younger son Jean, married the year after Claudine, in November 1871. In contrast to his brother and sisters, Jean brought to his marriage only his *vestiaire* and his rights to the succession of his mother.[21] The explanation for this oversight becomes apparent in the following act, registered in May 1873:

> On the 14th of May, 1873, registered a donation-partage . . . by Terrat, Claude, farmer at Espinasses Commune of Marlhes to his four children sole heirs:
>
> 1. Jean Terra, cultivator at Espinasse
> 2. Pierre Terra, *cafetier* at Monistrol
> 3. Marie, spouse of Jean-Marie Pacalon cultivator at Chaizes, commune of St-Romain-la-Chalme (Haute-Loire)
> 4. Claudine, spouse of Jean-Marie Play farmer at Peybert, commune of Marlhes
>
> For a quarter by preciput, and three-sixteenths for his part, to Jean Terra first named and for three-sixteenths to each of the others. Of all his goods consisting in furnishings and personal property [*mobilier*] described in a statement attached to the donation and estimated at five thousand sixty-six francs sixty-five centimes
>
> .    .    .    .    .    .    .    .    5066,65 F
>
> at 1% received fifty francs eighty centimes     50,80 F
>
> The recipients of the donation will pay to the donator an annual pension of two hundred forty francs in the proportion of their portions, payable every six months. To the act added cession to the profit of Jean Terra first named by his coheritors of all rights in the present donation meaning two thousand eight hundred fifty francs, that is for each nine hundred fifty francs payable in one year with interest of .5 percent.
>
> Passed before Jammes at Marlhes the 3rd of May 1873.[22]

The apparently neglected son, Jean, received by this act of donation the disposable quarter of his father's succession in addition to his normal share of one-quarter of the remaining three-quarters. The residences listed for each of the children, with only Jean remaining at Espinasse, suggest that Claude Terrat had been living with his younger son since Jean's marriage two years before, and that he would continue to live there until his death. In exchange for caring for his father, Jean received the disposable quarter of his father's succession. All of the children, according to their share in the succession, were responsible for paying an annual pension of 240 francs to their father.

The act of donation from Terrat to his children was followed by an act of cession from Pierre, Claudine, and Marie of their shares to Jean in return for payment in one year of the cash value of their shares, with .5 percent interest. Because much of Claude Terrat's personal property was probably in livestock and farm equipment, this cession was not an unmixed blessing for Jean: he had to convert into cash within a year property valued at more than 2,850 francs.

This succession of acts, beginning with Pierre's marriage in 1867 and ending with the donation of Claude's property to his four children in 1873, shows that in spite of the restrictions of French inheritance law Claude Terrat exercised considerable control over his succession, and especially over the timing of the transfer of property to his children. Claude Terrat lived a very long life for nineteenth-century Marlhes, reaching the age of seventy-nine before he died in 1880. Such a demographic circumstance could have led to long-delayed marriages for his children and argument over the division of the estate when Claude finally did die. In his sixties, however, Claude allowed his children to marry and provided each with a donation of money. They each in turn left the family farm, using the donation to establish themselves elsewhere. Both daughters married established farmers, one in Marlhes, the other in Saint-Romain-la-Chalm. A possible dispute between Pierre and Jean over succession to the farm rented by Claude was prevented by the large donation Pierre received at his marriage, enabling him to set up a café in Monistrol. Finally, Claude retired seven years before his death in favor of his younger son Jean, in return for an annual pension from his children. No reason is given for this decision, but it seems likely that his age and the desire to assure that the lease of the farm at Espinasse would go to his son at his death influenced him.

The combination of donations in marriage contracts, donations before death providing for the disposal of the free portion of Claude Terrat's estate, and the cession of rights by other heirs to the favored son illustrates both the extent of a nineteenth-century French peasant's control of his succession and the limits on that control. Terrat decided the timing of his succession and encouraged his older son to move away from Marlhes and establish himself in Monistrol by a large donation at marriage, leaving the farm to the younger son. His children followed his lead by ceding their rights in the succession to the favored heir in return for cash payment. When the acts are placed in order they reveal a clear inheritance strategy aimed at providing for each child while preserving the integrity of the family's wealth from one generation to the next. They provide a view of nineteenth-century French successions far different from that gained by reading the strict provisions of the legislation or the work of nineteenth-century critics such as Frédéric Le Play. Testamentary freedom under the Code was less than absolute, of course; it was not, however, nonexistent.

The interaction of parent and heirs in the Terrat succession suggests that the practice of inheritance under the Civil Code should be viewed from two directions, that of the provisions made by the parents for the disposition of their goods and that of the subsequent actions of heirs. The provisions of parents had their most important effect on the timing of the transfer of property; by marriage contracts and donations, the transfer could be made prior to the death of the parent and an early marriage or independence from the family of origin made possible for the child. By testaments in favor of surviving spouses, on the other hand, the transfer could be delayed until the death of both parents, the result of which could be a long period of dependency on his parents for the child during his twenties and early thirties. The action of heirs, in contrast, primarily affected whether the property remained intact or was divided among the heirs into separately cultivated farms. This decision determined the financial burdens on the farm, possibilities for capital investment and agricultural improvement, and the size of landholding during the next generation. This in turn affected the material basis for family life and the extent to which children remained attached to their native commune, and therefore the likelihood that they would emigrate or remain there during their own lifetimes.

The inheritance strategy of parents in nineteenth-century Marlhes is described by the data in table 26, compiled from *déclarations de mutations après décès* registered with officials of the Bureau d'Enregistrement.[23] The data have been divided into two groups, one representing the Second Empire covering the period from 1850 to 1865, the other illustrating practices under the Third Republic from 1883 to 1898. There seem to be only slight differences between the two groups, and a first general conclusion is that inheritance practices did not change appreciably between the middle and the end of the nineteenth century. The overwhelming strategy was a willingness to allow the strict equal inheritance provisions of the Code to run their course: 67 percent and 71 percent died intestate with no provision for the disposition of their inheritances. The intestacy of most successions is reflected in the disposition of successions: the two most important categories are those of equal division among children and lateral kin. Children were of course the normal heirs under the Code for intestate successions. In the absence of surviving children, lateral kin—brothers or sisters of the deceased—became the heirs under the Civil Code.

The major inheritance strategy during the nineteenth century in Mar-

Table 26. Successions in Marlhes

| | 1850–1865 | | 1883–1898 | |
|---|---|---|---|---|
| | N | % | N | % |
| TYPE OF SUCCESSION | | | | |
| Intestate | 190 | 67.1 | 150 | 71.4 |
| Own marriage contract | 18 | 6.4 | 13 | 6.2 |
| Child's marriage contract | 7 | 2.5 | — | — |
| *Donation entre vifs* | 3 | 1.1 | 6 | 2.8 |
| Written will | 55 | 19.4 | 36 | 17.3 |
| Oral will | 7 | 2.5 | 4 | 1.9 |
| Other | 3 | 1.1 | 1 | 0.4 |
| Total | 283 | 100.0 | 210 | 100.0 |
| DISPOSITION OF SUCCESSIONS | | | | |
| Equal to children | 137 | 48.4 | 113 | 53.8 |
| Share to spouse | 5 | 1.8 | 2 | 1.0 |
| Share to favored child | 12 | 4.2 | 7 | 3.3 |
| Share to spouse + equal to child | 31 | 11.0 | 30 | 14.3 |
| Share to spouse + share to favored child | 16 | 5.7 | — | — |
| Bequest | 1 | 0.4 | 3 | 1.4 |
| Lateral kin | 58 | 20.5 | 36 | 17.1 |
| Descendant kin | 15 | 5.3 | 14 | 6.7 |
| Survivor + other kin | 8 | 2.8 | 5 | 2.4 |
| Total | 283 | 100.0 | 210 | 100.0 |

Source: See note 23, chapter 8.

lhes was the pattern of intestacy and equal division among surviving children or, less frequently, lateral kin described above. This pattern so dominated that there is no social group within the rural community that did not have this as its majority pattern. Intestacy was not the preserve of the poorer elements in the rural community, those without much property to pass to their heirs. Nor was it the strategy of those whose fortunes were principally in movable rather than landed property. It was a strategy followed by large and small landholders, as well as farmers, day laborers, and weavers.

There are two possible explanations for the strength of intestacy in nineteenth-century Marlhes. It is possible that the disparity between the desired strategy of the peasantry and the possibilities under the Code was so great that most families abandoned any attempt to circumvent the

Code and simply submitted to it. This, however, suggests that Stephanois peasants were historically passive, without their own aims and means of pursuing them. This seems unlikely when considered in the light of probable Ancien Régime inheritance practices in the Velay. There is rather a convergence of the Ancien Régime strategy and the provisions of the Code for intestate successions. It was suggested earlier that the intention of the Ancien Régime practices in the Velay was to maintain the family homestead as well as the right of each child to live in it for as long as he or she wished. The requirement of the Civil Code for equal inheritance rights of all children assured this almost as well as a will could. Intestacy was a strategy designed to maintain the family homestead as a focus for the lives of the younger generation by assuring to all of them their right to live there during their own lives.

If intestacy was the majority strategy in nineteenth-century Marlhes, however, it was not the only one. An important minority of successions were governed by conscious acts of the parent to control the disposition of his or her succession. The most important type of act was a written will, making up 19.4 percent of successions under the Second Empire and 17.1 percent at the end of the century. With only a handful of cases in each category were those successions governed by provisions of the marriage contract of the deceased (usually in the form of a guarantee of use of a portion of the estate for life to the surviving spouse); oral wills; and the provisions of a child's marriage contract.

Once this second strategy has been discerned, however, we must guard against too quickly assuming that it conforms to historians' views of French peasants striving against the Civil Code to maintain the integrity of their property from generation to generation and that it is the opposite of the intestacy strategy already described. In fact, the differences between the two strategies are less profound than they seem to be. The one distinguishable group tending to follow the minority pattern of testamentary succession rather than the majority pattern of intestacy consisted of married males. Under the Second Empire, women, no matter what their marital status, tended to die intestate. Of one hundred twenty-nine women in the first period, ninety-eight died intestate. Only twenty-four made provision for the distribution of their succession, usually through wills, occasionally through the marriage contracts of their children. Of thirty-eight single males in this period, twenty-eight died intestate; sixteen of twenty-one widowers also died intestate. In sharp contrast, only twenty-seven of seventy-one married males died intestate. The successions of another twelve were controlled by their own marriage contracts; only one contributed to his child's marriage contract. Over 40 percent, twenty-nine, made wills disposing of their succession. Thirteen of these provided exclusively for their widows, while another fourteen provided for their widows and also bestowed shares on favored children.

A similar pattern exists for the later period, although it is less pronounced. A majority of successions in all groups were intestate, but again married males showed a greater tendency toward nonintestacy than any other group. Of sixty-five successions by married males, twenty-seven were not intestate. In contrast, only three of twenty-three single men made any provisions for their successions, and only seven of twenty-six widowers did so. Women also showed a tendency towards intestacy: nine of twenty-two single women's successions were not intestate; ten of thirty-five married women did not die intestate, and only four of thirty-nine widows made any provisions for the disposition of their successions. The pattern of provision for surviving widows by married men was strengthened in this period, particularly at the expense of favored children. There is only one case in which a child was favored, while twenty-six of the twenty-seven nonintestate successions of married males provided for their spouses. Ten of these twenty-six were the result of marriage contract provisions, but fourteen were from wills.

The estates of males, especially married and widowed males, did tend to be larger and more heavily landed than those of any other group in the population. The contrast is especially strong between married men and married women. Only fifteen of fifty-five successions of married women in the Second Empire, and only ten of thirty-five successions during the Third Republic, included landed property. Their successions were usually in personal property, at times very high amounts of personal property. On the other hand, among married men, only twelve of seventy-one successions under the Second Empire and twenty-one of sixty-five successions during the Third Republic did not include landed property. Women were passing on liquid assets to their heirs, while men were transmitting their patrimony, the land they had received from the generations before themselves.

Intestacy was not the preserve of any one social or economic group in the rural community, but the size of the succession did play a part in determining whether or not the succession would be governed by a will. Intestate successions were evenly distributed through the entire range of values of personal and landed property, but there is a slight relationship between the value of the succession and the decision to employ a will. During the Second Empire, while 19.9 percent of successions valued less than one thousand francs in personal property employed a will, 26.4 percent of those valued over one thousand francs employed a will. In the same period, 20.2 percent of successions with landed property with a revenue of less than one hundred francs per year used wills, while 16.7 percent of those with revenues more than this amount per year used them. A similar division exists in the Third Republic: 17.1 percent of those successions with less than one thousand francs in personal property value used a will, while 22.9 percent of those worth over one thousand francs used one. The division is sharpest in landed successions in this period: while only 12.8 percent of successions worth less than one hundred francs in annual revenue used a will, 33.9 percent of those worth over one hundred francs in revenue were governed by testaments.

However, the disposition of testamentary successions disproves any possible intentions by the peasants of Marlhes to conserve their patrimony from one generation to the next by the use of wills. The purpose, present at mid-century and gaining strength as time passed, was rather to provide for the widowhood of a surviving wife. Few successions went exclusively to spouses: this was possible only when there were no other legal heirs available, a very rare occurrence given the wide range of reserve heirs under the Civil Code. More than 10 percent of successions included a provision for either the use or ownership of a portion by the survivor. It was possible, of course, to will the use of a portion to the surviving spouse and also to favor one child after the death of the survivor. This was only rarely done in the middle of the century and was never done at the end of the period. More frequently, the will that provided for the surviving spouse contained no provision for the ultimate disposition of the property; after the death of the survivor, that portion was divided equally among the children. Successions in which provision was made for the spouse were also much more numerous than those in which the disposable quarter was given to a child (11 percent versus 4.2 percent in 1850–65; 14.3 percent versus 3.3 percent in 1883–98). Under the Second Empire many of these provisions for spouses were the result of the original marriage contract for the couple (sixteen of thirty-one) but a substantial portion were the result of wills (twelve of thirty-one). The pattern toward provisions in wills becomes even more pronounced under the Third Republic, as twelve of thirty were the result of marriage contracts while fifteen of thirty were in wills. The purpose of testamentary successions in nineteenth-century Marlhes, therefore, seems less to insure the inheritance of as much as possible of the estate by one child than to provide for the old age of a surviving spouse. Once this had been accomplished, many of these successions allowed the equal division of the estate among all of the children.

Particularly striking is the extent to which this was done by testament, controlled by the husband himself, rather than by marriage contract, the result of negotiations between the parents of the couple. The minority pattern of inheritance strategies in nineteenth-century Marlhes suggests that among a small group in the rural community the wife was being incorporated into the family of procreation. In Marlhes this seems to have preceded French legislation by at least a generation. In the original legislation of the Civil Code the surviving spouse could inherit in an intestate succession only in the case of a lack of collateral kin to the twelfth degree. It was not until the law of 9 March 1891 that the surviving spouse received any right to the succession of his or her spouse, and the right received was only to the use of a portion, not to permanent ownership. This right to use was enlarged by the law of 29 April 1925, but extended ownership was still not given. Only with the law of 3 December 1930 did the surviving spouse receive the right to ownership of a portion of the deceased spouse's estate.[24] While even at the end of the century it was rare for widows in Marlhes to receive the ownership of a portion of their husbands' successions, there does seem to have been a growing feeling that the material well-being of the widow was not the responsibility of her own family of origin (the position of the Civil Code) but could be charged to the succession of her husband and therefore to his family.

In this respect inheritance practices paralleled changes in the form of marriage contracts. Beginning around the middle of the century the regime of community of acquisitions replaced a dotal regime modified to allow the husband some control over the goods of his wife.[25] Under the dotal regime there was no community of property within the marriage; each partner brought a certain amount to the marriage as a dowry and retained the ownership of this during the marriage. In practice any profit of the marriage was owned and could be employed by the husband as he saw fit. While the purpose of the dotal regime may have been to guarantee the property of the wife, its effect was to emphasize the temporary nature of her membership in the family line of her husband, a membership that ended when her husband died. In this event she received her original dowry and no more; the patrimony, represented by her husband's *apports* and the profit of the marriage, was passed on to the next generation without any provision for the widow unless required by her marriage contract. The principal difference between this marriage regime and that known as the *communauté réduite aux acquêts* was that while property brought to the marriage by each partner remained individual property, the profit of the marriage was now to be divided equally between husband and wife. The position of the widow in the family of procreation was strengthened as her own estate grew from the addition of her half of the property acquired during her marriage.

These changes reflect the beginnings of a shift in emphasis from the vertical relationships of lineage, represented by the patrimony, toward the relationships within the conjugal unit itself, especially the relationship between husband and wife. It was at best a hesitant movement, discernible only among the small minority who used wills to control their successions. Further, its effect was not to permanently incorporate a widow into her husband's family but to extend her temporary membership, begun at marriage, until her death rather than until the death of the husband. The modest increase in testamentary provisions for widows between mid-century and the end of the century is significant, however, in that it coincided with the shift from dotal marriage contracts, under which the first group of successions examined here was made, to the regime of community of acquisitions, under which the second group was made. It was therefore the result of a genuine change in the position of the wife in the family rather than simply a substitution of testamentary provisions for those of marriage contracts. Under the dotal regime the widow of a peasant was likely to receive little other than well-used clothing, kitchen furnishings, and linen as her part of the succession, the residue of a lifetime of use of the trousseau she had accumulated prior to her marriage. With the community of acquisitions, in contrast, she received not only these goods but also half of the excess of the community over its original value at marriage. She was therefore in a better position to support herself during her widowhood than under a dotal regime. The increase in testamentary provisions for widows during the second half of the century argues that not only were the rights of the wife improving in the second half of the nineteenth century but also that her husband was more concerned with her future.

The patterns of inheritance in nineteenth-century Marlhes suggest several conclusions about the intentions of parents as they exercised their limited rights under the Civil Code. The majority pattern of intestacy, which extended throughout the rural community, was less a resignation of parents to the division of their estates by the Civil Code than a continuation of Ancien Régime practices that emphasized the preservation of the family homestead as a focus of the family in the next generation. The equal inheritance rights guaranteed under the Civil Code adequately fulfilled this intention. There is one element of discontinuity between the Ancien Régime and the second half of the nineteenth century—the use of the limited testamentary freedom of the Civil Code to provide for a surviving widow rather than to favor a child. This change seems to be the result of a shift in attitudes within the conjugal unit about the position of the wife and her relationship to the patrimony of her husband's family.

If the legal restrictions of nineteenth-century France reduced the power of parents over the disposition of their successions, this power, in somewhat attenuated form, was passed to their children. The Napoleonic Code insisted on the right of each child to an equal share in the ownership of the succession of his parents, but placed no restrictions on the disposition of these equal shares after the succession. The estate could be liquidated or divided; several heirs could cede their rights in the succession to another heir; or each heir could retain partial ownership of the entire succession. Therefore, the disposition of a succession was hardly achieved with the death of the parent; final control rested with the heirs, in their decision on which of these possible legal paths to follow.

Whichever strategy was pursued, it particularly affected the landed property in the succession. Some informal unregistered division of movable property probably took place in all successions. It was relatively easy to divide a sum of money, or the few personal items of clothing or furniture involved in the personal property successions of most of the peasants of nineteenth-century Marlhes. Even successions such as that of Claude Terrat, in which the movable property probably included livestock, could eventually be converted to cash or simply divided in kind. Division of landed property, in contrast, was a lengthy and complex process. It required debate among the heirs over the division of each part of the estate. Since the estate probably consisted of pastures, arable land, forest, and wasteland spread around the commune, its division meant numerous arguments over the comparability of different types of land and land located in different parts of the commune.[26]

The small size of landholding in nineteenth-century Marlhes suggests that at one time a genuine system of partible inheritance, with division of the landed portion of the estate by heirs, may have been the rule. By the nineteenth century, however, the younger generation of heirs followed a consistent, almost universal strategy that preserved the landed part of their inheritance intact through the refusal to divide the property after the death of the parent. Much less frequently the same objective was reached through the cession of portions to one heir in exchange for money payments. Between 1866 and 1896, only 87 cessions, 28 divisions and 9 liquidations were registered for persons or property in Marlhes; in the same period of time a total of 506 successions were registered.[27] Only in 7.3 percent of the cases, therefore, was the property either liquidated or divided physically; fully three-quarters of successions led to joint ownership by the heirs of the entire landed portion of the succession. In spite of the legal structure requiring division of ownership in France and the Stephanois region, the practice within that structure was one that maintained the integrity of landholding from generation to generation.

The preservation of landed property was a decision of heirs that testators could only encourage, as Claude Terrat did. The detailed analysis of successions in Marlhes suggests an important shift of control toward heirs with the revolutionary and Napoleonic legislation in France. This does not mean that parents lost all control over their estate to their children nor does it imply that parental authority within the family disappeared. Such an interpretation of the influence of inheritance legislation of the revolutionary period grossly oversimplifies the complexity of property transfers from one generation to the next as well as the nature of authority within the family. The effect of the new legislation was to divide power over the succession and its disposition and limit the basis of parental authority in the family. This authority came to rest principally on parental control of the timing of the property transfer—whether children would receive their shares prior to their father's death or at his death, or whether it would be delayed even longer by donation of use rights to the widow. In Marlhes most farmers continued to work their farms until they died: among those 506 successions between 1866 and 1896 there were only 57 (11.3 percent) donations before death. Such persistence could delay for years the marriage of a child unless the parent chose to provide for his child in a marriage contract. The father thus maintained some control over the age at marriage of his children through his control over the timing of the transfer of property needed for the establishment of a household. The same control allowed a minority of fathers in Marlhes to delay transfer of a portion of their estates even beyond their own deaths by providing use rights for their widows.

While the parent retained control over timing of the property transfer with the Napoleonic Code, he did lose control over the ultimate disposition of his succession. In Marlhes, however, this loss of control was compensated by the remarkable agreement of parents and heirs on the need to maintain the homestead as a place in which all children could live if they so decided. Both generations followed a unified strategy that was modified only by the minority tendency of married males to provide in wills for the remainder of the lives of their widows. This strategy, followed through the provisions of the Civil Code for equal inheritance by all children and completed by the joint ownership by children of that inheritance, focused not on the arable land of the patrimony but on the family home as the center of the adult lives of children. It was a strategy remarkable for its freedom of choice for children: to them was left the choice of whether to divide the family property into separate farms, to cede their rights to a brother or sister, or to retain their part-ownership of the whole property. This freedom was of course the intention of the framers of the inheritance legislation of the revolutionary period. In the view of the peasantry of the Stephanois region, however, it was a by-product of a strategy that achieved aims desired by both parents and children.

The ability of this strategy to achieve the traditional aim of the peasantry—maintenance of the *houstau*—suggests one explanation for its persistence through the nineteenth century. This interpretation of the pattern as an adaptation of nineteenth-century legislation to Ancien Régime social patterns provides only a partial accounting of the inheritance strategy, however. The coexistence of this strategy with a rural economy characterized by small landholding, high migration rates, and the incursion of industrial work as an alternative to agricultural work remains to be explained. The small size of landholding in nineteenth-century Marlhes and the difficulty of dividing landed successions equitably doubtless played a part in the decision not to divide. Nevertheless, the most important factor was the relationship between this inheritance strategy and the complex rural economy of the region. Two aspects of the rural economy were central: the proximity of the urban region and the possibility of nonagricultural employment in the rural community in the ribbonweaving industry. The first allowed migration from Marlhes and other rural communes to the industrializing cities without requiring abandonment of the rural community by the migrant. He could migrate from Marlhes to Saint-Etienne for several years and then return to his family home. Ribbonweaving provided heirs who could not be supported by the land with an occupation that allowed them to exercise their rights to live on the family homestead as adults.

Inheritance therefore provides an important link between the family structure described earlier and both landholding and participation in ribbonweaving. The joint ownership of farms in nineteenth-century Marlhes that resulted from inheritance practices provided the basis for membership in the household for kin of the householder, especially siblings and their heirs, nieces, nephews, and cousins. If the farm was large enough, these additional members could find occupations in the agricultural sector. Even if the farm was small, the weaving industry provided economic opportunity. This explains the failure of weavers to establish separate households: they chose to practice their trade while living in the family home. Through the mediation of shared ownership of homesteads both landholding and domestic weaving became forces in favor of extended family structure.

The transfer of property between generations appears therefore to have been a vital element in the family system of nineteenth-century Marlhes. The inheritance practices represented the most important way in which the growing administrative power of the French state was felt in the rural community. This political context was complemented by the economic context of the urbanizing rural economy. The next chapter, analyzing the intersection of the domestic economy of the peasant family and the developing rural economy, considers this economic context in more detail.

# Chapter 9
# Three Types of
# Family Economy

Work in the peasant family in Marlhes followed a strict division of duties between men and women. Du Maroussem indicates that "the working of the land, culture of all types, was reserved for men; never, except during harvests, did women intervene."[1] This division is confirmed by occupations given in census lists: the only agricultural occupation with a significant number of women in either the 1851 or 1901 census was that of *ménagère*,[2] a term that implied the household responsibilities of women. The tasks of women were domestic, "the making of butter and cheese"; and the axiom "outside work for men, indoor work for women" was carefully observed in the region.[3]

The family economy was, however, sensitive to two aspects of economic life in the region—the ability of the family to supply labor and the changing economic opportunities offered by the growing urban-industrial region in the nearby valley. The labor available varied through the developmental cycle of the family group, with the labor of both husband and wife available from marriage until the birth of the first child, when it was decreased by the reduced ability of the wife to work during childbearing. The low level continued for another fifteen years or more, until childbearing was completed and the wife was able to return to a full work level. At the same time, the growth of children added their strength to the family, and it was in the later years of the marriage, when childbearing was completed and before adult children had left the family, that the most labor was available.

This developmental cycle was common to all peasant families with nuclear structure. The economic opportunities available in nineteenth-century Marlhes required further allocation of labor between agricultural and industrial work throughout the life cycle, and it is the way this allocation was carried out that gives the family economy in Marlhes its particular characteristics. Three different family economies may be found in the village during the nineteenth century. One was common to all families at mid-century and featured an almost equal division of labor between agriculture and industry along the lines of sex. By the end of the century this form of domestic economy had given way to two other types: one that continued to divide labor between agriculture and industry, although with less emphasis on industry than at mid-century; and another that focused the entire family's labor on agricultural work. These variations in family economic organization were the result of the changes in the rural economy that occurred with the development of the urban-industrial region and the different ways these changes were felt by land-owning and landless families in the village.

Table 27 outlines the domestic economy typical of mid-century in Marlhes, indicating the labor available in the household and its allocation. The principal characteristics of this type of family economic organization were that only male members of the family worked in agriculture and the labor of women was almost exclusively devoted to domestic ribbonweaving. The labor available in the family for these activities varied, however, through the life cycle. The column in table 27 indicating agricultural Standard Labor Units indicates the variations in agricultural labor. From marriage until older children reached their mid-teens, the family was only able to provide one person, the head of household, toward the labor needs of the farm. It was only after children reached the age of fourteen or fifteen that they began to contribute substantially to the labor supply. When this occurred, the supply of agricultural labor in the family rose sharply, first to two persons, with two sons each contributing half as much work as their father, and then to three persons, when the sons reached adulthood.

The importance of this varying labor supply in the family group may be seen through a comparison with labor demands on peasant farms. The principal determinant of the demand for agricultural labor was the size of the farm. Most farms were not located in one place in the commune but spread over the entire commune, or even in other villages of the canton. This made their cultivation difficult and time-consuming, in-

**Table 27.** Labor Allocation in Subsistence Agriculture—Domestic Weaving Family Economy

| Family Cycle | Age of Head | Head | Wife | S | S | D | D | Agric. S.L.U. | Indus. S.L.U. | Total S.L.U. |
|---|---|---|---|---|---|---|---|---|---|---|
| Marriage | 30 | 1 | .8 | | | | | 1 | .8 | 1.8 |
| 1st preg. | 31 | 1 | .5 | | | | | 1 | .5 | 1.5 |
| 2d preg. | 33 | 1 | .5 | | | | | 1 | .5 | 1.5 |
| 3d preg. | 35 | 1 | .5 | | | | | 1 | .5 | 1.5 |
| 4th preg. | 37 | 1 | .5 | | | | | 1 | .5 | 1.5 |
| Chld. 14–16 | 45 | 1 | .8 | .5 | .5 | .5 | .5 | 2 | 1.8 | 3.8 |
| Chld. 18+ | 50 | 1 | .8 | 1.0 | 1.0 | .8 | .8 | 3 | 2.4 | 5.4 |

creasing the labor requirements of the farm. Much time was lost traveling from one parcel to another, and transportation of crops from field to storehouse was a major operation, sometimes involving crossing the entire width of the commune. Finally, the same equipment had to be maintained whether the farm was five hectares or fifty, increasing the labor invested in this activity per hectare.

The inefficient organization of most farms in Marlhes increased the labor requirements per hectare, but their small size kept the total labor required for agriculture low. At most, a five-hectare farm in Marlhes required the work of one or two persons, and it is possible that many farms did not need the full time of even one person. This conclusion is reached if we attempt to estimate the labor needs of a typical small farm in Marlhes. A five-hectare farm, in which three hectares are devoted to cereal farming and the remaining two hectares are used to raise milk cows or goats,[4] would probably require about 3,209 hours of labor per year, using labor estimates from the Federal Republic of Germany for cereal cultivation and from Belgium for livestock. At the amount of labor per person (or Standard Labor Unit) given in the German study, this type of farm would only require the labor of 1.07 persons.[5]

The weak point in this estimate is the figure for labor required by cereal cultivation on very small farms. Twentieth-century estimates on this vary from 136.49 hours per hectare in Belgium to the 931 hours per hectare on small farms in the Federal Republic.[6] It has seemed best to use the high German estimate here because of the inefficiencies of farming in nineteenth-century Marlhes and the difficulties of working the rocky mountain soil. The figure given above is no more than an estimate of the labor required to work a farm in Marlhes; it is, however, a suggestive estimate. Even with a very large margin of error, its import is clear: while most farms in Marlhes probably occupied the time of one person, with occasional assistance from a second, they did not provide full-time employment for persons beyond the head of household and one son. Only if the farm grew larger, over ten hectares, would it begin to place a regular demand on more than two members of the family.

Thus if a man married in his late twenties or early thirties, as did most males in nineteenth-century Marlhes, he faced a long period of twelve or fifteen years, until he was in his mid-forties, before his family was able to provide the full labor supply for his farm. Once that occurred, the family quickly became too large for the needs of most farms. The family farm in mid-nineteenth-century Marlhes was only rarely in balance between labor demand by the farm and labor supply from the family.

The imbalance between labor supply and demand created by the developmental cycle of the peasant family presented two different problems for the family. In the earlier years of the life of the household the labor supply needed to be expanded; in the later years it had to be decreased. A number of tactics were available to meet both of these strategic needs for the peasant family. Labor could be expanded by temporary reallocation of some labor, such as that of the wife or daughters, into agriculture; on a more permanent basis it could be met by hiring either day laborers or domestic servants or, finally, by family extension. The labor supply in the family could be reduced by the placement of sons as domestic servants in other households; by out-migration of children to the urban valley; or by strict adherence to nuclear family structure, encouraging children to form their own households when they married.

Both temporary reallocation of labor to agriculture and the hiring of day laborers were best suited to a farm on which the shortage of labor was felt only during specific periods of the year, such as harvest time. This is doubtless what many householders did, especially those whose holdings were relatively small. As du Maroussem indicated, the one instance in which women did engage in field work was during the harvest, and the number of *journaliers* listed in the 1851 census testifies to their importance in providing a temporary, elastic source of labor during peak demand seasons.

A second alternative was to hire domestic farm workers, engaged for an entire year with the promise to be fed and housed and paid a small salary at the end of the year.[7] Agriculture was the most important occupational group to engage domestics: in both 1851 and 1901 three-quarters of the households with a domestic present were headed by an agricultural occupation. Other groups also made use of domestics, however. In 1851 there were four domestics hired by sawyers to assist in sawmills, although there were none in this group in 1901. Weavers also employed an occasional domestic to assist in weaving; these households were headed by *passementiers*, skilled artisans, rather than by the *rubannières* who made up most of the weaving population in Marlhes. Shopkeepers and artisans such as masons also hired laborers as domestics. The overwhelming number of domestics, however, worked in agricultural households.[8]

Data presented in tables 28 and 29 suggest the importance of domestics in fulfilling the labor needs of the agricultural household for additional labor during the years of low labor supply in the family. Table 28, in which the presence of a domestic worker is cross-tabulated with the age of the householder, indicates that in spite of the relatively low proportion of households in Marlhes in 1851 that employed domestic workers, this tendency was strongest when the householder was in his middle years, between thirty-five and forty-four. Almost one-fifth (17.8 percent) of the households headed by a person aged thirty-five to forty-four included a domestic. In contrast to the concentration of households with a domestic in the middle age groups, those headed by persons in older age groups, over forty-five, show a decreasing tendency to have

**Table 28.** Presence of Domestic Servant by Age of Head of Household in Marlhes, 1851

|  | 15–24 | 25–34 | 35–44 | 45–54 | 55–64 | 65+ | Total |
|---|---|---|---|---|---|---|---|
| Domestic | 0 | 10 | 27 | 19 | 9 | 8 | 73 |
| present | 0.0% | 11.9% | 17.8% | 11.7% | 8.6% | 9.3% | 12.1% |
| Domestic | 14 | 74 | 125 | 143 | 95 | 78 | 529 |
| not present | 100.0% | 88.1% | 82.2% | 88.3% | 91.4% | 90.7% | 87.9% |
| Total | 14 | 84 | 152 | 162 | 104 | 86 | 602 |
|  | 2.3% | 14.0% | 25.2% | 26.9% | 17.3% | 14.3% | 100.0% |

Source: A.D.L. 49 M 85, *Liste nominative de recensement de la commune de Marlhes*, 1851.

a domestic present in the household. The pattern by age, therefore, was for households with domestics present to concentrate in the middle age group, between thirty-five and forty-four, those years when the householder's family was unable to meet the labor requirements of the farm.

Table 29 shows another side of this pattern, the tendency for larger farms to employ domestic servants more frequently than on smaller farms. Households with over five hectares of land show an increasing tendency to have domestic help for farm work, and the relationship is especially striking on larger farms, those with over twenty hectares, with 61.9 percent of farms of this size employing a domestic.

A third alternative was also available in Marlhes to expand the labor supply of the family farm—adding extended kin to the nuclear family. There are similarities between the use of domestics and family extension that make them appear to be two different solutions to the same problem, the temporary shortage of agricultural labor on the farm during certain times of the family developmental cycle. Both family extension and the use of domestics tended to occur most often when the householder was in his thirties and early forties, the period when the family was hampered by the reduced ability of the wife to work because of childbearing. The most frequent type of family extension in these age groups involved the addition of siblings or other lateral kin to the nuclear family. If these family members were male they could provide the additional labor needed to work the farm during the early years of the family's development. Family extension was also strongly correlated with landownership, as was the use of domestics at mid-century. The larger the farm, the greater the need for additional labor, yet in most cases the ability of the nuclear family to supply labor remained at the level outlined in table 27.

One of the principal characteristics of the use of domestic servants as

Table 29. Presence of Domestic Servant in Household by
Amount of Land Owned by Householder in Marlhes, 1851

| | Hectares | | | | |
| --- | --- | --- | --- | --- | --- |
| | 0–1 | 1–4 | 5–19 | 20+ | Total |
| Domestic present | 48 | 7 | 5 | 13 | 73 |
| | 10.0% | 11.7% | 12.5% | 61.9% | 12.1% |
| Domestic not present | 433 | 53 | 35 | 8 | 529 |
| | 90.0% | 88.3% | 87.5% | 38.1% | 87.9% |
| Total | 481 | 60 | 40 | 21 | 602 |
| | 79.9% | 10.0% | 7.0% | 3.0% | 100.0% |

Chi squared = 50.83 with three degrees of freedom; significance = .001; contingency coefficient = .279.

Source: A.D.L. 49 M 85, *Liste nominative de recensement de la commune de Marlhes*, 1851; Série P Non-Coté, *Matrice cadastrale de la commune de Marlhes.*

farm labor was the elasticity of this labor factor. Few servants expected to spend a lifetime on one farm, or even in domestic service. Hiring was only done for one year, and at the end of that period the landowner could discharge the domestic and reduce the farm's labor force. Family extension, on the other hand, was less easily adjustable, and the kin who extended the family could not be hired and fired with the same ease. The inheritance rights of siblings in the farm was the principal factor discouraging a high elasticity of extended kin on the family farm. These considerations placed limits on the freedom of movement of the householder in meeting his labor needs. It seems apparent, however, that both tactics were used by peasant families in Marlhes.

The allocation of labor in the peasant household in nineteenth-century Marlhes was intended, of course, to provide income for the family as well as to occupy each family member. It is unfortunately almost impossible to measure agricultural returns to the peasant family in this period. The consumption of goods produced by the family farm and the uneven participation of the peasantry in markets as sellers and buyers make it difficult to determine either income or expenditures on goods not produced on the farm. The best measure of independence for the peasant was the amount of land he controlled, either through ownership or rental. By this standard many peasant families in Marlhes were particularly disadvantaged. As we saw in chapter 3, the production of an average farm was not sufficient to support an entire family. Thus agriculture was not only an activity that did not occupy the entire labor force of the family, but—perhaps more important—could provide the sole basis for a family economy only in the rare cases of large landowners.

Domestic ribbonweaving was therefore a necessary supplement to agriculture in most households in the village at mid-century. This importance is reflected in table 27, showing the role of weaving in the family economy during the developmental cycle.[9] Domestic weaving recruited its workers primarily among women in the age groups from fifteen to fifty-five and in all civil statuses. Therefore, the household had a weaver at almost all times during its existence. A wife continued her work as a weaver after marriage, and only the coming of children reduced her ability to work in the trade during the fifteen years after her marriage. As children, daughters probably helped their mother by winding the silk for the weft on bobbins and assisting at the loom. The labor of the household devoted to weaving increased as daughters reached their teens and worked as weavers. The mother herself began to be able to work full time again, with her childbearing behind her. As the daughters reached adulthood, their contribution in labor increased and the family participated most heavily in weaving, limited only by the number of looms available.

The labor investment in domestic weaving was therefore always present, with a sharp increase as daughters reached their late teens, before they themselves married. The hardest years for the family were those during which children were being born and before they reached their mid-teens. After that the situation of the family quickly brightened, with increasing numbers of hands available for weaving work. Industrial income was lowest, therefore, during the head of the household's thirties and forties. It increased as he reached his middle and late forties, and in his early fifties it was very high; then it decreased again as daughters married and left home.

Only an approximation of the contribution of domestic weaving to family income can be determined from the available sources. Workers were paid by the task and prices changed from day to day, yet official reports during the domestic phase of ribbonweaving gave daily wages for weavers. In 1835 Alphonse Peyret suggested that daily wages for *compagnons* in Saint-Etienne were between 1.70 and 2.00 francs per day.[10] The Chambre de Commerce of Saint-Etienne in 1871 indicated that wages for women varied from 1.50 to 2.50 francs per day.[11] Wages in the countryside were probably lower than those in the city, and in the 1848 Inquiry on Industrial and Agricultural Work, the justice of the peace for Saint-Genest-Malifaux said that "workers in ribbons all work by the task, and cannot earn more than 50 centimes per day on the average, and their food."[12] In the neighboring canton of Bourg-Argental the justice of the peace reported that wages in ribbonweaving were 95 centimes for women and from 65 to 75 centimes for children.[13]

The wide variation of all estimates, their doubtful basis, and the lack of constant work in ribbonweaving make it difficult to place much faith in the absolute level of these figures. But they do furnish an order of magnitude, and we may safely estimate a daily wage of between 50 and 75 centimes for two-thirds of the year at mid-century for a domestic weaver in the countryside. At this rate a weaver would earn between 100 and 150 francs per year. The contribution of this amount to the family budget may be seen by comparing it with estimates in the 1848 Inquiry of the amount necessary to support an individual and a family of four. For the canton of Saint-Genest-Malifaux these estimates were 200 francs for a single worker and 500 francs for a family of four.[14] If a family member was weaving, the trade could provide 20 to 30 percent of the family's needed income. Thus weaving income could make up the difference between the needs of a family and the production of a farm but was not sufficient to support an individual or family by itself. The amount earned from weaving was about 50 francs short of the minimum required for an individual. In Marlhes this could be made up by the shares in family farms that many weavers held, shares providing a place to live in the family homestead and the economies of living in a larger group. It would be inviting disaster, however, for a landless family to attempt to live on the earnings of a head of household who worked as a weaver. Weaving fit into the domestic economy of Marlhes at mid-century only as a subsidiary to agriculture or as an artisanal occupation.

The principal components of the domestic economy at mid-century were the agricultural and industrial activities already described. Others were also available, however. Men could find occasional work as day laborers or undertake the temporary migrations that Olwen Hufton has described as such an important part of the traditional domestic economy of the poor in France.[15] Trips to the Plaine du Forez north of Saint-Etienne must have been made, especially at harvest time. These activities were not likely to bring in much income: a day laborer in Marlhes earned only 1.50 francs per day,[16] and it is not likely that many days' work were available in the village. The principal benefit of temporary migration was not the money income that it brought but the way it eased pressure on the resources of the family left behind. It was also possible for women to earn income through mercenary wet-nursing, caring for infants from the urban valley. It is impossible to document the income of a family in the Stephanois region from wet-nursing due to a lack of records. George Sussman, however, has found a fee of about 10 francs per month to be common in Normandy in the early nineteenth century.[17] If this is taken as an approximation of the fee in the Stephanois region, a family could earn up to 120 francs per year through this activity. In fact, the high mortality of nurslings made it difficult to continue earning this fee for an entire year. It was more likely that a smaller amount, perhaps only 10 or

20 francs, could be earned from this practice. All of these activities, however, provided helpful supplements to a family's income.

The family economy in Marlhes at mid-century was therefore a mixed subsistence and wage economy, characterized by the division of the family's labor between agricultural and industrial work and by the household as a locus of both production and consumption. Men worked in the fields and women carried on a number of wage-earning activities in the home, with domestic ribbonweaving the most important. The principal differences between social groups lay in the emphasis placed on wage-earning or agricultural work, with poorer families depending more heavily on weaving and wet-nursing than the families that owned larger amounts of land. In all families, however, the combination of agriculture and industry in the household could be found. In this family economy the household was a production as well as a consumption unit.

The differences between the family economies of landless and landowning peasants in Marlhes—only a question of emphasis at mid-century—became increasingly large as the century wore on, and by the end of the century the mixed subsistence and wage economy of mid-century had been transformed into two different forms of family economic organization. The most direct descendant of the mid-century domestic economy continued to mix agriculture and industrial wage earnings. However, this new family economy reflected the economic changes of the second half of the century. Agriculture became more market-oriented, drawing more labor and increasing the responsibilities of the *ménagère*. As factory work became more important in ribbonweaving, industrial wage earning became less important in the domestic economy. This mixed family economy, however, was increasingly confined to the poorer members of the village community, those without adequate land, among whom the agricultural improvements of the second half of the nineteenth century were only slightly felt. Here, more than anywhere else, the impact of the economic changes in the Stephanois region created differences in the family patterns of the peasants in Marlhes.

The agricultural work performed by men remained relatively stable throughout the nineteenth century. This work consisted of sowing and harvesting crops; plowing land for planting and again during its fallow year; maintaining equipment and buildings; feeding livestock; tending small gardens near the house; and gathering wood from the forests that the peasant either owned or used through communal rights. The shift in agriculture from a diverse cereal and husbandry agriculture to a more specialized agriculture aimed at production of milk products for the urban market caused little change in these tasks. Even if land was to be shifted from rye to oats, it was worked in the same way. The chores around the farm remained similar throughout the century, whether subsistence cereal production was combined with husbandry or fields previously used for rye were converted into artificial pastures for increased husbandry. Men's work in Marlhes remained associated with agriculture and the activities of plowing, harvesting, and maintenance that had characterized it for centuries. This continuity is reflected in table 30—the work of the male members of the family was allocated to agriculture, as it had been at the middle of the century.

A major difference between this agricultural-industrial family economy and its antecedent of mid-century lay in the work of married women. At mid-century their work consisted of a multitude of wage-earning tasks that could be carried out in the home: preparation of garden and dairy products for market, wet-nursing, and above all domestic ribbonweaving. The principal economic changes of the half-century reshaped these patterns of work for the wives of poorer peasants. Most important was the replacement of domestic by factory ribbonweaving. The wife ceased to work in a ribbonweaving factory when she married, as the labor demands of factory work made it necessary for her to choose between remaining in her household and going to the factory to work. During the twenty years after marriage the family had no participation in weaving. Instead, the wife and mother devoted her energies to childrearing and increased attempts to take advantage of the growing market for agricultural products through emphasis on preparation of milk and especially cheese. These activities may be considered agricultural, but in a different sense than the agricultural work of the male members of the household. The *ménagère* bore responsibility for turning the products of the family farm, and especially its small herd of goats and a few cows, into marketable products. Mercenary wet-nursing also continued to be an *industrie à point* for women in poorer families.

Table 30. Labor Allocation in Day Laborer—Factory
Weaving Family Economy

| Family Cycle | Age of Head | Head | Wife | S | S | D | D | Agric. S.L.U. | Indus. S.L.U. | Total S.L.U. |
|---|---|---|---|---|---|---|---|---|---|---|
| Marriage | 30 | 1 | .8 | | | | | 1.8 | — | 1.8 |
| 1st preg. | 31 | 1 | .5 | | | | | 1.5 | — | 1.5 |
| 2d preg. | 33 | 1 | .5 | | | | | 1.5 | — | 1.5 |
| 3d preg. | 35 | 1 | .5 | | | | | 1.5 | — | 1.5 |
| 4th preg. | 37 | 1 | .5 | | | | | 1.5 | — | 1.5 |
| Chld. 14–16 | 45 | 1 | .8 | .5 | .5 | .8 | .8 | 2.8 | 1.6 | 4.4 |
| Chld. 18+ | 50 | 1 | .8 | 1.0 | 1.0 | .8 | .8 | 3.8 | 1.6 | 5.4 |

Only when a daughter reached the age of fifteen and could enter the factory labor force did industrial work appear in the mixed economy of the turn of the century. Her stay in the factory was not likely to be permanent, lasting only until her own marriage when she took up the duties of a *ménagère*. As we have already noted, this brief appearance of factory work in the family developmental cycle reduced the effect on family structure that had been such a feature of the domestic weaving patterns of mid-century. In another way, however, the change from domestic to factory weaving and its concentration in a short part of the lives of daughters led to subtle alterations in the internal organization of the family. The household no longer encapsulated both the production and consumption of family members. With their work separated from that of the household, the earnings of young women were also separate. This definition of the ownership of a part of the family's earnings forced decisions about the disposition of wages on the family in much the same way that factory organization forced decisions concerning the work of the mother.

Estimating weaving income at the end of the century is easier than at mid-century, for the weavers worked not by the task but for fixed wages in weaving or spinning factories. Wages in these factories seem to have been higher than in the domestic weaving of mid-century: du Maroussem indicates that in spinning factories the maximum wage was 1.25 or 1.40 francs for older workers. Younger women probably received between 50 centimes and 1 franc per day, although he only indicates that their wages could reach the lowest levels.[18] In weaving factories wages were slightly higher than in spinning and were paid in two ways. In manually operated factories the wage was paid by the day at the rate of 1 or 2 francs per day. In factories in which looms were powered by steam or water, earnings ranged from 25 to 50 francs per month—the same wage, but paid by the month.[19]

If wages such as these were received for the entire year, they could provide a substantial income for the weaver and her family. A minimum wage of 25 francs per month over twelve months provided 300 francs annually for the family budget. In fact, because of the seasonality of demand for ribbons, a weaver or spinner could not work for the entire year. Even if she worked for two-thirds of the year, however, her income of 200 francs or more could be an important contribution toward meeting the expenses of the family.

Estimating family expenses at the end of the nineteenth century is more difficult than at mid-century, when the data of the 1848 Inquiry provide some information. No such evidence is available from the end of the century. However, the last quarter of the nineteenth century was a period of deflation,[20] and it is possible to use changes in the departmental price of a hectoliter of wheat between mid-century and the end of the century to correct the 1848 estimates for deflation. In 1848-60 the mean price of a hectoliter of wheat was 20.85 francs; by 1890-1900 this had decreased to 17.24 francs. When the ratio between these two price levels is applied to the 1848 figures for household expenses, estimates of 165 francs for an individual and 413 francs for a family are reached. Income from weaving could therefore make an even greater contribution to the needs of the family in the 1890s than it had a half-century earlier.

But did it? The principal difference between factory wages and the earnings of a daughter who worked in domestic weaving was that the extent to which she had contributed to the weaving of a particular ribbon for which the family was paid by the fabricant was no longer open to debate. Her earnings from factory work were obvious—the contents of her pay packet. As production became separated from the household, the ownership of the return for production became more clearly defined. To whom, then, did these earnings ultimately belong in Marlhes, the daughter or her parents?

The best place to look at the division of the earnings of a daughter is in the process of accumulation of a dowry, the sum of money that made marriage possible. The answer unfortunately is ambiguous, and it is difficult to find a steady progression in one direction between 1850 and 1900.

The accumulation of a sum of money for the purchase of household furnishings and farm tools was the most important task for a young couple before their marriage. Without these resources the newly married couple began their married life in absolute poverty, unable to work even a rented farm. Although most couples in Marlhes started with only a trousseau valued at a few hundred francs and another two or three hundred francs in cash, that could make the difference between economic success or failure for the new family. It was enough to furnish the house with linens and other necessities, purchase livestock, and acquire the plow and other tools needed to work the land.

The opportunities for acquiring this cash and property were limited in the rural Stephanois region. The parents of the couple were an obvious source: they might make a donation at marriage to their son or daughter. In the 1867 marriage contract of Jean-Baptiste Frappa and Jeanne Marie Bergeron, for example, the bride herself brought liquid property valued at 200 francs. The principal wealth of the couple was a donation of 1,300 francs in cash from the father of the bride.[21] Other relatives were another source. They too may have provided donations for nieces or nephews at marriage. When Pierre Moine married Catherine Moulin in Marlhes in 1867, Catherine brought not only 300 francs in property and 300 francs in cash to the marriage, but also the successions of her three aunts by their donation.[22]

The final and most significant source of dowries in Marlhes was the personal savings of the couple. Most married couples found themselves beginning their marriage in the situation of Jean Quiblier and Antoinette Tranchand, whose total property in their marriage contract amounted to a little over 600 francs. Jean owned only his clothing and 300 francs in cash; his principal wealth was his future right to his father's succession. Antoinette owned only household linens, her clothing, a loom for weaving ribbons, and 300 francs in cash.[23] This marriage depended less on Jean's inheritance than on the small sums of money saved by the young couple in the years before their marriage.

A dowry that came from personal savings could be accumulated only if the profits of the child's work were at least shared by the family with the child. One type of work that probably featured this sharing was domestic service, available for a few years to both young men and young women. A position could occasionally be found for a teen-ager as a maid or domestic servant on a farm in the area. The family studied by du Maroussem, for example, had earned its entire fortune at marriage through domestic service: the wife had accumulated 250 francs as a maid in a chateau in the canton, while the husband worked as a domestic for an elderly gentleman in the region and saved 600 francs by the time of his marriage.[24] Such earnings took a long period of time, however; the annual wage for this type of work during the Second Empire was only 50 francs for a farm domestic, 80 francs for a servant.[25] The principal value of placement of a child as a domestic accrued to the parents of the child, for the burden on the household was reduced with the departure of the child for the household of his or her employer, who housed, clothed, and fed the domestic. The small salary could become an adequate dowry in four or five years only if carefully saved. But domestic service did provide young men and women with opportunities to earn the money necessary to marry and establish their own households.

The economic structure of the region also provided another opportunity for young women—ribbonweaving. All young women throughout the period, except the daughters of large landowners at the end of the nineteenth century, followed this pattern of industrial work to accumulate a dowry.

While it is clear that young single women worked in large numbers in ribbonweaving throughout the nineteenth century, it is less clear what happened to their earnings. Certainly a part must have been paid to their parents, if for no other reason than to contribute to their own upkeep. Weavers lived at home and were fed from the family pot; they must have contributed something to the family budget. A report on the region for the Inquiry on the Situation of Workers by the Chamber of Deputies in 1871 indicates this pattern, stating that "until the time of their marriage children assist their parents."[26]

However, there is also strong evidence that at least a part of the earnings of young women remained their own, to be saved for their dowries. Perhaps the best evidence for this is the almost universal pattern in marriage contracts for the bride herself to have several hundred francs' worth of personal property or cash. While occasionally a young couple received a donation from their parents, the vast majority had no other resources at marriage than their own savings. There is even a case, in 1894, of a marriage contract in which a bride listed as one of her assets a loan of 400 francs she had made to her parents.[27] While few young women were able to accumulate very large dowries on their own, most dowries did come from their own efforts. Individual work as a teen-ager and young adult was more important in providing the means to marry than a donation from parents.

The implications of the pattern of individual accumulation of dowries among the poorer families in Marlhes are ambiguous. It does indicate that individual economic activity existed in the peasant household, with earnings saved by the daughter for her own account rather than contributed to a common family fund. This does not necessarily indicate that a spirit of individualism and self-expression was the reason for this individual saving. Even at the end of the century parents could determine the type of activity their daughter undertook. Du Maroussem claims that the decision to place a child in domestic service or in weaving rested with the father of the family.[28] Whether the choice was made by father, mother, or both parents, it was a limited choice for most parents in Marlhes—for if they could not provide work on their own farms for their children, they had to place them in some form of employment, whether domestic service or ribbonweaving. A limitation on the authority of many parents therefore was their own poverty and lack of a farm that would support and employ their entire family. Without that basis for parental authority, their choices in the future of their children were limited.

Poorer parents also lacked instruments to enforce decisions made for a child. Among larger landowning families, the ability of the parents to establish their daughter with a donation at marriage gave them leverage over her conduct before that event. The inheritance provisions of the Civil Code may have diminished this authority, but it did not disappear entirely; a father could control the timing of his children's marriages, if not their eventual succession to his wealth. Parents who owned little or no land enjoyed no such leverage. Their own poverty meant that they had little wealth with which to endow their daughters, and their control over their children prior to marriage was reduced. Each child, whether a son or a daughter, of a family with little or no land knew that if he or she was to acquire the economic means to establish a household, it would be through his or her own efforts, not through a donation from a parent. The work as a domestic servant or ribbonweaver that was the lot of most young people in nineteenth-century Marlhes may have had some benefits for the family economy, either by removing a person from the household or by adding to income through the contributions of the child. It also provided the child with the means to marry and, from the point of view of the child, that must have been its primary purpose.

We know, therefore, that at least part of daughters' earnings remained under their control both at the middle and at the end of the century. But we do not know if there was a deepening of this pattern as the century wore on and factory weaving made the exact amount of the daughter's contribution more obvious. What does seem clear is that with the greater clarity in accounting introduced by the advance of industrialism, families persisted in the allocation of a part of their daughters' earnings toward the accumulation of a dowry, universally recognized as a necessity for marriage. Rather than indicating that an amorphous spirit of individualism was growing in the industrial conditions of the mixed economy of the Stephanois region, the individual saving of children in Marlhes seems to have been an adaptation of the family group to the economic reality that required most children to earn their own dowries before their marriage.

A complete break with the typical activities of the family economy of mid-century was made by a limited group of families in late nineteenth-century Marlhes, those that owned enough land to support and occupy all members of the family. These families, no more than 25 or 30 percent of those living in the village, turned away from the wage-earning possibilities offered by the ribbonweaving trade and focused their labor solely on the market agriculture that prospered in the last quarter of the nineteenth century. These families preserved the identity between production and consumption typical of mid-century. Their do-

**Table 31.** Labor Allocation in Agricultural Property Owner Family Economy

| Family Cycle | Age of Head | Head | Wife | S | S | D | D | Agric. S.L.U. | Indus. S.L.U. | Total S.L.U. |
|---|---|---|---|---|---|---|---|---|---|---|
| Marriage | 30 | 1 | .8 | | | | | 1.8 | — | 1.8 |
| 1st preg. | 31 | 1 | .5 | | | | | 1.5 | — | 1.5 |
| 2d preg. | 33 | 1 | .5 | | | | | 1.5 | — | 1.5 |
| 3d preg. | 35 | 1 | .5 | | | | | 1.5 | — | 1.5 |
| 4th preg. | 37 | 1 | .5 | | | | | 1.5 | — | 1.5 |
| Chld. 14–16 | 45 | 1 | .8 | .5 | .5 | .5 | .5 | 3.8 | — | 3.8 |
| Chld. 18+ | 50 | 1 | .8 | 1.0 | 1.0 | .8 | .8 | 5.4 | — | 5.4 |

mestic economic organization, outlined in table 31, reflects the complete dedication of the family's labor supply to agriculture. As with the poorer members of the village community at the end of the century, male work remained much the same in these families as it had been during the Second Republic—devoted to agriculture and field work—and the wives of property holders no longer worked in ribbonweaving but in agricultural work. The distinctive feature of these households was the devotion of the labor of daughters to work on their parents' farm, not to factory ribbonweaving, as occurred in other families at this time. The agricultural-factory labor economy of the poor in the late nineteenth century represented a partial shift of labor from wage earning to agriculture; among the landowning families of that period, this withdrawal was complete as even daughters remained at home to work on the farms of their parents.

What lay behind this shift away from the mixed economy typical of mid-century, and why did the families of landowners develop differently from those of land-poor peasants? First of all, we may emphatically reject any notion that the changes in women's work in property-owning families were part of a process of increasing female domesticity among these wealthier peasants. With only a few exceptions, the wives and daughters of peasants in Marlhes were a necessary part of the labor force for working the farm. As table 31 makes clear, the work first of the wife and then of the daughter was necessary: without their contribution the family would be lacking the arms necessary to work the farm. In particular, the increased importance of market farming, and especially the increase in the importance of the sale of dairy products, made the work of the women of the family, who prepared milk and cheese for sale, even more vital. The labor requirements of the larger farms of these families increased, especially in the areas reserved for women—"the making of butter and cheese," in du Maroussem's words.[29]

Thus, increased labor demands on the farms of the turn of the century provide a partial explanation for the increased dedication of women's work to the nonindustrial sector. But these factors were also at work on the families of the landless at this time, and their daughters provided the labor force for the weaving and spinning factories that developed in the countryside. Why the particular trait of landowners' families, the absence of ribbonweaving among their daughters?

The answer seems to lie in the growing shortage of available labor in the countryside in the years of the Third Republic.[30] The rural exodus that became apparent in those years on a national level was also becoming an important fact in the Stephanois countryside. The pull of the urban-industrial valley remained strong and it became increasingly difficult for villages to keep native sons and daughters at home. An indication of this increasing pull of the city is the declining population of Marlhes itself: more than 2,200 persons had lived in the village in 1861, after the creation of the commune of Saint-Regis-du-Coin. This total declined slowly but steadily, with only a few upswings, during the next half-century, and by 1911 the population of the village was only 1,671 persons. The canton of Saint-Genest-Malifaux, the principal region in which farmers in Marlhes could recruit domestic servants and day laborers, lost 15 percent of its population in that half-century.[31] The lure of the city with its better living conditions and higher wages drew those who in the past supplied the additional labor needed to work larger farms in the village.

This labor shortage was apparent in the decreased tendency to use domestics on farms at the end of the century and in the weakening of the relationship between landholding and use of domestic labor that was present at mid-century. In 1851, 12.1 percent of all households employed a domestic, while in 1901 only 9.2 percent included one. As is evident from tables 32 and 33, the tendency toward use of domestics to meet the labor requirements of the family farm in periods of low family labor supply continued at a reduced level, with 13.8 percent of households headed by a person aged twenty-five to thirty-four and 13.2 percent of those headed by a person aged thirty-five to forty-four including a domestic servant. But the relationship between landholding and the presence of a domestic worker was much weaker in 1901 than in 1851. Most significantly, the 1901 data show a change in the place of domestic labor on large farms: of the ten farms over twenty hectares in 1901, only one employed a domestic. The shortage of a cheap labor supply in the countryside as a result of the rural exodus is the explanation for this reduced use of domestic service on larger farms at the turn of the century.

The householder still had to provide labor to work his land, however, especially as he moved more and more toward a market-oriented agriculture.[32] The solution came from within his family, with the labor of

Table 32. Presence of Domestic Servant by Age of Head of Household in Marlhes, 1901

|  | 15–24 | 25–34 | 35–44 | 45–54 | 55–64 | 65+ | Total |
|---|---|---|---|---|---|---|---|
| Domestic present | 0 | 9 | 14 | 6 | 6 | 4 | 39 |
|  | 0.0% | 13.8% | 13.2% | 7.6% | 6.3% | 5.3% | 9.2% |
| Domestic not present | 5 | 56 | 92 | 73 | 88 | 72 | 386 |
|  | 100.0% | 86.2% | 86.8% | 92.4% | 93.7% | 94.7% | 90.8% |
| Total | 5 | 65 | 106 | 79 | 94 | 76 | 425 |
|  | 1.2% | 15.3% | 24.9% | 18.6% | 22.1% | 17.9% | 100.0% |

Source: A.D.L. 49 M 353, *Liste nominative de recensement de la commune de Marlhes*, 1901.

Table 33. Presence of Domestic Servant in Household by
Amount of Land Owned by Householder in Marlhes, 1901

|  | Hectares | | | | |
|  | 0–1 | 1–4 | 5–19 | 20+ | Total |
|---|---|---|---|---|---|
| Domestic | 31 | 3 | 4 | 1 | 39 |
| present | 8.6% | 9.7% | 17.4% | 10.0% | 9.2% |
| Domestic | 330 | 28 | 19 | 9 | 386 |
| not present | 91.4% | 90.3% | 82.6% | 90.0% | 90.8% |
| Total | 361 | 31 | 23 | 10 | 425 |
|  | 84.9% | 7.3% | 5.4% | 2.3% | 100.0% |

Chi squared = 2.03 with three degrees of freedom; significance = .16; contingency coefficient = .069.

Source: A.D.L. 49 M 353, *Liste nominative de recensement de la commune de Marlhes*, 1901; Série P Non-Coté, *Matrice cadastrale de la commune de Marlhes.*

not only his wife but also his daughters being used to meet the requirements of the farm. These farmers employed their daughters to watch their herds of sheep and cows and to assist their mother in preparing dairy products, rather than as domestic or factory weavers. The landholder family economy of the turn of the century, focused exclusively on agriculture, therefore represents the response of the family unit to the increased agricultural opportunities created by urban development and the labor shortage created by the opportunities for migration to the cities.

The movement of landholders' daughters from weaving to agriculture during the second half of the nineteenth century presents a counterpoint to the wage earning of poorer peasants' children at this time. If the explanation of this shift lies with the labor needs of the farm, it is evidence of the ability of parents to allocate the labor of their family as they needed and saw fit. In nineteenth-century Marlhes it was these larger landowning families who reflected most accurately du Maroussem's claim that "the family group is one; it is necessary to have a master."[33] At mid-century, when there was no necessary conflict between domestic weaving and occasional agricultural work by daughters and when domestic servants were plentiful, these young women worked in the weaving trade. At the end of the century, however, when it became impossible to continue the combination of industrial and agricultural work and the family was faced with a shortage of available outside labor, the claims of the farm took precedence and daughters worked at home, not in the new spinning and weaving factories.

The three distinct types of family economic organization found in nineteenth-century Marlhes and described in this chapter indicate the interrelationships that existed between economic development and the basis of family life for the peasants of Marlhes. The organizational changes of ribbonweaving, from a domestic to a factory trade, engendered conflicts within the family economy and choices as to whether a family member would work in the trade. The development of market agriculture caused a reallocation of family labor to serve the needs of the family in that sector. The labor shortage in the countryside that resulted from rural-urban migration in the second half of the century prompted further reallocation of family labor among the larger farmers who at mid-century depended on hired labor.

The focal point of the family's responses to these external stimuli was the work of its female members, the wife and daughters of the householder. The fluidity of women's work in the peasant family in Marlhes and the apparent ease with which the family shifted the effort of its female members should not hide from us the importance of this work in all three of these types of family economy. Both in meeting family labor needs and in providing needed money income, the work of wives and daughters was vital and formed an integral part in the calculations of the parents as they pursued their goals of economic survival.

It is obvious that a view of the peasant domestic economy as a common economic unit under the control of the head oversimplifies the situation in nineteenth-century Marlhes. The families of larger landholders at the end of the century came closest to this ideal, working in a family economy in which "production and family life were inseparably intertwined [and] the household was the center around which resources, labor and consumption were balanced."[34] To a certain extent this also describes the mixed economy of mid-century in Marlhes, since domestic weaving allowed the close association of production and consumption in the household. It is among the poor majority at the end of the century that this ideal is least applicable, and a family wage economy, with shared consumption but not production, came into existence. This type of economic organization of the family, which was to become common in nineteenth-century cities,[35] appears first in Marlhes among the poorest members of the village community.

The family economy in Marlhes also casts doubt on the assumption of an emphasis in peasant families on supporting as many members as possible rather than maximizing production.[36] It was a struggle for these small farmers to support a nuclear family, and most families were forced by the small size of their landholding to supplement agricultural earnings with industrial work. Under such conditions there could be no question of supporting additional family members from the proceeds of the family farm. The principal pattern in the region seems to have been one of removing additional persons from the family of origin as quickly as possible, either through placing children as domestics when they reached their teens or through the migration of children to the industrial valley. This pattern was modified only by the inheritance patterns of the region which gave each child a share in the land owned by his parents, a right he or she retained throughout life. The economic realities of the countryside, however, imposed a strict limit on the ability of these additional kin to remain on the family farm. If they did so, they had to support themselves through some activity other than farming.

The opportunities for additional work were best in the middle of the century. Domestic ribbonweaving provided an alternative for women. The earnings of a domestic weaver approached the amount required to support an individual in the middle of the nineteenth century, and this accounts for the tendency of domestic ribbonweaving to encourage family extension and discourage migration. In this case, the limits of the domestic economy, the inheritance patterns of the region, and the presence of industrial work combined to make it possible for sisters of householders to remain in the region on the family farm yet still support themselves.

For men the situation was different. The only activity available for a man who did not have his own farm was occasional work as a day laborer on the farms of others. The best alternative for a brother was not remaining in the countryside but joining the migrants heading down the slope to the factories and mines of the valley.

The principal change in possibilities of supplemental work in the second half of the century affected women. Ribbonweaving declined in importance and required factory work. As a consequence, sisters of householders were less able to remain in the countryside and their rates of migration rose. The need for additional male labor on the family farm did not change, as the increased demand for agricultural labor in animal husbandry was met by the conversion of wives from ribbonweavers to agricultural workers, preparing dairy products for marketing.

The domestic economy of the peasant family in nineteenth-century Marlhes therefore was principally characterized by the need for each individual to provide his or her own means of support. Only the economies of living in a large group, as opposed to living alone, encouraged the extension of the family group by the addition of a sibling or more distant kin of the householder. These same economic constraints encouraged children to earn their own fortunes. The economic situation of the peasantry and its interaction with the family developmental cycle and needs provided the basis for the family life of the peasants of Marlhes.

# Chapter 10
# The Stages of Life

The family developmental cycle that looms so large in the preceding chapters was the complement of an individual developmental cycle determined by the relationship of the individual to the family group. Even today, family position largely determines individual status: infancy, childhood, adolescence, and adulthood are defined not only by age but also by one's role in a family group. In a modern French village studied by Laurence Wylie, for example, adolescence is defined not only as being a certain age, but also as a period in which family responsibilities are minimal and a certain amount of irresponsible behavior is not only condoned but expected.[1]

The definition of the stages of life through one's relationship to the family group was even stronger in the past. The theme of "the ages of life," an indication of this relationship, is common in early modern French literature and art. Yet these ages, so important in determining perceptions of status by an individual and society, were not immutable over time. The translator of a popular sixteenth-century Latin text, *Le Grand propriétaire de toutes choses*, suggests this change through the differences between Latin and French terminology: "It is more difficult in French than in Latin, for in Latin there are seven ages referred to by various names, of which there are only three in French: to wit, childhood, youth and old age."[2] A comparison of modern ideas of the stages of life, particularly the notion of a period of adolescence, as in Wylie's village, indicates the changes that have occurred since that period.[3]

What were individual and social perceptions of status in Marlhes during the nineteenth century? While no direct evidence exists of this, it is possible to reconstruct a series of "ages of life" determined by changes in attitudes toward the individual and the apparent importance of certain events in the individual's lifetime. Five stages seem to have been perceived both by the individual and by the broader society in which he lived. There was a period of infancy, in which the society and the family recognized the fragile nature of the infant's life with an apparent fatalism toward the survival of the child. This was succeeded by childhood, with dramatically different popular attitudes toward the individual. The child was educated and given basic skills that would help in later life, especially if that life involved movement into the industrial economy of the cities. Around the age of twelve or thirteen, this period of childhood gave way to adolescence, although not in the modern sense of lack of responsibility: the adolescent was expected to work and contribute to the family income as well as accumulate the financial resources for marriage. This event moved the individual into adulthood, with complete independence from the family of origin and the establishment in most cases of a completely separate household. Adulthood meant family responsibilities: for men the duties of a householder, for women childbearing and childrearing and participation in the maintenance of the household's economic position. Finally, after the death of the spouse, a poorly defined period of old age came about, marked by a lessening of family responsibilities but a continuation of the necessity to work to support oneself. These five stages of life defined, in terms of family role and position, the status of the individual.

The focus of the family group for the vast majority of families in nineteenth-century Marlhes was the conjugal pair of husband and wife. Only among the few larger landowners was the family group likely to extend beyond the conjugal pair and their children, including most often retired parents of the husband or wife. In the most populous social group, nuclear family structure was the rule, and the allocation of the labor force and the economic resources of the family group depended on the husband and wife and left little room for additional adult family members.

The nuclear family group was likely to be relatively large in nineteenth-century Marlhes, however, and the child born into the family was probably one of four or five children. Even with the high infant mortality characteristic of the village population, a child would grow up with three or four brothers and sisters. While these births were spread over a period of fifteen or twenty years, the birth of children began a period of great strain on the family group. Whether a child lived or died in infancy, the birth threatened the life of the mother and meant that her ability to work was reduced. At the actual birth of the child this may have been temporary, lasting only a few months. If the child lived, however, it meant an increase in the household responsibilities of the mother, caring for the child, and a long-term reduction in her contribution to the family economy. An average woman in Marlhes, married at age twenty-five and married for 18.5 years, would have almost six children in that period, given the fertility rates described in chapter 5. The reduction from childbearing in the ability of the mother to work lasted almost as long as most marriages, and each succeeding child added to the demands children made on the time of the mother. It is not surprising that du Maroussem called the early childbearing period the most difficult for the peasant family, during which rent payments for the farm fell behind and the debts of the household increased.[4]

The care of the children was the responsibility of the mother, and she received little assistance from other family members. The nuclear structure of most families in Marlhes meant that there was no grandparent available to assist in childraising. The high mortality and low life expectancy in the commune, as well as the frequency with which one parent was from a commune other than Marlhes, made it difficult even to find a grandparent with whom the child could be left.[5]

The absence of other family members besides the parents who could care for infants frequently led to tragic results. I have already suggested that a partial explanation for the high level of infant mortality in Marlhes was the inability of parents, especially poor parents, to devote undivided attention to child care and to dedicate family resources to protecting the fragile life of the infant. This inability is apparent in the continued prevalence of mercenary wet-nursing in the village on the eve of the Great War: the economic situation of many households made it impossible for these parents to subordinate all other objectives, such as the possibility of earning income, to the welfare of their own children.

We must, however, carefully formulate our description of the attitudes of these parents and this peasant society toward their young children. Certainly a fundamental element in this must have been an appreciation of the fragility of a new life. Newborn children died in large numbers in the village, even at the end of the century; to the deaths of native children must be added the deaths of nurslings. If our ancestors in rural Europe were more familiar with the lives of infants than we are today, they were also better acquainted with their deaths.

But why did this acquaintance not lead to the kind of emotional stress that today accompanies the death of a young infant? One argument would link the apparent fatalism of Marlhes peasants to an unwillingness to invest emotionally in a child that is not likely to live long. Certainly infants in Marlhes do not seem to have been the subject of intense emotional involvement on the part of their parents. Even the birth of a child was greeted more with ritualized celebration than with spontaneous joy.[6] The evidence of continued wet-nursing appears particularly damning in understanding parents' attitudes. This must, however, be placed in context.

One aspect is, of course, the economic importance of wet-nursing for the peasant family. Although the practice of wet-nursing appears to make a solid case for the failure of these parents to care for their children,[7] this kind of argument fails to consider the economic decision making of the peasant family. Living close to the subsistence level and frequently below it, the peasant family needed to utilize every possible source of income. Thus it was to the advantage of the adults for the mother to work, even if, as in the case of wet-nursing, her work meant weaning the infant. Yet those adults may also have felt that it was to the advantage of the infant, over the long run, for family income to be as high as possible.

It was then a choice between long-run advantages for the child and the short-run disadvantages of early weaning, inadequate substitute foods, and death. In our terms, this was no choice. Yet we must be careful about attributing to peasants our own medical knowledge. In Marlhes (and probably in much of pre-twentieth-century rural Europe) the principal connection between child care and infant mortality lay in diet and the absence of adequate substitute foods for the child after weaning. In terms of modern medical knowledge, which tells us that the substitute foods used for infants could lead to infection or hypothermia, weaning was dangerous. That peasant parents of the middle and late nineteenth century made their decisions on the basis of this level of knowledge would be a difficult argument to make. The short-run dangers of weaning and mothers working were probably not as apparent to these peasants as they are to us. We should beware of applying "sacrifice tests" formulated on the basis of mid-twentieth-century knowledge and attitudes to nineteenth-century peasants.

Thus infants in Marlhes were probably not the centers of attention that children in the mid-twentieth century are in Europe and America: there were too many of them and parents knew too well that their lives were fragile. The economy of Marlhes also placed parents in the position of choosing increased family income or increased child care. Given their lack of knowledge of the potential harmful effects of choosing income, and their certain knowledge of the benefits for the entire family of this choice, is it surprising that this was the way most families, especially poorer ones, decided? Parents in Marlhes did not dislike their infant children, nor were they indifferent to their survival. The framework for their decisions about childrearing and the information they had to make choices were, however, different from our own.

The importance of parents' perception of the fragility of infant life in forming their attitudes toward a child becomes apparent in the alteration of attitudes that occurred in the next phase of life, childhood, when the future of the child was much more secure. This phase continued to be marked by a lack of spontaneity in parent-child relations, but is remarkable for the willingness of parents to sacrifice family income in order to educate their children.

Education in the broadest sense took place both at home and in schools. Most important for those who remained in Marlhes during their adult lives was the training in farming or weaving and housekeeping that was instilled through assisting parents at work in the household. Sons probably began helping their fathers with farm work as soon as they were physically able, and learned through example the ways of farming the piece of rocky soil worked by the family and the care of the livestock that was becoming increasingly important in the rural economy. Daughters also received training at home. At the middle of the century, when domestic weaving was still an important part of the family economy, daughters were able to assist their mothers at weaving. Young girls could reduce the down time of the loom between orders by helping wind the silk for the weft of ribbon onto bobbins. As they grew older, they helped with the weaving itself, relieving their mother on the loom. The decline in domestic weaving led to a different type of work in the home, but daughters continued to receive the training needed to prepare dairy goods. Throughout the period, the skills children would need to run a farm household successfully were learned from their fathers and mothers.

The nineteenth century also saw a rapid increase in children's formal schooling in the basic skills of industrial society—writing, reading, and arithmetic. Marlhes was, indeed, remarkable in rural France for the extent to which these skills were taught to its sons and daughters; this is perhaps the most important expression of the place of children in the family. The real beginning of primary education in nineteenth-century Marlhes was the Guizot Law of 1833, which forced the commune to upgrade the quality of its facilities for primary education. The ambivalent attitude in the Municipal Council is reflected in a statement by the mayor in 1840, bemoaning the disadvantages of soil and weather in the commune and claiming that "the inhabitants of the commune can hope to obtain a school that meets their needs only by means of assistance [from the state]."[8] In spite of this financial concern, the commune supported primary education, imposing an additional three centimes on the landed, personal, and movable taxes of the commune.[9]

It is difficult to determine the extent of education in the communal school at this time. The only solid information on the student body and the course of studies indicates that this primary education aimed at only bare literacy for most students. A discussion in the Municipal Council of subventions for poorer parents declared that there were three types of student in the primary school of the commune. The first was those who were learning only to read. The second included those who were learning to read, write, and do arithmetic. In the third group, finally, were those learning reading, writing, arithmetic, "the elements of the French language," and the legal system of weights and measures.[10] The discussion does not indicate how many students there were in each of these categories, but it seems likely that the first and second drew most of the students. Beginning in the 1830s and 1840s, education in Marlhes seems to have been limited to the teaching of reading, writing, and arithmetic. As will be seen, it was only moderately successful at this, achieving minimal levels of literacy.

Education was, however, surprisingly widespread in the community. The Council discussion cited above also indicated the number of students attending the communal school: there were 134 students attending out of 180 children of the proper age for attendance. These figures give some indication not only of school attendance but also of the ages at which it was thought that children should attend school. The 180 possible students represented only about 40 percent of the population in the age groups between five and thirteen in this period. Schooling was limited to only a few years, three at most, for children in Marlhes.

While education was limited to several years in childhood, a large proportion of those of the proper age did in fact attend. The 134 pupils were a relatively high proportion of the 180 possible. This high attendance was remarkable in a rural village where many parents themselves had little education. Further, sending a child to school was a double cost to the family, for his work on the farm was lost and the school itself required payment, in 1841 fixed at between 1.00 and 1.75 francs per month, depending on the course of instruction followed. Only for the poorest families was this waived, provided they were certified by the Municipal Council as indigent.[11]

The early 1840s saw the building of another school, this one located in the hamlet of Coin, several kilometers east of the bourg of Marlhes. The building was not large, with two classrooms and space for only about sixty students.[12] It was not built as a communal school, but was probably established by the Petits Frères de Marie, a Catholic teaching order. There is an indication of this in the statement by Jean François Celles in 1852 that he was the *instituteur* in the free school of Saint-Regis-du-Coin. Listing his qualifications as required by the Falloux Law, he stated that he was a Marist and had taught in several of their other schools in the region.[13] It is probable that Marists were hired as teachers for the public school in Marlhes as well.

Beginning in the early 1860s, the commune began to consider the reconstruction of the school building in the bourg. In 1862 the Municipal Council decided to construct a new building; this was completed in 1866. At the same time, the director of the school began boarding students in the new school building, making it possible for them to stay overnight and avoid long walks home.[14]

From the late 1850s until the Ferry Laws in the early 1880s, the public school for boys in Marlhes was staffed by Marists, as the commune hired members of this religious order as public school teachers. At the same time, there were several other schools in the commune. We have already noted the free school in Saint-Regis, although this was no longer in Marlhes after 1858. Several other free schools are mentioned in the last third of the nineteenth century. A request from the hamlet of Joubert, near the border with Jonzieux, that a communal school be established there was initially rejected on the grounds that there was a free school in the hamlet of L'Allier, larger and more centrally located than Joubert.[15] Later, in 1883, there is an indication of a free school for girls in the bourg directed by the religious congregation of the Soeurs Saint-Joseph. There is no indication of how long this school had been in existence; in 1884 it was transferred to the commune and became a public school supported by the commune.[16]

As the opportunities for education expanded in Marlhes in the first years of the Third Republic, the proportions of the school-age children attending school also rose from the levels of 1841. Of the 144 students registered in the public school for boys in the bourg in 1884, 115 were between the ages of six and thirteen. These 115 students were a large proportion of the 189 boys in this age group listed in the 1881 census. Since there was also a private school for boys in the hamlet of L'Allier at this time, it seems that most boys were attending school, perhaps for as long as six or seven years.

Certainly much of the improvement in educational opportunities was the result of the legislation of the nineteenth century, beginning with the Guizot Law of 1833 and continuing to the Ferry Laws of the 1880s. The high attendance in nineteenth-century Marlhes of children of primary school age indicates, however, that this legislation found considerable support among the Marlhes peasants, for they sent their children to school in spite of the cost of education and the loss of the child's work on the family farm.

A motivation for this surprising devotion to education becomes apparent in the aftermath of the Ferry Laws of the 1880s, which required the laicization of the public schools in each commune. In Marlhes this attempt of the Third Republic to remove Catholic brothers and sisters from the educational process led to a strong resistance from the population. The principal form of resistance was the refusal of the population to send their children to the new laicized schools required by the Ferry Laws, and the continued strong attendance at schools taught by members of religious congregations. There is an indication that 160 students attended the *école communale* in 1882; and two years later, in the national Inquiry on Primary Education, the Ecole Publique de Garçons in Marlhes is listed as having a total of 144 students.[17] At the same time the Municipal Council was adding to the staff of this school, approving the addition of one assistant in 1882 and another in 1884; in each case, the large number of students was cited as the reason.[18] Yet ten years later, in response to a prefectoral letter asking the advice of the commune on a proposal to suppress a position of assistant in the Marlhes school for boys, the Municipal Council noted that the position was completely useless because of the small number of students attending, which, they noted, had never passed five.[19] The reason for this decline in the student population is clearly indicated in a statement made in 1902 by the mayor: under pressure from the departmental administration to construct a separate building for a public school for girls, the mayor noted that "the commune possesses a large building for the boys' school in which 180 students were formerly taught, but since laicization the maximum number of students had been 5; now there was only 1."[20] The enforced laicization of teachers in primary schools required by the Ferry Laws led to a wholesale withdrawal of students from the public school and their placement in free schools taught by religious congregations. The Catholic schools that continued to provide most of the primary education in Marlhes probably required tuition from parents, and it is a measure of the strong Catholicism of the area that parents would rather pay than send their children to the schools of the Republic.

Training in Catholicism was not, however, the only goal of the schools, and the best evidence of this is the success of the schools in teaching basic skills to their students. The literacy of the population of Marlhes in the second half of the nineteenth century was remarkably high, at least insofar as it can be measured by signatures on marriage acts.[21] Data on this subject are given in table 34, which tabulates separately marriages in the periods from 1841 to 1870 and 1871 to 1898. In both periods the literacy of men was greater than that of women, but the increase in educational opportunities for women in the last quarter of the century is apparent in the dramatic increase in the literacy of women between the two groups. Whereas only 54.6 percent of women married between 1841 and 1870 could sign their names, 84.8 percent could do so in the period 1871 to 1898. The increase in the literacy of males was less spectacular, from 76.2 percent to 92.4 percent, but the initial level was much higher. By the end of the nineteenth century, most children in Marlhes, both sons and daughters, were receiving at least basic instruction in writing.

Whether this represents a conscious effort of parents to educate their children or was only a by-product of the desire to provide good training in Catholicism, it is clear that most children received a basic primary education at considerable cost to their families. For those who remained in Marlhes throughout their lives, this was not particularly useful. The economy of Marlhes, however, was oriented toward the growing urban regions of the valley of Saint-Etienne, and increasingly throughout this period the basic rudiments of reading and writing were necessary for children who attempted to earn their livings in that urban environment. The high migration rates found for children and young adults in Marlhes and the attraction of Saint-Etienne for the mountain region suggest that many persons experienced the urban environment at some time during their lives. The literacy skills provided by the system of primary education in nineteenth-century Marlhes provided the basis for participation in urban industry and life for the migrants from Marlhes to Saint-Etienne.

**Table 34.** Proportions Signing Marriage Certificates in Marlhes

A. 1841–70

| | | Wife Signed | | |
|---|---|---|---|---|
| | | Yes | No | Total |
| Husband Signed | Yes | 250 64.4% | 138 35.6% | 388 76.2% |
| | No | 28 23.1% | 93 76.9% | 121 23.8% |
| Total | | 278 54.6% | 231 45.4% | 509 100.0% |

B. 1871–98

| | | Wife Signed | | |
|---|---|---|---|---|
| | | Yes | No | Total |
| Husband Signed | Yes | 280 88.3% | 37 11.7% | 317 92.4% |
| | No | 11 62.3% | 15 57.7% | 26 7.6% |
| Total | | 291 84.8% | 52 15.2% | 343 100.0% |

Source: A.C. de Marlhes, *Registres de mariages*, 1841–98.

The best way to view the widespread participation in the educational system of Marlhes during the nineteenth century is as a form of capital given to each child by his or her family during childhood. At expense to the family, most children received not only the traditional training at home in the farm work and weaving that characterized the rural household, but also literacy skills that provided the basis for participation in the growing urban society on their doorsteps. The amount of this capital received by children in Marlhes from their families of origin was not as great as in other groups in nineteenth-century Europe; bourgeois children, for example, received extensive secondary and even university educations from their families. But the peasants of Marlhes were severely limited in their ability to provide their children with any kind of assistance in their lives. The spread of primary education throughout the rural community, even to the poorest groups for whom the sacrifice needed to educate a son or daughter was greatest, testifies to the importance of education among the residents of Marlhes. The increase in educational opportunities during the nineteenth century was at least partially associated with the great increase in urban opportunities for children and the recognition of the need children would have for basic literacy skills if they followed an urban occupation. In spite of the material limitations on most families of Marlhes, these skills were provided.

The development of education among the peasants in Marlhes was similar to the spread of primary education that Roger Thabault noticed in his study of a village in the west of France during the nineteenth century. In Mazières-en-Gatine the impulse toward education came from parents who saw employment possibilities for their children other than working the soil. The increase in the number of minor administrative positions in the 1860s and 1870s and the practical use of the knowledge gained in school by children who worked as tradesmen encouraged parents to educate their children.[22]

In Marlhes, the increase in primary education and the principal breakthrough in literacy came in the 1840s and 1850s, with continuing progess throughout the remainder of the century. Although this was earlier than in Thabault's village, the growth of primary education in Marlhes owed its strength to the development of the nearby urban region. Parents provided their children with education in increasing numbers in the last two-thirds of the nineteenth century, as the rapid expansion of the urban region increased both the opportunities and the education required for young men and women from the countryside.

Education ended abruptly in Marlhes around the time children reached their thirteenth birthday. The transition from childhood to youth was celebrated by a religious ceremony,[23] but the entry to youth was more than a religious passage, for it marked the economic coming of age of the child and a change in the child's relationship to his or her parents. In the most concrete terms this transition to youth meant the beginning of the work life of the child. In the family du Maroussem studied in Saint-Genest, for example, the oldest daughter was sent to work in a spinning factory at the age of fourteen, while the oldest son was working at the same age as a shepherd on a farm in the region.[24] For boys the entry into the work force frequently meant placement outside the family as a farm domestic. This was particularly common at midcentury; it continued at the end of the century, but decreased in importance. For girls the domestic weaving common in most households at mid-century allowed them to remain at home, assisting their weaver mothers. The decline in domestic weaving in the last third of the century required a shift in work patterns for girls. The poorer families in the commune placed their daughters as workers in weaving factories, while on larger farms daughters remained at home, helping their parents by tending livestock and preparing dairy products.

The most important social aspect of these different patterns of work for youths in nineteenth-century Marlhes was the continued supervision of both boys and girls by either their parents or representatives of parental authority. For young men who worked as domestic farm workers, supervision by their parents was replaced by supervision by the farm household into which they moved as domestics. Girls who worked as domestic ribbonweavers remained in their families of origin, under the supervision of their parents. Even at the end of the century, when domestic weaving had declined and daughters were working in factories, they remained under their parents or nuns brought by factory owners to watch over the moral development of their workers.[25] The types of employment available for a youth in the countryside invariably continued the subordinate position of the youth either to his parents or to a representative of the parents.

Only in the case of migration to the urban industrial valley did youths escape their parents, and even in this case it seems likely that the subordinate position of youths continued. Migration to Saint-Etienne for the mountain resident was not definitive migration such as a move to Paris. Marlhes was only twenty-two kilometers from Saint-Etienne, and the frequency of migration in the region almost guaranteed that a son who left his family at age eighteen or nineteen to seek his fortune in the industrial city would find an aunt or uncle in the city. No study of urban residency patterns exists for Saint-Etienne that would provide definitive evidence on the ways these kin supervised their nephews, but it seems probable that even migration to Saint-Etienne did not free the youth from the control of the older generation.

In spite of this universal supervision of the youth, the beginning of work did mean the beginning of the separation of the child from the family of origin. In the early teens this was limited, but as the child grew he or she began to be able to earn more and more. A daughter could weave ribbons herself as she learned the techniques from her mother and could take orders herself from the *commis.* A son was able to begin working for himself as a day laborer, and on many farms this was an economic necessity as the family farm could not provide work for the growing family. The increase in independence of children was greatest for those sent out to work as domestics. The child was for the first time in his life living away from his parents, and at the end of each year received a sum of money, however small, that remained his own.

The most important aspect of this gradual separation of youths from their families of origin was the growing adult responsibility of the youth. Principal among these new cares was the necessity to earn the financial basis for marriage. The poverty of most families in Marlhes made it incumbent on the child to earn the money needed to establish a new household, and it was work as a domestic servant or ribbonweaver that provided most individuals with this opportunity. Almost as soon as children left the world of childhood and became workers, they were faced with the responsibility of making their own way in the world.

Youth in nineteenth-century Marlhes was therefore a period of gradual change in the relationship of a son or daughter to the peasant family. The period between the entry into the work force and marriage was marked by a continuation of the supervision of the youth by the older generation. The family or its surrogates provided the framework of authority for the youth, and this phase of the individual's life cycle was not marked by a period of complete independence. Within this framework of continued supervision, however, the youth began to look toward the establishment of a family independent of the family of origin.

The explanation for this pattern among youths in nineteenth-century Marlhes lies primarily in the tenuous economic base of the peasant household. The approach of most families toward their children emphasized their future independence; parents pushed children toward independence by placing them as weavers or domestics. As the family grew during its developmental cycle the larger number of adults could not be supported nor find employment on most of the farms in Marlhes. Only by encouraging children to work on their own could the family economy remain in balance with the resources it possessed.

The combination of continued supervision of youth and growing independence from the family of origin that characterized this phase of the individual life cycle is reflected in the courtship patterns of the rural community. An example of this may be seen in the individual initiative and parental control that marked the formal courtship of Marie Philomène Boudarel by Claude Chorain in 1867. This courtship was minutely described by the sacristan of Marlhes, Jean Chatelain, in a report for a Stephanois folklorist, Victor Smith.[26] The courtship began through an intermediary, known in the region as a *balendraud*, because Marie did not live in Marlhes but in the nearby commune of Saint-Romain-la-Chalm (Haute-Loire). The *balendraud* determined if the girl and her family were interested in the match. If so, the young man was invited to Sunday dinner by the girl's parents. This was repeated for several succeeding Sundays, until finally the young man extended a return invitation to the girl's parents to come to Sunday dinner at his parents' home. If this invitation was accepted, according to the account, "le mariage est presque conclu." The dinner of both families was frequently the time when the date for signing the marriage contract was decided.[27]

In this description the different roles of parents and their children in courtship are clearly indicated. Even in the Chorain and Boudarel families, both relatively wealthy, the initiative for the match came not from parents but from the children. It was Claude Chorain, not his parents, who approached the Boudarel family through the *balendraud*. The role of the parents was significant, however: Claude clearly was under scrutiny by the parents during the series of Sunday dinners, and it was the parents of Marie Boudarel who accepted the Chorains' dinner invitation, and with it the match. This courtship process shows children with the initiative, as we would expect given the necessity for youths in this region to accumulate their own means to marry. Yet parents also played an important part in approving the marriage, and the final arrangements were made at a meeting of both sets of parents as well as the young couple.

The formal courtship described by Chatelain was, however, probably preceded by a long period of informal courtship on which he is unfortunately silent. Other sources, however, allow a reconstruction of these informal courting practices, and they also reflect the tension between individual arrangements made between youths and continued supervision by parents. While traditional forms of community control over courtship had declined in Marlhes by the nineteenth century, the practices that were followed allowed youths to meet and court in a freedom that was limited by the nearness of parents to supervise the process.

The most common type of courtship in many rural areas of western Europe was the gathering of all members of a village or hamlet on a winter evening, known as a *veillée*. During these meetings women talked and sewed, men told stories, and young people talked and danced.[28] The custom declined throughout Europe in the late nineteenth century, however, and the evidence suggests that *veillées* were not frequent in Marlhes during the period under study here. The informants of folklorist Paul Fortier-Beaulieu from Marlhes in the 1920s and 1930s told him that the custom was unknown in the village, suggesting that if it ever existed there it had disappeared before the middle of the nineteenth century, when these women were in their childhood.[29] The frequent exogamy of marriages in Marlhes also suggests that this custom had fallen into disuse. If such a system of courtship was the rule in a peasant community, most marriages would take place between neighbors. These marriages were the exception, not the rule, in Marlhes. Many marriages included a young man or young woman from a commune other than Marlhes, and only rarely were marriages between neighbors from the same hamlet. The absence of any evidence attesting to the existence of *veillées* and the failure of marriages to conform to the pattern the custom was most likely to produce suggest that young men and women found other places to meet in nineteenth-century Marlhes.

Probably the most important were gatherings of the rural community for fairs, markets, and traditional communal feasts. For many members of the rural community, especially young people, these provided more social contact than economic exchange. Their importance for courting is described by one of Fortier-Beaulieu's informants: "These are occasions for young men and women to become acquainted. People allow young women to go out on these days, but a little later 'on va les chercher.' When they [young men and women] have already met, the young man goes to look for the girl at her house and takes her out to dance. Often they dance through the night. Monday morning, one still finds some couples in the streets, who go to the cafés and say, 'Give us something to wake us up . . . we have laughed much, we have danced.' Sometimes the father accompanies his daughter."[30] Unfortunately there is no indication of the type of father who was most likely to accompany his daughter, but the import of this witness is clear: the fairs and market days provided a recognized opportunity for young people to meet each other, and if they had already met, they could further their acquaintance during the festivities. As in the formal courtship described earlier, this informal courtship combined opportunities for individual initiative of youths with a distant supervision by parents.

During the nineteenth century the great fairs that provided the occasion for these meetings occurred about once every other month in Marlhes. A number of neighboring communes also held fairs, and those of Saint-Genest-Malifaux and Le Chambon-Feugerolles, for example, were easily reached by young men in search of entertainment on an afternoon. Traditional holidays provided further chances for young couples to meet. These holiday celebrations seem to have attracted young men from all over the region. Fortier-Beaulieu indicates that "in all regions, people follow the holiday celebrations. One Sunday people will meet in one place, and a week later they will meet in another." There also were dances held in the auberges and cafés of the bourgs. There is no indication in any record of the frequency of these dances, only that they existed and were an important meeting place for young people.[31] Young women seem to have been less likely to venture far from home for a holiday or dance than young men. One of Fortier-Beaulieu's sources told him that until the beginning of this century, it would have caused a scandal for a young woman to go to a dance in another town.[32] Young men, in contrast, seem to have enjoyed considerable freedom of movement from town to town as the fairs and holiday celebrations occurred. The supervision extended over young women was stronger than that given young men.

The fairs and holiday festivals provided the principal location for the continued courting of a young woman by a young man after they had met. The heavy work load required of young men and young women by the family economy left them little time during the week for courting, either formally or in the informal meetings known as "fréquentation aux champs." One of Fortier-Beaulieu's sources told him: "Twenty years ago, girls worked a lot. They helped to plow, they tended livestock. There could be no question of meeting in the fields during the week. On Sundays, people met occasionally in the meadows."[33] While this source mentions only agricultural work, certainly neither domestic nor factory ribbonweaving left much opportunity for such meetings. The fairs and festivals, therefore, seem to have been the principal places in which young people could socialize.

Thus the informal courtship of youths in nineteenth-century Marlhes was less encumbered by explicit community or family restrictions on the behavior of the young couple than those characteristic of traditional peasant communities in western Europe. It was not, however, a situation of complete freedom for the youths. Parents obviously were concerned about the courting of their children, as indicated in both the informal practices of accompanying daughters or only allowing them to walk without supervision at fairs for a short while, and the formal consent to a suitor evident in the Chorain example.

The tensions that might have resulted from these conditions of youthful individual initiative in courting and continued parental supervision were tempered by the economic conditions within which courtship occurred. Two characteristics of the rural economy replaced parental control with economic constraint, especially among the landless families that we would expect to show the least signs of parental authority. The differentiation of agricultural and industrial occupations by sex meant that the full impact of the industrial work in the countryside was not felt in nuptiality patterns. Only the prospective bride worked as a ribbonweaver; her future husband worked in agriculture, and throughout the period under discussion the establishment of a household required the acquisition or rental of a farm. Also, saving the funds needed to establish the new household could be a time-consuming process, one that continued to hold the age at an elevated level. The tie between land and marriage in nineteenth-century Marlhes was tenuous but surely existed. The factor governing access to land was not the inheritance pattern familiar in Ancien Régime peasant communities, but the economic constraints of a poor region in which saving required a long period of time.

These economic constraints changed little during the period under study here. For the children of most families in Marlhes, the economic changes of the last third of the century altered only the means available for them to achieve their goal of saving for marriage. Factory weaving replaced domestic weaving, but did not greatly increase the earning capacity of a young woman. For young men there were even fewer changes: domestic service and agricultural day labor remained the principal employments of young men from the middle through the end of the century.

The stability of nuptiality patterns in Marlhes throughout this period is the result of this continuity of the economic foundations of marriage.

        The marriage that followed courtship marked the definitive shift for the individual from the family of origin to the family of procreation, in which adult life would be spent. The best indication of this is the pattern of household structure in the village. The majority of households in Marlhes were nuclear in structure, indicating that marriage meant the establishment of a new household separate from the families of origin of the newly married couple. The conjugal couple became the center of a new family, not an adjunct to an already existing family. For the majority of the families in Marlhes, this transition was a necessity of the family economy, which could not support or employ many additional family members. For most of these people, marriage meant the beginning of almost complete independence from parents, with the establishment of a household that was separate from the family of origin both physically and economically. The new husband and wife entered into full maturity both in their family roles and in the community.

Even among larger landholders, similar patterns of individual independence with marriage may be found. Again this is indicated by the patterns of family structure already described. Not all larger landowning families were three-generation families, of course. Even for this type of family structure, however, the stem family, in which the younger married couple remained in a subordinate position to the older parents, was very rare. Most three-generation families in Marlhes were headed by members of the younger generation, and the parents of the householder were frequently widows or widowers living in retirement. Even in these extended families, therefore, marriage meant the entry into leadership of the household for the newly married husband and his wife. These households were distinguished from those of their poorer neighbors not through the respective roles of the conjugal pair, for the newly married couples in extended families also entered into maturity in their family roles and in the community. Rather, the difference lay in the residence arrangements, themselves largely the product of the differences in economic resources of the different types of households.

Thus marriage marked the fruition of the increasing individualism of young people that characterized the years between the ages of twelve or thirteen and the late twenties, when marriage became a possibility. The independence from the family of origin that came about at marriage made this an important turning point in the lives of young men and women. It did not, however, free them from family bonds, for they entered immediately into a new family. The domestic economy of the new household was as narrowly based as that of the family of origin, and the new couple had to work together if they were to succeed. Almost immediately children were born, and the family economy felt the strains of this phase of family life. The independence from the family of origin that began with marriage was only a part of the transition for the young couple from the family of their parents to the new demands of their own family.

Old age was little different from most of adult life for men and women in Marlhes. The nuclear family structure that predominated in the region meant that there was little chance for retirement for a parent after his child had married. Only among the small proportion of the families in Marlhes with extended structure involving three generations was there a tendency toward this retirement pattern. The overwhelming pattern in three-generation households was for the oldest generation to retire at least from heading the household. Stem families, in which the older generation continued to lead the household, made up only 32 percent of the three-generation households in Marlhes in 1851 and only 22 percent in 1901.[34] The extended member frequently was a parent of the head of household, with 68 percent in 1851 and 78 percent in 1901 of the vertically extended families in this group. This type of extension depended on the amount of land owned by the household, and it seems likely that this was a pattern among larger landowners, with the control of the family farm being passed onto the younger generation at the time of marriage while the parents continued to live on the farm but in a reduced role.

More often the principal consequence of advancing age was the reduction of the size of the nuclear family in the household, as children grew up and either left to establish their own households at marriage or migrated to other communes or the industrial valley. When this was the case, the working patterns of a lifetime continued until the man or woman was either incapacitated or died. Men continued to work in the fields, although as men became very old they may have given up part of the land that they rented. At the middle of the century, women continued to work as domestic ribbonweavers well into old age, supporting themselves as they had throughout their lives. Toward the end of the century, as domestic weaving declined, animal husbandry and the preparation of dairy products for sale at markets in the region became the most important aspect of the work of older women, as it was for married women. For the majority of the population of Marlhes, old age may have meant a slackening of work, but it did not mean retirement from work altogether; the continual economic pressure on the resources of the household required that men and women continue to work until they were physically unable to do so.

The most significant aspect of old age for most people was the death of a spouse. The high death rates of Marlhes and the disparity between men's and women's ages at marriage ensured that widowhood would occur sometime in the late forties or early fifties for many people, and many widows and widowers lived ten or fifteen years after their spouses died. When this occurred, it placed a severe stress on the balance of work in the household, and for many the only alternative was a quick remarriage. Van Gennep reports that this was a necessity: "Isn't a peasant with livestock and children who becomes a widower required to marry without delay?"[35] A traditional story in the region told of a widow at the funeral meal for her husband who, when told by her neighbor at the table, "Have patience, poor woman," immediately thought of the tailor in the bourg named Patience and responded happily, "I would take him willingly, but do you think he will have me?"[36]

In spite of this perhaps apocryphal story, a substantial proportion of widows and widowers did not remarry, and they appear in increasing proportions in older age groups. For all but a very small proportion of these, their families, in one form or another, continued to provide them in old age with companionship. A high proportion of widows and widowers in Marlhes lived in the extended families of their children. In 1851, 20 percent of widowers and 24 percent of widows lived in three-generation families. In 1901 the proportion for men was 18 percent, and for widows an astonishing 43 percent. Widows and widowers made up the majority of the parents who extended families: in 1851 only three of the thirty-four parents living with their children were still married; in 1901 only four of thirty-eight parents living with married children were not widows or widowers. By far the more important part of these were widows, and many of them may have been the beneficiaries of testamentary provisions by their husbands.

A small proportion of widows and widowers found places in the households of their brothers or sisters. Members of this group also tended to be women. In 1851 there were two widows who were the sister of the head of the household, but there were no brothers. In 1901 only one widow living in the household of her brother could be found, and again there were no brothers. This suggests that the pattern of a widow returning to her family of origin after the death of her husband did not exist to any great extent in the village. If the general pattern was to maintain throughout life an interest in the parental homestead through not dividing the inheritance, the reason for this does not seem to have been to retain a place to return to after the death of one's spouse. The inheritance share was most important before marriage and in case of permanent celibacy, providing the basis for the adult lives of those who did not leave the family of origin. For those who established their own households, the break was definitive.

The largest proportion of widows and widowers continued as heads of their households after the death of their spouses. Of 70 widowers in

Marlhes in 1851, 51, or 73 percent, were heads of household. Of 118 widows, 75, or 64 percent, were heads of household. A similar pattern existed in 1901: 14 of 17 widowers (82 percent) and 37 of 69 widows (54 percent) were heads of household. For the majority of men and women in Marlhes, the death of a spouse did not lead to immediate retirement. Men continued to act as the heads of their households, while women stepped into the shoes of their dead husbands and took over household leadership.

A much smaller group of widows and widowers lived alone. Single-member households included only 14 percent of the widowers and 9 percent of the widows in 1851, and in 1901 the figures were even lower: there were no widowers living alone, and only 7 percent of the widows in 1901 lived by themselves. Also insignificant was the frequency of widows or widowers as lodgers: in 1851 there were two widowers and seven widows (3 percent and 6 percent respectively of the total) living as lodgers, and there were none in 1901. Living alone, either as a lodger or in a separate household, was not a frequent pattern of habitation for widows and widowers in nineteenth-century Marlhes.

Therefore, most of the householders who were widows or widowers lived with their children. Even in poorer families characterized by nuclear family structure, parents were not abandoned in their old age. An outline of the nuclear family remained, headed by the widowed parent and including at least one unmarried child. In 1851, 41 of 70 widowers (59 percent) and 64 of 118 widows (54 percent) lived with unmarried children, and in 1901, 14 of 17 widowers (82 percent) and 32 of 69 widows (46 percent) lived with at least one. Both the nuclear and stem families in Marlhes included in their developmental cycles a phase in which old people were able to continue to enjoy the companionship and support of their children.

From the child's point of view there was an important difference in the two arrangements, for the stem family allowed the child to marry and, most frequently in Marlhes, to take over control of the household. In nuclear families, however, this did not happen, and the child or children who stayed with the parent remained under the authority of the parent and was not able to marry. In an ironic reversal of roles, the stem family provided more freedom for the child and quicker accession to his or her marriage than the nuclear family. Stem family arrangements were likely to lead to conflicts between the householder's mother and his wife over household duties. The nuclear family, on the other hand, was more likely to produce conflicts centering on the decision of the child to marry and the responsibility of the child toward his or her widowed mother.

The relationship of the individual to the family in old age was marked by increased dependence of the individual on the family, especially on adult children, and the remarkable response of all types of families to this need. The rural economy was important in defining this aid: the narrow limits set by the relative poverty of the greater part of the rural peasantry could not be broken no matter how strong a desire children may have had to support their parents. As a result, the blissful retirement envisioned by Le Play in the patriarchal or stem family was reserved for very few. For most old people, the economic demands of the family economy required that they continue to work until they became physically incapacitated or died. Within these limits, however, the family remained the most important framework for old age. The fortunate few turned their farms over to their grown sons upon the death of a spouse, and were able to enjoy a period of respite from the farm and industry duties that had been their life's work. Although work continued for most, at least one child remained at home, continuing the skeleton of a nuclear family for the aging person. In spite of the frequency with which young men and women left their families of origin, both extended and nuclear families provided needed services for aging parents.

The relationship between the individual and the family in Marlhes was far from constant; it varied significantly depending on the age of the individual and the developmental stage of the family group. The family was most important for the individual at either end of life, in childhood and old age. Young children, of course, depended almost totally on their families of origin for material support and personality development. The family fulfilled these needs to the limits of its resources, providing children with a modest amount of capital during the first decade of their lives. With a universality that made Marlhes one of the most literate rural villages in nineteenth-century France among both men and women, children received the rudiments of an education. This literacy may not have been necessary to a career as a farmer or ribbonweaver if the child remained in the rural commune. In the event of migration to the industrial valley, however, education provided a basis for integration into the urban society. At times the cost to the family was relatively high, both in terms of the cash outlay for tuition and the lost work of young children on the farm. Virtually all families in nineteenth-century Marlhes chose to provide their children, both sons and daughters, with this fundamental capital.

The period between the end of childhood at the age of twelve or thirteen and old age, around sixty, was, in contrast, marked by the decreasing importance of the family for the individual and growing independence of the individual from his family of origin. The late teens and early twenties were a period of growing independence from the family for both sons and daughters, culminating in their marriages. In spite of this decreased importance of the family of origin in the life of the youth, however, the family group remained an important point of reference for the individual. Even in the case of those who migrated from Marlhes to the industrial valley, the absence of definitive migration and the short distance from Marlhes to the industrial region, reinforced by equal inheritance and the failure of heirs to divide their inheritances, meant that the family remained a focal point in the lives of young adults.

Marriage transformed the relationship of the individual to the family group. The overwhelming majority of peasants in Marlhes established their own households instead of remaining in the households of their parents. The family group was largely defined by the conjugal pair rather than any larger kinship group, and in the period immediately following marriage the new family depended on the new husband and wife rather than on their families of origin. Their joint efforts maintained the family economy and provided for the growing number of children that characterized the households of Marlhes. Again, however, it is important to note the communality of the new family group, as the conjugal pair cooperated in maintaining the family in spite of the heavy and varied demands that the rural economy imposed on the relatively small labor force available in the family.

Finally, as the individual grew older, he or she came once again to depend heavily upon the family, now represented more and more by the adult children who remained at home in their families of origin. Most remarkable in this phase is the response of the family to the needs of the aged person, a response that indicates better than any other evidence the solidarity of the family group in Marlhes and the strength of the relations between parents and children. For the overwhelming majority of older persons in Marlhes, the family provided the framework of their lives in old age, both in the material sense of providing support and in the emotional sense of providing companionship. This was true for both nuclear and extended family patterns in Marlhes, the family structures characteristic of both the poorer and wealthier sections of the rural community. Especially in widowhood, when the family of procreation of the individual had been broken by the death of a spouse, the skeleton of the nuclear family remained, with one or more children remaining celibate at least until the death of the remaining parent. For wealthier landed members of the community, the death of the husband was the signal to turn over leadership of the household to the younger generation, although the widow remained a member of the household of her son or daughter. For the overwhelming majority of the older persons in Marlhes, the family provided an economic and social setting for old age.

The relations of individuals to their families in Marlhes remained relatively constant throughout the entire period under study here. The economic changes of the late nineteenth century that reorganized the agricultural and industrial work of the rural population seem to have had remarkably little effect on the ways individuals used their families and on the places individuals took in their families. The patterns of family re-lations described here were primarily dependent on the level of economic resources available to the individual peasant family, not on the structure of the work in agriculture and industry that provided those resources. As factory weaving replaced domestic weaving and industrial employment declined in importance in the rural community, the family group main-tained its level of resources by reallocating the labor of some family members from one type of work to another. The peasant family and its individual members were able to adapt economic changes in the Stephanois countryside to their central aims of accumulating resources and maintaining the family group.

# Chapter 11
# Conclusion: Marlhes in Perspective

I chose to study the village of Marlhes because its social and economic structure reflected a phase in the long process of upheaval and change that took place in Europe during the last three centuries—the transition from a rural, agricultural, peasant society to an urban, industrial society. With its dependence on the nearby urban center and the importance in the local economy of wage-earning and domestic textile work, Marlhes bridges these two forms of socioeconomic organization. In particular, I have been interested in the families of the peasants of Marlhes and in how they dealt with the economic development that occurred in the Stephanois region: the decline and reorganization of ribbonweaving, the increased market orientation of agriculture, and the growing importance of wage earning for the peasant household.

The argument of this book is that these symptoms of the modern world were integrated into the patterns of behavior of the peasant families in Marlhes. The family economy—the unit of labor supply and consumption in peasant society—was the means for this integration, and this facet of family life changed most dramatically in the nineteenth century in Marlhes. Other characteristics of the peasant family were altered in less visible ways. Family structure, reproductive behavior, inheritance practices, and relations within the family continued to bear the unmistakable imprint of the past. The peasant family pursued a consistent set of goals: maintenance of the conjugal family unit and preservation of the homestead or *houstau* for a wider kin network. We must guard against an excessive formalism in stating these elements of continuity: the stem family as it existed in nineteenth-century Marlhes was different from that found in traditional peasant societies, and the high reproductivity of the village population, so similar to Ancien Régime patterns, was a response to the opportunities of the industrial valley rather than high mortality conditions. In sum, however, there does not appear to have been a major disjunction between the peasant families of traditional Europe and the families we have found in Marlhes.[1]

The reason for the successful integration of changing economic conditions and structures into the peasant family in Marlhes lies in the local conditions that interacted with the more general processes of industrialization and urbanization in the region. The social structure of Marlhes in the early nineteenth century was dominated by a class of smallholders who maintained a link to the land but were forced to earn family income through wage earning in industrial occupations. The deindustrialization of the countryside and the increased market orientation of agriculture therefore created conditions similar to what had gone before. The family unit remained intact, even though it was forced to alter its allocation of labor and find new sources of income.

The flexibility of the peasant family that we found in Marlhes was a fundamental characteristic of rural life during the eighteenth and nineteenth centuries, a period in which the peasant family of traditional Europe came under heavy pressure from capitalism and industrialism. While at first sight each local study of this process of decline of the peasantry appears to reveal even more complex patterns of diversity, the localism of European rural society in this period provides a framework for interpretation. The general processes that mark European history in the nineteenth century interacted with existing local conditions and were in turn marked by those local conditions. Industrialization, urbanization, and the growth of political participation did not produce the same results everywhere. It has become apparent, for instance, that the development of domestic rural industry did not have the same effect on social structure in every part of Europe. In areas such as the Zurich highlands, Flanders, and Leicestershire it created a new landless social class of proletarians, leading to radical alteration of family life, demographic behavior, and political activity.[2] Yet it is also apparent that local conditions—"social, geographical, and legal restraints" in the words of Lutz Berkner—determined how rapid this process would be and to what extent rural society would actually be changed. In the Austrian Waldviertel, for example, legal restrictions on settlement prevented the textile industry from dominating the economy and textile activity was integrated into the life of what remained essentially a farming community. Proto-industrial work did not therefore disrupt social relations or alter family patterns in this part of Europe.[3] In other areas, such as the Pays de Caux in France, the textile industry spread into an area where most peasants were already landless. It did not create a new social structure: such a structure had already been in existence before the spread of the textile industry.[4] Similarly, in Marlhes the opportunities for wage earning from the urban economy made it possible for the existing class of smallholders to earn income and support their families. In every case local conditions determined the response to the general process of proto-industrialization and economic development.

Thus, the area in which Marlhes was probably most typical was its uniqueness: the ability of a particular area to take a general process—in the case of Marlhes, the decline of rural industry and the development of nearby markets for agricultural products—and turn it to the uses of the local peasantry. This examination of Marlhes has shown this process of local adaptation of the large-scale processes of eighteenth- and nineteenth-century European history to the particular situation of a local area. The local flavor of the peasant remained even after he had become a Frenchman, and this localism colored the meaning of being a Frenchman.

The integration of economic development into peasant family patterns was to a large extent the result of the ability of the peasant family to bend but not break under the pressure of new economic structures. The pressure in the countryside, however, was light compared to that felt in the growing urban centers of nineteenth-century Europe. The tie to the land that maintained the peasant family in Marlhes would be lost in an urban setting, and this study provides no assurance that when rural families were transplanted to mill towns they did not bend so far that they broke. Some evidence does suggest that country dwellers brought their rural behavior with them into industrial cities: Michael Anderson has found that in Preston in Lancashire, a town experiencing rapid industrialization in the early nineteenth century, patterns of rural family behavior, especially the importance of kin in times of crisis, persisted among both Englishmen and Irishmen who came to the city.[5] But further inquiry into the patterns of life of newcomers to the cities of industrializing Europe is necessary before we can generalize about this experience. It would, however, be surprising if the adaptability found in Marlhes did not remain a central element in the social history of Europeans during the century of upheaval and change between the French Revolution and the Great War.

# Appendix 1
# Vital Events in Marlhes, 1815-1910

| Year | Births | Deaths | Marriages |
|------|--------|--------|-----------|
| 1815[1] | 91 | 57 | 13 |
| 1816 | 77 | 85 | 22 |
| 1817 | 90 | 89 | 9 |
| 1818 | 91 | 65 | 10 |
| 1819 | 66 | 87 | 28 |
| 1820 | 95 | 60 | 12 |
| 1821 | 77 | 81 | 26 |
| 1822 | 79 | 65 | 13 |
| 1823 | 80 | 65 | 19 |
| 1824 | 99 | 71 | 23 |
| 1825 | 87 | 63 | 21 |
| 1826 | 100 | 66 | 16 |
| 1827 | 100 | 63 | 29 |
| 1828 | 120 | 74 | 22 |
| 1829 | 101 | 69 | 27 |
| 1830 | 113 | 82 | 26 |
| 1831 | 107 | 63 | 15 |
| 1832 | 96 | 54 | 25 |
| 1833 | 106 | 56 | 9 |
| 1834 | 93 | 84 | 25 |
| 1835 | 93 | 84 | 16 |
| 1836 | 95 | 50 | 20 |
| 1837 | 100 | 59 | 13 |
| 1838 | 86 | 79 | 15 |
| 1839 | 104 | 71 | 8 |
| 1840 | 97 | 82 | 25 |
| 1841 | 101 | 70 | 22 |
| 1842 | 103 | 67 | 18 |
| 1843 | 105 | 68 | 23 |
| 1844 | 107 | 66 | 12 |
| 1845 | 110 | 60 | 18 |
| 1846 | 99 | 83 | 16 |

| Year | Births | Deaths | Marriages |
|------|--------|--------|-----------|
| 1847 | 83  | 83  | 22 |
| 1848 | 98  | 77  | 16 |
| 1849 | 104 | 65  | 19 |
| 1850 | 90  | 76  | 24 |
| 1851 | 96  | 77  | 21 |
| 1852 | 99  | 57  | 21 |
| 1853 | 80  | 74  | 17 |
| 1854 | 98  | 104 | 24 |
| 1855 | 80  | 100 | 12 |
| 1856 | 110 | 81  | 12 |
| 1857 | 85  | 70  | 18 |
| 1858 | 78  | 62  | 20 |
| 1859 | 75  | 58  | 12 |
| 1860 | 67  | 71  | 17 |
| 1861 | 69  | 55  | 9  |
| 1862 | 71  | 77  | 10 |
| 1863 | 66  | 49  | 13 |
| 1864 | 78  | 71  | 25 |
| 1865 | 85  | 93  | 12 |
| 1866 | 77  | 61  | 11 |
| 1867 | 88  | 65  | 23 |
| 1868 | 75  | 66  | 15 |
| 1869 | 80  | 66  | 18 |
| 1870 | 72  | 70  | 9  |
| 1871 | 68  | 76  | 10 |
| 1872 | 72  | 63  | 10 |
| 1873 | 80  | 64  | 16 |
| 1874 | 69  | 45  | 13 |
| 1875 | 71  | 57  | 16 |
| 1876 | 82  | 52  | 12 |
| 1877 | 66  | 104 | 13 |
| 1878 | 63  | 73  | 7  |
| 1879 | 79  | 49  | 12 |
| 1880 | 63  | 44  | 14 |
| 1881 | 63  | 47  | 10 |
| 1882 | 64  | 36  | 4  |
| 1883 | 55  | 54  | 10 |
| 1884 | 60  | 40  | 12 |
| 1885 | 65  | 44  | 13 |
| 1886 | 70  | 38  | 14 |
| 1887 | 47  | 61  | 18 |
| 1888 | 63  | 51  | 12 |

| Year | Births | Deaths | Marriages |
|------|--------|--------|-----------|
| 1889 | 53 | 45 | 11 |
| 1890 | 57 | 81 | 9 |
| 1891 | 51 | 30 | 13 |
| 1892 | 61 | 45 | 10 |
| 1893 | 53 | 45 | 7 |
| 1894 | 57 | 30 | 13 |
| 1895 | 42 | 41 | 8 |
| 1896 | 54 | 54 | 8 |
| 1897 | 53 | 33 | 13 |
| 1898 | 51 | 38 | 13 |
| 1899 | 58 | 44 | 14 |
| 1900 | 56 | 44 | 12 |
| 1901 | 59 | 39 | 12 |
| 1902 | 43 | 38 | 12 |
| 1903 | 55 | 36 | 16 |
| 1904 | 57 | 35 | 8 |
| 1905 | 58 | 35 | 13 |
| 1906 | 45 | 39 | 12 |
| 1907 | 51 | 42 | 6 |
| 1908 | 37 | 35 | 17 |
| 1909 | 39 | 35 | 12 |
| 1910 | 41 | 29 | 13 |

# Appendix 2
# Estimation of Rates of
# Out-Migration

The estimated rates of out-migration used in chapter 6 have been calculated using raw data collected by manual tracing of each individual listed in the 1851 and 1901 censuses for Marlhes to the following census listing available (1856 and 1911 respectively).[1] The tracing was carried out by searching for each individual listed in the second census in an alphabetical listing of the first census. A new variable, indicating whether or not the individual was present in the second census, was then added to the original record of each individual in the first census. This allowed the cross-tabulation of whether or not an individual was present in the later census with values of other variables in 1851 and 1901. In chapter 6 cross-tabulations by age, occupational group, and family structure have been employed.

Whether or not an individual can be found in a later census list depends not only on migration rates but also on mortality rates, since some individuals who cannot be found have died rather than migrated during the period between censuses. Therefore, before migration rates could be calculated it was necessary to correct the raw data of the migration variable for mortality. The life tables presented in chapter 4 have been used for this purpose. Probabilities of surviving five or ten years were calculated for each age group using the stationary population $(L_x)$ column of the respective life tables. This column gives the number of persons in each five-year age group in a population that is not growing or declining (a stationary population) and with the given mortality schedule. These figures can be used to project the population in 1851 or 1901 ahead to the next census, 1856 or 1911. For example, in 1851 there were a total of 6,255 persons aged twenty-five to thirty-four in the stationary population. These persons would be thirty to thirty-nine in 1856, and a total of 5,885 persons are in that age group in the stationary population. Thus, .941 of those aged twenty-five to thirty-four in 1851 survived to 1856. When multiplied with the number of persons aged twenty-five to thirty-four found in the 1851 census list for Marlhes, this gives an estimate of the number of persons aged thirty to thirty-nine who should be found in the 1856 census. The number actually found in the second census was subtracted from this estimate of the number of survivors to arrive at an estimate of the number of out-migrants. This was then divided by the number of years between censuses (five or ten) to arrive at an estimate of the annual number of migrants. The final rate was calculated by dividing this annual number of out-migrants by the original population at risk to migrate, the number in that age group in the first census list.

The large size of the first age group used, from birth to age twenty-four, and the wide range of mortality rates from birth until age twenty-four required special attention to the survivorship probabilities used to calculate this line on each table. A special survivorship rate was calculated for this group using the life tables and the age structure of this part of the population in 1851 and 1901. The population was divided into six age groups, those aged less than one year, those aged one to four, and the four five-year groups from ages five to twenty-four. The number of individuals in each of these age groups was then converted to a number indicating its proportional share of a model population of 1,000. These numbers were multiplied by survivorship rates for each age group calculated from the appropriate life table in the manner described above. The sum of these results indicates the number of individuals from that population of 1,000, with an age structure identical to that of Marlhes in 1851 or 1901, who would survive for the necessary five or ten years. Converted to an individual rate by dividing by 1,000, these totals provide a survivorship rate for the zero to twenty-four population group in the emigration tables. The values reached were .969 for 1851 and .921 for 1901.

This method of estimating migration rates provides detailed data by age, sex, marital status, family structure, and occupational group in the population. However, there are problems with these measures that must be discussed prior to their analysis. A relatively minor difficulty arises from the use of a single life table for the entire population to estimate mortality. The small number of individuals in the commune made it advisable to calculate a life table for the entire population based on an adequate number of individuals rather than life tables by sex that would have been based on low numbers of cases and therefore susceptible to large error. While undoubtedly there were some differences in mortality by sex, these were probably not large and the effect of this on the estimated rates used here should be minimal.

A more serious problem is the comparability of the rates derived for the five-year period 1851–56 with those for the ten-year period 1901–11. The 1906 census lists for the department of the Loire have not been preserved, so the longer period between censuses could not be avoided. As T. H. Hollingsworth has pointed out, the different period lengths could create spurious differences in the rates, because of return migration:[2] an individual might migrate from Marlhes to Saint-Etienne and remain there for seven years, then move back to Marlhes. He would be counted as a migrant if a five-year period existed between lists, but as a nonmigrant if a ten-year period was used.

Without a doubt there was return migration between Marlhes and Saint-Etienne, but it will affect the results given here only if the duration of time spent in Saint-Etienne was between five and ten years—that is, long enough to be counted as migration in the shorter period of five years but not so long as to be counted as migration in the longer period of ten years. Four situations that would produce such return migration may be outlined. Two describe unsuccessful and successful migrants. First, an individual might leave Marlhes and go to Saint-Etienne in search of work, but be unable to find it and have to return to his family farm in Marlhes. In this case, he or she might remain in the city for a year or two and then return, but it is doubtful that an unemployed person would or could remain in the city for five years and then return. Second is the case of the successful migrant who finds work in the city but retires to Marlhes after a career as a miner or steelworker. In this case the period outside Marlhes between migration and return will probably be longer than ten years. In neither case will the return migration affect the comparability of the results found here.

Two other instances that may affect the comparability of the rates are more serious, and arise from types of migration in which the move is not intended to be permanent, as in the two cases described above, but from its outset is intended to be temporary. Such temporary migration existed in the case of youths moving to Saint-Etienne to earn a dowry and returning to Marlhes to marry and live, and in that of placement outside the commune as a domestic servant or shepherd on a farm. The first of these was an important pattern in the Lyonnais in the eighteenth century, and there is little doubt that it was going on in nineteenth-century Marlhes.[3] The question, then, is how significant it was, and to what extent it will affect the comparability of migration rates for the two periods. A rough estimate of its importance may be obtained by a comparison of places of birth and places of residence given in marriage records in Marlhes. Of the 852 couples married in Marlhes between 1841 and 1898, only five men and two women indicated that they were born in Marlhes but lived in Saint-Etienne at the time of their marriage.[4] This is, of course, only an approximation of the extent of the pattern of temporary migration, yet it seems so minor from this estimate that it should not seriously affect the comparability of the results given here.

A second type of temporary migration that could affect the comparability of the results here is that of youths who are placed in domestic service outside the commune of Marlhes. While this employment may have lasted five years, it would only infrequently last ten years. Because of this, the migration rates for domestic servants and shepherds should be higher in 1851–56 than in 1901–11. In fact, the reverse seems true: in 1856, 43 of the 108 farm domestics and 29 of the 107 shepherds listed in 1851 could be found. In 1911 only 6 of the 45 domestics and neither of the 2 shepherds listed in 1901 could be found. The results run in the opposite direction than that expected by the bias of the method used. If there is a problem of comparability between these two sets of results, it does not stem from the inherent bias of the longer period between the later lists.

The cases in which the different periods between lists in the two sets of migration rates used here could produce distorted results seem, therefore, to be of minor importance. This does not mean that the possibility of bias in the results can be discounted completely, but that any bias that does exist should not be great enough to impede comparison over time of migration from Marlhes.

# Appendix 3
# Estimation of Probabilities of
# Family Extension

## A. Probability of Survival of Parents until Marriage of Their Children (Vertically Extended Family)

The probabilities of different members of the family surviving to create an extended type of family structure have been calculated using the following assumptions:

1. Age at marriage: twenty-five for women, thirty for men.

2. Mortality schedules: Marlhes, 1849–53 for 1851, Marlhes, 1899–1903 for 1901.

3. Each couple has four children. For convenience in the calculation, we assume that these children were all born at the same time, at marriage, and that the length of a generation is thirty years.

It is possible, therefore, to calculate the following probabilities of a male and female who survive to marry surviving to ages sixty and fifty-five, when their oldest child would have married and had a child.

a. 1851. Females: $l_{55}/l_{25} = 430/666 = .645$
Males: $l_{60}/l_{30} = 336/624 = .538$

b. 1901. Females: $l_{55}/l_{25} = 482/623 = .724$
Males: $l_{60}/l_{30} = 436/599 = .727$

The probabilities of different combinations of survival of the parents can be calculated from these:

$P(f)$ = probability of father surviving to see grandchild
$Q(f)$ = probability of father not surviving to see grandchild
$P(m)$ = probability of mother surviving to see grandchild
$Q(m)$ = probability of mother not surviving to see grandchild

a. 1851
$P(f) \times P(m) = .645 \times .538 = .347$
$P(f) \times Q(m) = .645 \times .462 = .298$
$Q(f) \times P(m) = .355 \times .538 = .191$
$Q(f) \times Q(m) = .355 \times .462 = .164$

b. 1901
$P(f) \times P(m) = .774 \times .727 = .563$
$P(f) \times Q(m) = .774 \times .273 = .211$

$Q(f) \times P(m) = .226 \times .727 = .164$

$Q(f) \times Q(m) = .226 \times .273 = .062$

Using these probabilities of survival, it is possible to calculate how many, out of 1,000 couples married, would survive to see their grandchildren. In 1851, 347 couples would survive; 298 fathers only would survive, and 292 mothers only would survive. In 1901, 563 couples survive; 211 fathers only survive; and 164 mothers only survive. Assuming that couples do not separate, this means that in 1851 there were a total of 836 possible extended family parents available, and in 1901 there were 938 parents available.

The probability of survival for children from birth to age thirty was .624 in 1851 and .599 in 1901. Out of 4,000 children born to 1,000 sets of parents, a total of 2,496 will survive in 1851 and 2,396 in 1901. Therefore the possible percentages of vertically extended or three-generation households are:

1851: 836/2496 = 33.5 percent

1901: 983/2396 = 39.1 percent

## B. Probability of Formation of Laterally Extended Households

The assumptions are the same as above. The probability of children surviving to age thirty is .624 in 1851 and .599 in 1901. Therefore, the probabilities of different numbers of children surviving to age thirty are:

|  | 1851 | 1901 |
|---|---|---|
| all four: | $(.624)^4 = .152$ | $(.599)^4 = .128$ |
| three: | $(.624)^3 = .243$ | $(.599)^3 = .215$ |
| two: | $(.624)^2 = .389$ | $(.599)^2 = .359$ |

At least two children must survive to age thirty in order for an extended family to be formed. Out of 1,000 sets of four children in 1851, therefore, all four survive in 152 cases; three survive in 243 cases; and two survive in 389 cases. Of the 1,000 cases, therefore, 784 have enough survivors to form a laterally extended family. In 1901, the total is 702 cases.

# Notes

Abbreviations Used in the Notes

A.N.                Archives Nationales de France, Paris
A.D.L.              Archives Départementales de la Loire, Saint-Etienne
A.C. de Marlhes     Archives Communales de Marlhes
DCCM                Déliberations du Conseil Municipal de Marlhes


Chapter 1

1. François Guizot, *Democracy in France*, pp. 76–77.
2. Frédéric Le Play, *L'Organisation du travail*, pp. 154–55.
3. Pierre du Maroussem, *Fermiers montagnards du Haut-Forez*, pp. 434–35.
Unless otherwise indicated, I have made all translations from French works.
4. See Talcott Parsons, "The Kinship System of the Contemporary United
States," for the best expression of the majority view. Sidney Greenfield,
"Industrialization and the Family in Sociological Theory," p. 313, finds no
relationship between industrialization and family structure, but this remains a
minority view. See also the essays in Harold Christensen, ed., *Handbook of
Marriage and the Family*; the recent historical studies by Peter Laslett, *The World
We Have Lost*; and Edward Shorter, *The Making of the Modern Family*.
5. Neil J. Smelser, *Social Change in the Industrial Revolution*; Michael
Anderson, *Family Structure in Nineteenth Century Lancashire*.
6. Charles Tilly, ed., *An Urban World*, pp. 2, 3.
7. David Landes, *The Unbound Prometheus*, pp. 18–19; Rudolf Braun,
*Industrialisierung und Volksleben*; Franklin F. Mendels, "Industrialization and
Population Pressure in 18th Century Flanders," pp. 18, 89, 90; Lutz K. Berkner,
"Family, Social Structure and Rural Industry," p. 286; J. D. Chambers, *The Vale
of Trent, 1670–1800*; Joan Thirsk, "Industries in the Countryside," pp. 85–86;
Herbert Kisch, "The Textile Industries in Silesia and the Rhineland"; Joel
Mokyr, *Industrialization in the Low Countries, 1795–1850*, chapters 2 and 3;
Peter Kriedte, Hans Medick, and Jurgen Schlumbohm, *Industrialisierung vor der
Industrialisierung*; Charles Tilly and Richard Tilly, "Agenda for European
Economic History in the 1970's" pp. 184–98; David Levine, *Family Formation
in an Age of Nascent Capitalism*, chapter 2; and the articles in "Aux origines de
la révolution industrielle," especially those by Pierre Deyon and Serge Chassagne.
8. Jan de Vries, "Peasant Demand Patterns and Economic Development."
9. Walter Minchinton, "Patterns of Demand, 1750–1914"; Jerome Blum, *The
End of the Old Order in Europe*, pp. 241–42; Folke Dovring, "The
Transformation of European Agriculture"; E. L. Jones, ed., *Agriculture and
Economic Growth in England, 1650–1815*.

10. Charles Tilly, ed., *The Formation of National States in Western Europe*; Louise A. Tilly, "The Food Riot as a Form of Political Conflict in France."

11. Blum, *End of the Old Order*, pp. 206, 240; Roger Thabault, *Education and Change in a Village Community*; Eugen Weber, *Peasants into Frenchmen*, chapter 18; Antoine Prost, *Histoire de l'enseignement en France, 1800–1967*, p. 159.

12. J. E. Dufour, *Dictionnaire topographique du Forez et des paroisses du Lyonnais et du Beaujolais formant le département de la Loire*, pp. 331, 542; Lucas, *Structure of the Terror*, p. 336.

13. Théodore Ogier, *La France par cantons et communes*, pp. 361, 359.


Chapter 2

1. Etienne Fournal and Jean-Pierre Gutton, *Cahiers de doléances de la province de Forez*, pp. 295, 308, 318, 334, 349. See especially the Cahiers for Saint-Galmier and Saint-Bonnet-les-Ouches, pp. 308 and 334, both of which describe certain features as a "remain" of feudalism.

2. J. Barret, *Usages locaux du canton de Saint-Genest-Malifaux recueillis et mis en ordre par M. J. Barret, juge de paix du canton*, pp. 60–64. In general, the "feudalism" of the late eighteenth-century Stephanois region seems to have been limited to seigneurial rights, as has been suggested for France as a whole by Alfred Cobban, *The Social Interpretation of the French Revolution*, chapter 5; there is no evidence in the Stephanois region to support Albert Soboul's view that a feudal type of economic and social organization existed, even at the end of the Ancien Régime, and certainly not during the nineteenth century. See Soboul's "The Persistence of Feudalism in the Rural Society of 19th Century France," p. 70.

3. A.D.L. Série P Non-Coté, Matrice cadastrale de la commune de Marlhes; Barret, *Usages locaux*, p. 65; du Maroussem, *Fermiers montagnards du Haut-Forez*, p. 466.

4. While reporting 40 hl/h in 1882, Planfoy reported only 20 hl/h in 1892. A.D.L. 55 M 19, *Statistique Agricole Décennale de 1882*; A.D.L. 55 M 46, *Statistique Agricole Décennale de 1892*.

5. A.D.L. 55 M 8, *Tableau des cultures de la commune de Saint-Genest-Malifaux*, 22 janvier 1837; A.D.L. 55 M 12, *Statistique Quinquennale de 1852*, Canton de Saint-Genest-Malifaux; A.D.L. 55 M 19, *Statistique Agricole Décennale de 1882*; A.D.L. 55 M 46, *Statistique Agricole Décennale de 1892*.

6. Returns calculated from seed requirements given in A.D.L. 55 M 21, *Statistique Agricole Annuelle de 1884*.

7. B. H. Slicher von Bath, *The Agrarian History of Western Europe A.D. 500–1850*, appendix, table III, pp. 332-33. See also Fernand Braudel, *Capitalism and Material Life, 1400–1800*, p. 81.

8. Michel Morineau, *Les Faux-Semblants d'un démarrage économique*, pp. 27, 29.

9. A.N. F[12] 1569, *Statistique de la République du 29 Thermidor An IX*, p. 6; Joseph Duplessy, *Annuaire du département de la Loire*, p. 266.

10. "Météorologie," pp. 160-61, 157.

11. Cited in Lucas, *Structure of the Terror*, p. 6.

12. A.N. F¹² 1569, *Statistique de la République*, p. 6. See also Duplessy, *Annuaire*, p. 259.

13. Ibid., p. 265.

14. Locard-Denoel, "De l'état de l'agriculture dans l'arrondissement de Saint-Etienne et de la nécessité de l'améliorer," p. 296. Compare Marc Bloch, *Caractères originaux de l'histoire rurale française*, p. 52.

15. Duplessy, *Annuaire*, p. 259; A.D.L. 55 M 9, *Statistique Agricole de 1841*; A.D.L. 55 M 12, *Statistique Décennale de 1852*; G. Touchard-la-Fosse, *La Loire historique, pittoresque et biographique*, p. 262; Locard-Denoel, "De l'état de l'agriculture," p. 283.

16. Cited in Lucas, *Structure of the Terror*, pp. 6–7.

17. A.D.L. 55 M 8, *Tableaux des cultures de la commune de Saint-Genest-Malifaux*, 22 janvier 1837.

18. A.N. F²⁰ 565, *Statistique Annuelle, Arrondissement de Saint-Etienne, 1854*; Agriculture, Céréales.

19. Société Impériale d'Agriculture, Industrie, Sciences, Arts et Belles-Lettres, *Compte rendu du commice agricole de Saint-Genest-Malifaux tenu au 1 et 2 août 1863*, p. 5.

20. M. le Baron de Saint-Genest, "Culture des montagnes, défrichements des terrains de bruyère et leur mise en prairie"; for Courbon, see the award in Société Impériale d'Agriculture, *Commice agricole du 2–3 août 1863*, p. 5.

21. A.D.L. 55 M 12, *Etat des animaux domestiques existants dans l'arrondissement de Saint-Etienne*; A.D.L. 55 M 14, *Statistique Agricole de 1857*; A.D.L. 55 M 18, *Statistique Agricole de 1881*; A.D.L. 55 M 46, *Statistique Agricole Décennale de 1892*.

22. A.D.L. 55 M 14, *Statistique Agricole de 1856*; A.D.L. 55 M 46, *Statistique Agricole Décennale de 1892*; A.D.L. 55 M 190–91, *Statistique Agricole de 1905*.

23. A.D.L. 55 M 12, *Etat des animaux domestiques*.

24. While apparently urban residents consumed less milk and cheese than was normal in a rural diet, these foods remained an important part of urban diets throughout the century. See Cecile Dauphin and Pierrette Pezerat, "Les consommations populaires dans la seconde moitié du XIXe siècle à travers les monographies de l'école de Le Play," p. 543.

25. "Enquête sur l'industrie laitière," p. 119.

26. Ibid., p. 118.

27. A.D.L. 55 M 12, *Etat des animaux domestiques*.

28. E. L. Jones, "Introduction."

29. Between 1801 and 1831, Saint-Etienne grew from 16,259 to 33,064 persons; from 1831 to 1851, it grew to 56,003; in 1854 the four communes of Beaubrun, Montaud, Outre Furens, and Valbenoite were added to the commune. Between 1861 and 1891, it grew from 92,250 to 133,443. These figures are based on data in Charles Pouthas, *La Population française pendant la première moitié du XIXe siècle*, p. 98; Jacques Schnetzler, "Un Demi-siècle d'évolution démographique dans la région de Saint-Etienne (1820–1876)," p. 172; Jacques Meaudre, "La Poussée urbaine à Saint-Etienne, 1815–1872," pp. 102–10.

30. Schnetzler, "Demi-siècle d'évolution démographique"; Meaudre, "Poussée

urbaine"; Jean Merley, "La Contribution de la Haute-Loire à la formation de la population stéphanoise au milieu du XIXe siècle," pp. 165–80; D. Tenand, "Les Origines de la classe ouvrière stéphanoise," pp. 69–78.

31. Louis-Jean Gras, *Histoire économique générale des mines de la Loire*, 1:159.

32. Ibid., 1:247, 283.

33. Ibid., 2:757.

34. Ibid., 2:791–851.

35. Louis-Jean Gras, *Histoire économique de la métallurgie de la Loire*, pp. 10, 14.

36. Ibid., p. 54

37. Ibid., p. 65.

38. Ibid., pp. 62, 239, 278.

39. Ibid., pp. 285, 364.

40. Louis-Jean Gras, *Les Routes du Forez et du Jerez*, p. 24; Lucas, *Structure of the Terror*, pp. 23–24.

41. Lucas, *Structure of the Terror*, pp. 24–26.

42. Gras, *Routes du Forez et du Jerez*, p. 139.

43. Ibid., pp. 141, 144; A. L. Dunham, *The Industrial Revolution in France, 1815–1848*, p. 17.

44. Gras, *Routes du Forez et du Jerez*, pp. 198–209.

45. Ibid., p. 197.

46. Dunham, *Industrial Revolution in France*, p. 23.

47. M. Crozier, "Demande d'une loi sur les chemins ruraux," p. 50.

48. Louis-Jean Gras, *Histoire du commerce local et des industries qui s'y rattachent dans la région stéphanoise et forezienne*, pp. 85–87.

49. A.D.L. 58 M 15, *Tableau des foires du département de la Loire au 6 mai 1807*.

50. A.D.L. 58 M 16, *Tableau des foires et marchés en activité dans le département de la Loire au 31 juillet 1837*.

51. Du Maroussem, *Fermiers montagnards du Haut-Forez*, p. 470.

52. Ibid., p. 469.

53. Ibid., p. 470.

54. "Enquête sur l'industrie laitière," p. 119.

55. Gras, *Histoire du commerce local*, pp. 423–24.

56. A.D.L. 58 M 16, *Etats des foires du département au 17 mai 1819*; A.D.L. 58 M 17, *Etats des foires et marchés au 1 juin 1876*.

57. See M. Levy-Leboyer, "La Croissance économique en France au XIXe siècle," pp. 788–807.

58. A.D.L. 58 M 15, *Tableau des foires du département de la Loire au 6 mai 1807*; 58 M 16, *Etats des foires du département au 17 mai 1819*; Duplessy, *Annuaire*, pp. 408–9; A.D.L. 58 M 16, *Rapport du 4 juin 1823 sur les marchés*; *Rapport du 30 avril 1830*; *Tableau des foires et marchés en activité dans le département de la Loire au 31 juillet 1837*.

59. *Délibérations du Conseil Municipal de Marlhes*, séance du 26 mai 1872. Extract in A.D.L. 58 M 43.

60. A.D.L. 58 M 43.

61. A.N. F$^{12}$ 1569; Louis-Jean Gras, *Histoire de la rubannerie*, p. 410.

62. Lucas, *Structure of the Terror.*

63. "Notice sur l'industrie de l'arrondissement de Saint-Etienne au commence-ment de 1828," p. 15.

64. A.N. F¹² 1569, *Statistique de la République, 29 Thermidor An IX,* pp. 5–6.

65. Duplessy, *Annuaire,* pp. 392–93; A.N. C 956, *Enquête sur le travail agricole et industriel du 25 mai 1848.*

66. This description of the organization of the trade has been drawn from Duplessy, *Annuaire,* pp. 394–97; Alphonse Peyret, *Statistique industrielle du département de la Loire,* pp. 11–27; Philippe Hedde, *Indicateur du commerce, des arts et des manufactures de Saint-Etienne, Saint-Chamond, et Rive-de-Gier,* pp. 29, 75–82; Philippe Hedde, *Revue industrielle de l'arrondissement de Saint-Etienne, suivie de l'indicateur du commerce, des arts et des manufactures de Saint-Etienne,* pp. 31–33; L. R. Villermé, *Tableau de l'état physique et morale des ouvriers employés dans le manufacture de coton, de laine et de soie,* 1:341–54.

67. Charles Tilly, *The Vendée,* p. 54.

68. This is only a rough measure of the volume of production of the trade, since all it measures is the raw silk bought and sold in the city of Saint-Etienne itself. It does not include silk bought by Stephanois fabricants in Lyon, nor does it take into account the cotton used as the weft in the cheaper ribbons called *mélangés,* which in some years could make up a large part of the ribbons produced in the region. The dispersed organization, the refusal of fabricants to report their volume of business even to their own trade associations, and the failure of records of fabricants to survive to this century make the volume of silk the only quantitative measure of the activity of the trade from year to year.

69. Lucien Thiollier, "Rubanier," p. 80, n. 1.

70. A.D.L. 88 M 22.

71. The best study of this is J. Ploton, "La Moulinage de la soie à Dunières, 1718–1914."

72. A.D.L. Série P Non-Coté, *Matrice cadastrale des propriétés bâtis de la commune de Marlhes, Augmentations, Années 1884, 1890.*

73. A.D.L. 88 M 21, *Rapports, Procès-Verbal des établissements industriels.*

74. A.D.L., Archives de la Chambre de Commerce, Carton 81, Dossier 4, Pièce 68.

75. A.D.L., Archives de la Chambre de Commerce, Carton 81, Dossier 4, Pièce 59.

76. A.D.L., Archives de la Chambre de Commerce, Carton 81, Dossier 4, Pièce 34.

77. A.D.L. 49 M 85, 49 M 260, 49 M 387, *Listes nominatives de recensement du canton de Saint-Genest-Malifaux,* 1851, 1881, 1911.

## Chapter 3

1. Du Maroussem, *Fermiers montagnards du Haut-Forez,* p. 404.

2. Gilbert Garrier, *Paysans du Beaujolais et du Lyonnais,* 1:130–31.

3. A.N. F¹¹ 2705 42 Loire, *Enquête Agricole Décennale de 1862.*

4. Du Maroussem, *Fermiers montagnards du Haut-Forez*, p. 465.
5. Garrier, *Paysans du Beaujolais et du Lyonnais*, 1:178.
6. Paul Bois, *Paysans de l'Ouest*; Tilly, *Vendée*.
7. Saint-Genest, "Culture des montagnes," p. 88.
8. "Enquête sur l'industrie laitière," p. 120.

Chapter 4

1. The family histories of the Courbon and Servie families are drawn from the families reconstituted from the birth, death, and marriage records in A.C. de Marlhes. For more information see chapter 5, note 14.
2. Calculated according to the method in Louis Henry and Michel Fleury, *Nouveau manuel de dépouillement et d'exploitation de l'état civil ancien*, pp. 103–5.
3. See Garrier, *Paysans du Beaujolais et du Lyonnais*, 1:93; Etienne Gautier and Louis Henry, *Crulai, paroisse normande*, p. 65; Jean Ganiage, *Trois villages de l'Ile de France*, p. 103.
4. Marcel Lachiver, *La Population de Meulan du XVIIe au XIXe siècle*, pp. 85, 87.
5. For the harvest year in the Loire, see Duplessy, *Annuaire*, pp. 266–67.
6. The infant death rates in these tables were calculated by the method described in Henry and Fleury, *Nouveau manuel*, pp. 108–9. Child death rates were calculated using the method for periods described in Louis Henry, *Manuel de démographie historique*, pp. 122–24. Other death rates have been calculated using the average number of deaths in each age group during 1849–53 and 1899–1903 respectively. A brief explanation of the functions of a life table may be found in Henry S. Shryock, Jacob S. Siegel, and Associates, *The Methods and Materials of Demography*, 2:429–33.
7. Gautier and Henry, *Crulai, paroisse normande*, p. 163; Ganiage, *Trois villages de l'Ile de France*, p. 105; Daniel Scott Smith, "A Homeostatic Demographic Regime," table 1.
8. Gautier and Henry, *Crulai, paroisse normande*; Ganiage, *Trois villages*; Smith, "Homeostatic Demographic Regime."
9. For the West Mortality pattern, see Ansley Coale and Paul Demeny, *Regional Model Life Tables and Stable Populations*, introduction.
10. Smith, "Homeostatic Demographic Regime," table 4.
11. Etienne van de Walle, *The Female Population of France in the Nineteenth Century*, p. 74.
12. An estimate of the development of infant and child mortality in Paris during the nineteenth century suggests that child mortality responds to improvements in health conditions before infant mortality. See Etienne van de Walle and Samuel H. Preston, "Mortalité de l'enfance au XIXe siècle à Paris et dans le département de la Seine," pp. 101–2.
13. Departmental estimates are taken from van de Walle, *Female Population of France*, table 8.1, pp. 191–95.
14. Gautier and Henry, *Crulai, paroisse normande*, p. 191, indicate a

pessimistic estimate of 27.7 years, an optimistic estimate of 32.19 years, and a mean estimate of 30.3 years.

15. The model table used is a Model West Level 8 Male table. See Coale and Demeny, *Regional Model Life Tables*, p. 9.

16. Data on wet-nursing in Marlhes is drawn from the death records of 327 nurslings who died in the village between 1841 and 1900. On the dangers presented by early weaning, see M. W. Beaver, "Population, Infant Mortality and Milk," p. 245; and John Knodel and Etienne van de Walle, "Breast Feeding, Fertility, and Infant Mortality," pp. 109–31. For a general argument of the impact of child care on infant mortality, see Jean-Louis Flandrin, "L'Attitude à l'égard du petit enfant et les conduites sexuelles dans la civilisation occidentale," pp. 173–77.

17. Yves Lequin, *Les Ouvriers de la région lyonnaise (1848–1914)*, 1:437.

18. The nearest doctor even at the end of the nineteenth century appears to have been in the industrial valley, based on an examination of the 1901 census for the canton of Saint-Genest-Malifaux in A.D.L. 49 M 353.

19. An attempt has been made to calculate $_1q_0$ for landowning and non-land-owning families using reconstituted marriages between 1841 and 1880. The rates obtained were .196 for landowners and .158 for nonlandowners, considerably lower than the rates obtained for the entire population of Marlhes that have been used in the life tables above. The reason for the probable error is the low number of cases provided in the reconstituted families as well as the possibility of a bias in those families that could be reconstituted.

20. Drawn from family reconstitution.

21. Duplessy, *Annuaire*, p. 167.

22. Ulysses Rouchon, *La Vie paysanne en Haute-Loire*, 1:20.

23. Antoine Limousin, *Enquête de 1848*, p. 46.

## Chapter 5

1. The indices are standardized measures of these rates, using the well-documented Hutterite population of the early twentieth century as the standard. The measures were developed by Ansley J. Coale and are described by him in "The Decline of Fertility in Europe from the French Revolution to World War II." The fertility measures express the performance of the subject population as a percentage of the performance of the married Hutterites after standardizing the age structure of the female population. Thus the $I_g$ of .880 in Marlhes in 1851 means that the married population of Marlhes had 88 percent of the births that would be expected if that population had the same age structure and the same age-specific marital fertility rates as the Hutterites. The measures are mathematically related: $I_f = I_h (1 - I_m) + I_g (I_m)$. That is, total fertility equals the sum of the illegitimacy rate times the proportion not married plus the marital fertility rate times the proportion married.

The female age at first marriage has been estimated using the method developed by John Hajnal for calculating singulate mean age at marriage from the age distribution of the female population. See John Hajnal, "Age at Marriage and Proportions Marrying." Strictly speaking, this method assumes a closed population; the figures given are, therefore, only approximations.

2. The term "natural fertility" is used here to indicate the absence of any conscious effort at family limitation through contraception. See Louis Henry, "Some Data on Natural Fertility," p. 81.

3. John Hajnal, "European Marriage Patterns in Perspective."

4. For France, see Etienne van de Walle, "Alone in Europe," pp. 276–77.

5. Between 1851 and 1891, $I_g$ for a sample of 33 villages in the department of the Loire fell from .768 to .512, indicating that much of the department experienced the fertility transition by 1891. See James R. Lehning, "Demographic, Economic and Cultural Factors in the Decline of Marital Fertility."

6. Van de Walle, *Female Population of France*, p. 345.

7. A.C. de Marlhes, *Registres des actes de mariages*, 1841–98.

8. Hajnal, "European Marriage Patterns," p. 109.

9. A.D.L. 49 M 85, 49 M 260, 49 M 353, *Listes nominatives de recensement de la commune de Marlhes*, 1851, 1881, 1901.

10. Domestic ribbonweaving acted to depress out-migration, while its decline and the rise of factory organization in the weaving industry made its work force one of the most likely groups to migrate by the end of the nineteenth century. See chapter 6 below.

11. Hajnal, "European Marriage Patterns," p. 102.

12. See James C. Davis, *A Venetian Family and Its Fortune*, 1500–1900, especially chapter VI for a noble family of Venice; see Pierre Goubert, "Historical Demography and the Reinterpretation of Early Modern French History," pp. 21–22, for a summary of the complexities of marriage in peasant society in early modern France.

13. Franklin F. Mendels, "Proto-Industrialization"; Tilly and Tilly, "Agenda for European Economic History"; Braun, *Industrialisierung und Volksleben*; Paul Deprez, "The Demographic Development of Flanders in the 18th Century"; Levine, *Family Formation*. See however the recent article by Serge Chassagne, "La diffusion rurale de l'industrie cotonnière," pp. 109–10, which finds no change in nuptiality patterns with the spread of rural industry in the Mauges region in western France.

14. Marriages between 1841 and 1880 have been reconstituted using the method described in Henry and Fleury, *Nouveau manuel*. Only Type MF families (those in which the date of birth of the wife, date of marriage, and an end of observation are known) have been retained for analysis here. A fuller analysis of these reconstitution results will be published at a later time. Type MF families represent 253 of the 641 marriages in Marlhes between 1841 and 1880, or 39.5 percent of the marriages in this period. The rates in table 11 are based on 224 first marriages of males and 242 first marriages of women.

Families have been linked with nominal listings of landholders in 1851, 1881, and 1901 that I have drawn from the 1834 *matrice cadastrale de la commune de Marlhes*, in A.D.L. Série P Non-Coté. This record of the land tax is described more fully in chapter 3 above. Families have been allocated as property owners if they fulfilled either of the two following qualifications: (1) they were indicated in the *matrice cadastrale* as owning at least one hectare of land; (2) the occupation listed on the marriage act noted that the individual was a landowner.

15. Mendels, "Proto-Industrialization"; Braun, *Industrialisierung und Volksleben*; Levine, *Family Formation*.

16. Gautier and Henry, *Crulai, paroisse normande*, p. 245; Ganiage, *Trois villages*, p. 56.

17. A.C. de Marlhes, *Registres des actes de naissances*, 1841–1901.

18. Cities in the Stephanois valley had the following illegitimacy ratios in 1851: Outre Furens, 3.2; Beaubrun, 33.9; Montaud, 13.3; Valbenoite, 23.8; Saint-Chamond, 61.7; Le Chambon-Feugerolles, 7.3; Rive-de-Gier, 30.6. Calculated from reports of municipal administrations in A.D.L. 48 M 33, *Mouvement de la population pour l'arrondissement de Saint-Etienne*, 1851. For comparative data see the appendix to Edward Shorter, "Illegitimacy, Sexual Revolution, and Social Change in Modern Europe."

19. Gautier and Henry, *Crulai, paroisse normande*, p. 135; Ganiage, *Trois villages*, p. 92; Lachiver, *Population de Meulan*, p. 175.

20. See chapter 6 below.

21. See *Le Moniteur de Saint-Etienne* during the spring of 1903 and during 1905 and 1906 for the many outbreaks of violence during the application of the Law on Congregations and the inventorying of church goods. These incidents occurred both in rural villages such as Marlhes and in urban working-class districts such as the Soleil quarter in Saint-Etienne.

22. See the discussion of the seasonality of marriages in chapter 4 above.

23. See note 14 above.

24. For an analysis of fertility in northern France, see Louis Henry and Jacques Houdaille, "Fécondité des mariages dans le quart nord-ouest de la France de 1670 à 1829," and Jacques Houdaille, "Fécondité des mariages dans le quart nord-est de la France de 1670 à 1829."

25. Henry, "Some Data on Natural Fertility," p. 84.

26. Henry and Houdaille, "Fécondité des mariages," pp. 909–19.

27. Ibid., p. 921.

28. A.C. de Marlhes, *Registres des actes de décès*.

29. Eva J. Salber et al., "The Duration of Post-Partum Amenorrhea," pp. 348–49.

30. Knodel and van de Walle, "Breast Feeding, Fertility and Infant Mortality," pp. 118–22.

31. Emmanuel Le Roy Ladurie, "L'Amenorrhée de famine (XVIIe–XXe siècle)."

32. Etienne van de Walle and Francine van de Walle, "Allaitement, stérilité et contraception," p. 694.

33. Paul Fortier-Beaulieu, *Mariages et noces campagnards*; Arnold Van Gennep, *Le Folklore de l'Auvergne et du Velay*; Louis Gachon, *L'Auvergne et le Velay*.

34. Philippe Ariès, *Histoire des populations françaises*, pp. 344–72.

35. Data for Canada calculated from J. Henripin, *La Population canadienne au debut du XVIIIe siècle*, p. 60. Data for Crulai calculated from Gautier and Henry, *Crulai, paroisse normande*, p. 97. The figure for southern France is given in Jean-Louis Flandrin, *Familles*, p. 252, and is based on P. Valmary's study of the parish of Thezels in Bas-Quercy. It refers to the number of children born if a woman is married from twenty to forty-four years of age.

36. A.D.L. 49 M 85, *Liste nominative de recensement de la commune de Marlhes,* 1851.

37. The given data is the age specific marital fertility rate and the number of married and total women in each age group. The Total Fertility Rate (*TFR*) is equal to the sum of the product of the marital fertility rate for each age group times the number of married women in each group divided by the number of women in each group, multiplied by the width of the time interval, five years. Or, $TFR = 5\Sigma f(M/W)$, where $f$ = the marital fertility rate, $M$ = the number of married women, and $W$ = the number of women in each age group.

38. For calculation of Gross Reproduction Rates and Net Reproduction Rates, see George W. Barclay, *Techniques of Population Analysis,* p. 213; calculation of the intrinsic growth rate has been made using the equation $r \cong \log_e NRR/T$, in Ansley J. Coale, "The Calculation of Approximate Intrinsic Rates," pp. 94–97.

39. J. Bourgeois-Pichat, "The Population of France since the 18th Century," p. 506. He uses a mean length of generation of twenty-eight years, which is probably too low for the eighteenth and nineteenth centuries. If this is the case, the NRRs he has calculated would be too high.

40. David Levine, "The Demographic Implications of Rural Industrialization," appendix.

41. For a theoretical description of this kind of a model, see Lutz K. Berkner and Franklin F. Mendels, "Inheritance Systems, Family Structure and Demographic Patterns in Western Europe, 1700–1900." Daniel Scott Smith has examined the homeostatic nature of pre-decline demographic patterns in "A Homeostatic Demographic Regime."

42. For literacy in Marlhes see chapter 10 below.

## Chapter 6

1. Meaudre, "Poussée urbaine," p. 29, and Tenand, "Origines de la classe ouvrière stéphanoise," p. 88, indicate that about 50 percent of the growth of the population of Saint-Etienne in the nineteenth century was due to in-migration and that, depending on the period, 55 to 60 percent of the in-migrants came from a region within forty kilometers of the city.

2. Tenand, "Origines de la classe ouvrière stéphanoise," indicates that Marlhes was one of the heaviest contributors to the population of Saint-Etienne.

3. A.C. de Marlhes, *Registres des actes de mariages,* 1841–98.

4. Merley, "Contribution de la Haute-Loire," pp. 165–80, and "Eléments pour l'étude de la formation de la population stéphanoise à l'aube de la Révolution industrielle," pp. 261–77.

5. A.D.L. 49 M 143, *Recensement de 1861;* A.D.L. 49 M 353, *Recensement de 1901.*

6. Calculated using data from A.D.L. 49 M 24, 49 M 85, 49 M 260, 49 M 320, *Recensements de 1841, 1851, 1881, 1891,* and A.C. de Marlhes, *Actes de naissances et décès,* 1842–51 and 1882–91.

7. See appendix 2 for a description of the procedure used to calculate these out-migration rates.

8. In 1851 there were 203 individuals in shopkeeping and artisanal trades, 27

in forestry; in 1901 there were 171 in shopkeeping and artisanal trades, 19 in forestry.

9. For a more complete description of family structure in Marlhes see chapter 7 below.

10. Frédéric Le Play, *L'Organisation de la famille*, pp. 8–10.

11. See the explanation given by Pierre Merlin, *L'Exode rural*, p. 45 and chapter 4.

12. A.N. F²⁰ 594, *Statistique annuelle de 1858, prix et salaires*; Pierre Guillaume, *La Compagnie des Mines de la Loire (1846–1854)*, p. 138; Claude Chatellard, "La Misère à Saint-Etienne entre 1870 et 1914," pp. 87–88.

13. See Talcott Parsons, "Kinship System," and William J. Goode, *World Revolution and Family Patterns*.

14. See A. Redford, *Labour Migration in England, 1800–1850*, for an early study based on this hypothesis; and P. Deane and W. A. Cole, *British Economic Growth, 1688–1959*, for a more recent one. The difference between these two interpretations is examined, along with evidence for nineteenth-century Lancashire, in Michael Anderson, "Urban Migration in Nineteenth Century Lancashire."

15. Eugene Litwack, "Geographic Mobility and Extended Family Cohesion."

## Chapter 7

1. A.D.L. 49 M 85, *Liste nominative de recensement de la commune de Marlhes*, 1851, fols. 19, 28, 32.

2. This point has been made numerous times by Lutz K. Berkner: see "The Stem Family and the Developmental Cycle of the Peasant Household"; "The Use and Misuse of Census Data for the Historical Analysis of Family Structure"; "Household Arithmetic." It continues to be ignored in studies of family and household structure, however. The most glaring example is the collection of essays in Peter Laslett and Richard Wall, eds., *Household and Family in Past Time*. It is similarly ignored by Jean-Louis Flandrin in his otherwise excellent *Familles*, chapter 2. A notable exception may be found in Etienne van de Walle, "Household Dynamics in a Belgian Village, 1847–1866," based on Belgian population registers.

3. See above for the family structure and members of the Barralon family; landholding is from A.D.L. Série P Non-Coté, *Matrice cadastrale de la commune de Marlhes*.

4. A.D.L. 49 M 85, 49 M 353, *Listes nominatives de recensement de la commune de Marlhes*, 1851, 1901.

5. See Berkner, "Stem Family."

6. Le Play, *L'Organisation du travail* and *L'Organisation de la famille*, for the emotional characteristics of patriarchal, stem, and nuclear families. Parsons, "Kinship System," and Talcott Parsons and Robert F. Bales, *Family, Socialization and Interaction Process*, discuss the nuclear family group as a psychological unit.

7. Shorter, *Making of the Modern Family*, p. 205. Shorter himself does not argue that household structure implies an emotional atmosphere; in fact, he specifically dissociates himself from this view, saying, "The nuclear family is a

state of mind rather than a particular kind of structure or set of household arrangements."

## Chapter 8

1. Le Play, *L'Organisation de la famille*, p. 26; Bloch, *Caractères originaux*, vol. 2; Walter Goldschmidt and Evalyn Jacobson Kunkel, "The Structure of the Peasant Family," p. 1062; Lutz K. Berkner, "Inheritance, Land Tenure, and Peasant Family Structure"; and the essays in Jack Goody, Joan Thirsk, and E. P. Thompson, eds., *Family and Inheritance*.

2. Le Play, *L'Organisation de la famille*; H. J. Habakkuk, "Family Structure and Economic Change in 19th Century Europe," pp. 1, 4.

3. See Mendels, "Proto-Industrialization," and Tilly and Tilly, "Agenda for European Economic History," for the development of rural industry and its impact. Changes in the nature of wealth are best summarized in Adeline Daumard et al., *Les Fortunes françaises au XIXe siècle*; see also Pierre Leon, *Géographie de la Fortune et structures sociales à Lyon au XIXe siècle (1815–1914)*.

4. For an interpretation emphasizing the importance of the Empire in the centralization of the French state, see Robert Holtman, *The Napoleonic Revolution*. Other studies suggest that continuity through the revolutionary period is the proper interpretation: see Alexis de Tocqueville, *The Old Regime and the French Revolution*, especially part 2; L. Tilly, "Food Riot"; Denis Richet, *La France moderne*; and C. Tilly, "Food Supply and Public Order in Modern Europe." Notaries were in many cases the mediators between local traditions and the Civil Code: see Theodore Zeldin, *France, 1848–1945*, especially chapters 4 and 10.

5. See the map of customary regions of France and the area of written law in Jean Yver, *Egalité entre héritiers et exclusion des enfants dotés*.

6. Ibid., p. 155.

7. Ibid., p. 160.

8. Jean Merley, *La Haute-Loire de la fin de l'Ancien Régime aux débuts de la Troisième République (1776–1886)*, pp. 230–31.

9. *Gazette Nationale ou le Moniteur universel*, no. 69, dimanche le 10 mars 1793, p. 660.

10. Ibid. See also Jacques Godechot, *Les Institutions de la France sous la Révolution et l'Empire*, p. 438.

11. Ibid., p. 661.

12. The relevant legislation is: law of 29 Germinal An XI on successions; law of 13 Floréal An XI on donations and wills; decree of 20 Pluviôse An XII on marriage contracts. See *Bulletin des Lois*, No. 274, 279, An XI; No. 135, An XII.

13. A.C. de Marlhes, *Actes de mariages*, 1867, no. 20; 1870, no. 6; 1871, no. 10.

14. Ibid.

15. A.C. de Marlhes, *Actes de décès*, 1880, No. 16.

16. See the Act of Donation quoted below.

17. A.D.L. Enregistrement, 9607, *Actes Civils Publics*, 22-10-1867.

18. See the Act of Donation quoted below.

19. A.D.L. Enregistrement, 9609, *Actes Civils Publics*, 20-4-1870.

20. Marie's marriage contract apparently was made in the Haute-Loire; I have not been able to locate either her marriage certificate or the registration of her marriage contract.

21. A.D.L. Enregistrement, 9609, *Actes Civils Publics*, 19-10-1871.

22. A.D.L. Enregistrement, 9611, *Actes Civils Publics*, 14-5-1873.

23. *Déclarations des mutations après décès* were made by the family of the deceased to the local notary; in Marlhes this meant the notary in either Marlhes or nearby Saint-Genest-Malifaux. The notary was responsible for collecting inheritance taxes from the family and registering the act with the Bureau d'Enregistrement for the region. This section is based on the registrations of two sets of *mutations*: all those of persons living in Marlhes registered between 1850 and 1865, found in A.D.L. Enregistrement, 2816–21, *Déclarations mutations par décès*, totalling 283 cases; and a similar group for the period from 1883–98, found in A.D.L. Enregistrement, 9649–56, *Déclarations mutations par décès*, totalling 210 cases.

24. H. Vialleton, "Famille, patrimoine, et vocation héréditaire en France depuis le code civil," especially p. 589.

25. Fortier-Beaulieu, *Mariages et noces campagnards*, pp. 125–26.

26. There is a fictional description of such a debate that has the ring of truth in Emile Zola's *La Terre*.

27. Based on A.D.L. Enregistrement, 9642–56, *Declarations mutations par décès*, and A.D.L. Enregistrement, 9606–29, *Actes Civils Publics*. Because of possible underregistration, these figures may underestimate the extent to which successions were divided. They are so heavily weighted in one direction, however, that even a substantial underregistration would not alter the conclusions. Because of the necessity for establishing responsibility for payment of the *contribution foncière*, underregistration should be relatively low.


## Chapter 9

1. Du Maroussem, *Fermiers montagnards du Haut-Forez*, p. 421.

2. A.D.L. 49 M 85, 49 M 383, *Listes nominatives de recensement de la commune de Marlhes*, 1851, 1901.

3. Du Maroussem, *Fermiers montagnards du Haut-Forez*.

4. The amount of land devoted to cereals in Marlhes remained very close to 60 percent of the total area throughout the period under study. See A.D.L. 55 M 14, *Statistique Agricole de 1856*; A.D.L. 55 M 190–91, *Statistique Agricole de 1905*.

5. The 3,209-hour figure is calculated as follows: cereals require 931 hours per hectare, according to a study of nonmechanized peasant farming in the Federal Republic of Germany, B. Van Deenen et al., *Materialien zur Arbeitswirtschaft*, cited by S. H. Franklin, *The European Peasantry*, pp. 17–20. Three hectares therefore require 2,793 hours per year (3 × 931). Milk cows require 208 man-hours per cow, according to a study in Belgium described in Folke Dovring, *Land and Labour in Europe, 1900–1950*, appendix 4, p. 399. If the two remaining

hectares of a five-hectare farm are used to support two milk cows, this adds 416 hours to the annual labor requirement of the farm. The total of these two is therefore 3,209 hours per year. At 2,992 hours of work per Standard Labor Unit, the five-hectare farm requires 1.07 persons.

6. Dovring, *Land and Labour in Europe*, p. 399, gives the figure of 136.49 hours per hectare for wheat, oats, and mixed grains. Franklin, *European Peasantry*, p. 18, gives the figure of 931 hours per hectare in Federal Germany, citing Van Deenen, *Materialien zur Arbeitswirtschaft*.

7. A.N. F¹¹ 2705 42 Loire, *Enquête Agricole Décennale de 1862*, arrondissement de Saint-Etienne.

8. A.D.L. 49 M 85, 49 M 383, *Listes nominatives de recensement de la commune de Marlhes*, 1851, 1901.

9. The allocation of labor of family members in the table is based primarily on the patterns of recruitment described in chapters 2 and 3.

10. Peyret, *Statistique industrielle de 1835*, p. 30.

11. Chambre de Commerce de Saint-Etienne, *Enquête commerciale sur les traités de 1860*, pp. 13, 14.

12. A.N. C 956, pièce 224, *Enquête du 25 mai 1848 sur le travail industriel et agricole*, canton de Saint-Genest-Malifaux, question 7.

13. A.N. C 956, pièce 170, *Enquête du 25 mai 1848*, canton de Bourg-Argental, question 7.

14. A.N. C 956, pièces 224, 170, *Enquête du 25 mai 1848*, cantons de Saint-Genest-Malifaux and Bourg-Argental, question 8.

15. Olwen Hufton, *The Poor of Eighteenth Century France*, 1750–1789, chapter 3.

16. A.D.L. 55 M 12, *Statistique Quinquennale de 1852*, canton de Saint-Genest-Malifaux. The rate is 0.75 francs for a day laborer who was fed by his employer, and 1.50 francs for one who was not.

17. George D. Sussman, "Parisian Infants and Norman Wet Nurses in the Early Nineteenth Century," p. 641.

18. Du Maroussem, *Fermiers montagnards du Haut-Forez*, p. 473.

19. Ibid., p. 476.

20. See Landes, *Unbound Prometheus*, chapter 5, for the deflation of the late nineteenth century. The data on prices in the Loire that follow are drawn from Gras, *Histoire du commerce local*, pp. 592–669.

21. A.D.L. Enregistrement, 9607, 25-2-1867.

22. A.D.L. Enregistrement, 9607, 21-1-1867.

23. A.D.L. Enregistrement, 9607, 21-1-1867.

24. Du Maroussem, *Fermiers montagnards du Haut-Forez*, p. 431.

25. A.N. F¹¹ 2705 42 Loire, *Enquête Agricole Décennale de 1862*.

26. A.N. C 3025, *Rapport de Sous-Commission C*, pièce 159, question 6.

27. A.D.L. Enregistrement, 9627, 9-8-1894.

28. Du Maroussem, *Fermiers montagnards du Haut-Forez*, p. 412.

29. Ibid., p. 421.

30. See Zeldin, *France, 1848–1945*, pp. 171–73; and Merlin, *L'Exode rural*, pp. 7–16.

31. A.D.L. 49 M 143, *Recensement du canton de Saint-Genest-Malifaux de*

*1861*; A.D.L. 49 M 387, *Recensement du canton de Saint-Genest-Malifaux de 1911.*

32. The labor needs of the larger landowners were probably even greater than those of the smaller landholders, since on larger farms increased market orientation probably meant a greater emphasis on raising cattle and milk cows rather than goats. This cannot be proven from available data, but seems likely. Evidence given in Dovring, *Land and Labour in Europe*, appendix 4, indicates that dairy cows required much more labor than cattle or goats: in Belgium milk cows required 208 man-hours per animal, while other cattle required only 78 man-hours and sheep and goats only 12.49.

33. See, among many, the following: Habakkuk, "Family Structure and Economic Change"; Goldschmidt and Kunkel, "Structure of the Peasant Family"; William Parrish and Moshe Schwartz, "Household Complexity in 19th Century France."

34. Louise A. Tilly and Joan Wallach Scott, *Women, Work and Family*, p. 12.

35. Ibid., pp. 15, 104–5.

36. See Franklin, *European Peasantry*, pp. 19–20.

## Chapter 10

1. Laurence Wylie, *Village in the Vaucluse*, p. 99.

2. Philippe Ariès, *Centuries of Childhood*, p. 25.

3. Lawrence Stone has recently suggested that adolescence, "as a distinctive age-group with its distinctive problems," existed in early modern England, at least among the upper classes he has studied (*The Family, Sex and Marriage in England, 1500–1800*, p. 377). This does not mean, of course, that its distinctive features and problems have not changed.

4. Du Maroussem, *Fermiers montagnards du Haut-Forez*, p. 432.

5. This is in contrast to nineteenth-century Lancashire, where mothers were able to work in factories because childraising was carried out by resident grandparents. Michael Anderson, *Family Structure in Nineteenth Century Lancashire*, pp. 55–67, 143–46.

6. For the rituals surrounding birth and baptism, see the descriptions in Van Gennep, *Folklore de l'Auvergne et du Velay*, pp. 20–21, and Gachon, *L'Auvergne et le Velay*, p. 175.

7. Flandrin, "L'Attitude à l'égard du petit enfant," pp. 175–79; Shorter, *Making of the Modern Family*, pp. 203–4. Shorter's statement that "by the late eighteenth century, parents knew, at least in a sort of abstract way, that letting newborn children stew in their own excrement or feeding them pap from the second month onwards were harmful practices," because of the spread of medical personnel in Europe, does not seem to fit the circumstances in Marlhes, where Flandrin's emphasis on the fatalism toward infant death that permeated Christian thought seems more applicable.

8. DCMM, séance of 29 mai 1840.

9. DCMM, séances of 5 janvier 1834, 9 juin 1834.

10. DCMM, séance of 3 août 1841.

11. DCMM, séance of 3 août 1841.

12. The building, with an indication that it was built in 1841, is described in the report for Saint-Regis-du-Coin to the 1884 Inquiry on Primary Education in A.N. F¹⁷ 2921, *Enquête sur la situation materielle des écoles primaires en 1884*.

13. DCMM, séance of 9 mars 1852.

14. DCMM, séances of 6 mai 1860, 23 septembre 1860, 20 avril 1862, 16 décembre 1866. It is interesting to note that the three principal buildings on the place of Marlhes today were all constructed during the Second Empire: the town hall, the church, and the school.

15. DCMM, séance of 12 juin 1877.

16. DCMM, séances of 18 novembre 1883, 10 février 1884.

17. DCMM, séance of 20 mai 1882; A.N. F¹⁷ 2921, *Rapport pour Marlhes*, 21 juin 1884.

18. DCMM, séances of 20 mai 1882, 28 décembre 1884.

19. DCMM, séance of 21 mai 1894.

20. DCMM, séance of 25 mai 1902.

21. National averages for literacy in 1871–75 were 78 percent for men and 66 percent for women. See M. Fleury and P. Valmary, "Les Progrès de l'instruction élémentaire de Louis XIV à Napoléon III d'après l'enquête de Louis Maggiolo (1877–1879)," p. 87. Marlhes was particularly advanced for its part of the country, falling south of the line from the Bay of Mont-Saint-Michel to Lake Geneva that separated the more literate north of France from the south. On the correspondence between signatures and true literacy, see Kenneth A. Lockridge, *Literacy in Colonial New England*, p. 7.

22. See Thabault, *Education and Change*, pp. 125–27. Compare Patrice Higonnet's interpretation of education as a force from the outside acting on the rural community in *Pont-de-Montvert*, especially chapter V.

23. See Gachon, *L'Auvergne et le Velay*, pp. 176–77 for First Communion ceremonies.

24. Du Maroussem, *Fermiers montagnards du Haut-Forez*, p. 433.

25. Such was the case in the largest rural weaving factory in the region, the usine Colcombet at Saint-Didier-la-Seauve in the Haute-Loire, where Soeurs Saint-Joseph from Le Puy not only supervised workers after working hours but also supervised the work itself. Xavier de Monter, *Notice sur l'usine hydraulique et à vapeur de la maison Colcombet frères et Cie*, pp. 6, 10.

26. Victor Smith, "Un mariage dans le Haut-Forez en 1873." This is a published transcription of an original manuscript included in the collection of Victor Smith's papers in the Bibliothèque de l'Arsenal (Paris), Côte 6860. The references that follow refer to the published transcription. The document does not name the couple being married, and the date of the marriage was changed by Chatelain. The information that it is the marriage of Claude Chorain is from his grandson, currently adjoint of the commune of Marlhes, who was told this by his grandmother. Interview with Claude Chorain, 8 July 1975.

27. Smith, "Marriage dans le Haut-Forez," pp. 548–49.

28. For a description of *veillées*, see Shorter, *Making of the Modern Family*, pp. 124–25.

29. Fortier-Beaulieu, *Mariages et noces campagnards*, map 1, between pp. 16 and 17.

30. Ibid., p. 49.

31. Ibid., p. 52.

32. Ibid., p. 29.

33. Ibid., p. 66.

34. A.D.L. 49 M 85, 49 M 383, *Listes nominatives de recensement de la commune de Marlhes*, 1851, 1901. The other statistics cited in this section are also based on this source.

35. Van Gennep, *Folklore de l'Auvergne et le Velay*, p. 75.

36. Ibid.

## Chapter 11

1. For a general argument along these lines, see Hans Medick, "The Proto-Industrial Family Economy."

2. Braun, *Industrialisierung und Volksleben*; Mendels, "Industrialization and Population Pressure"; Levine, *Family Formation*.

3. Berkner, "Family, Social Structure, and Rural Industry," p. 194.

4. Ibid., p. 346.

5. Anderson, *Family Structure in Nineteenth Century Lancashire*.

## Appendix 1

1. The commune of Marlhes was reduced in size in 1858 by the creation of the commune of Saint-Regis-du-Coin. These series of events, therefore, do not relate to the same areas or population size before and after that year. Source: A.C. de Marlhes, *Registres de décès, naissances et mariages*.

## Appendix 2

1. The census lists are found in A.D.L. 49 M 85, 113, 353, and 387, *Recensements de 1851, 1856, 1901, et 1911*.

2. T. H. Hollingsworth, "Historical Studies of Migration," p. 88.

3. Maurice Garden, *Lyon et les lyonnais au XVIIIe siècle*, especially chapter 3.

4. A.C. de Marlhes, *Registre des actes de mariages*, 1841–98.

# Bibliography

I. Primary Sources

A. *Archives Nationales de France, Paris*

Series F$^{12}$: Commerce et Industrie
  1569: Statistiques industrielles, Loire, An IX.
  2413: Industrie de coton, des rubans et de la soie, An III–1855.
  2419: Dévidage des fils de lin, de coton et de soie, 1811–67.
  4476A–F: Situation économique et sociale des départements, 1830–66.
  4477, 4478A–B: Situation économique, 1866–1868.
  4511B: Situation économique, 1869–1886.
  4711: Rapports des inspecteurs sur l'exécution de la loi de 1841, 1841–66.
  4718: Correspondance avec les préfets relative au travail des enfants, 1855–71.
  4722–23: Enquête de 1867.
  4724–26: Statistique de travail des enfants, 1869–73.
  4728–29: Loi de 1874, Réponses au questionnaire du 31-8-1874.
  6195: Avis des chambres de commerce sur les traités avec l'Angleterre et la Belgique, 1872–73.
  6196: Renouvellement des traités de commerce, 1876–94.
  6197: Renouvellement des traités de commerce, 1886–92.
  6220: Angleterre: Traité de 1860.
  7600: Crise industrielle de 1848: Réponses des Chambres consultatives des Arts et Manufactures à la circulaire du 3 juin 1848.

Series F$^{11}$: Subsistances
  2705, 2717: Enquêtes agricoles décennales: questionnaires, 1862, 1882.

Series F$^{20}$: Statistiques
  561: Commission de Statistique Cantonale: Agriculture 1852–54.
  565: Statistique Agricole, 1854.
  571: Statistique Agricole, 1855.
  578: Statistique Agricole, 1856.
  586: Statistique Agricole, 1857.
  594: Statistique Agricole, 1858.
  603: Statistique Agricole, 1859.
  608: Statistique Agricole, 1859–60.
  613: Statistique Agricole, 1853.
  616: Statistique Agricole, 1855.
  620: Statistique Agricole, 1860.

626: Statistique Agricole, 1861.

715: Tableaux par régions des consommations d'une famille des ouvriers, 1844.

Série C: Assemblée Nationale

956: Enquête sur le travail agricole et industriel du 25 mai 1848.

B. *Archives Départementales de la Loire,*
*Saint-Etienne (Cour Fouriel)*

Series M: Personnel et Administration Générale

37 M 3–7: Epidémies, Cholera, 1831–32, 1835, 1848, 1854–65, 1884.

40 M 55: Cylindrage des rubans, 1837–1852.

40 M 89: Lacets (fabriques de) 1869–78.

40 M 114: Usines de soieries, 1817–87.

40 M 117–18: Teintureries, 1823–1891.

40 M 143–46: Industries diverses, 1820–93.

40 M 94: Moulins, 1814–77.

40 M 112: Scieries, 1822–94.

46 M 19: Formation de communes: Planfoy.

46 M 24: Formations de communes: Saint-Regis-du-Coin.

48 M 23–130: Mouvement de la population, 1841–1902.

49 M 24, 52, 85, 113, 143, 172, 202, 231, 260, 290, 320, 353, 387: Listes nominatives de recensement du canton de Saint-Genest-Malifaux, 1841–1911.

55 M 4–6: Commissions de Statistiques Agricoles, 1837–1901.

55 M 8–191: Statistique Agricole, 1832 to 1905.

56 M 3–4: Etats relatifs aux industries textiles, 1810–15, 1824–57.

56 M 7–10: Statistique sommaire des industries principales 1876–89.

57 M 1–6: Correspondances, renseignements, concours et commices agricoles, 1840–1900.

57 M 17–19 Questionnaires, 1850–1900.

58 M 15–21 Etats des foires et marchés, 1806–1902.

58 M 26: Tableaux des foires et marchés, arrondissement de Saint-Etienne, 1902.

58 M 43: Foires et marchés, commune de Marlhes.

66 M 11: Code rural, 1835.

66 M 13: Renseignements agricoles, 1844.

66 M 16: Loue d'ouvriers agricoles, 1833–63.

66 M 14: Travail agricole, 1848–49.

66 M 20: Bétail, 1813–54.

72 M 1–3, 5 Condition des soies de Saint-Etienne, An XI–1889.

81 M 21: Métiers à la Zurichoise, An XI.

88 M 15–16: Etats des établissements industriels visités, 1850–91.

88 M 17–18: Rapports, 1850–95.

88 M 18–23: Procès-Verbaux, 1878–1902.

90 M 1: Enquêtes et renseignements divers sur la situation des ouvriers, 1849–1916.

Archives de l'Enregistrement

I. Bureau du Chambon-Feugerolles
2659–62: Actes Civils Publics, 1841–65.
2930–31: Tables des Testaments, Donations et Depositions éventuelles, 1841–65.
2937–40: Tables des contrats de mariage, 1841–65.
2958–59: Tables des baux à ferme et à loyer, 1841–65.
2960–61: Table des baux écrits, 1870–90.

II. Bureau de Saint-Genest-Malifaux
9606–29: Actes Civils Publics, 1865–99.
9638–41: Actes sous signatures privées: baux d'immeubles, 1882–98.
9642 to 9656 Déclarations Mutations par Décès, 1867–98.

Archives de la Chambre de Commerce de Saint-Etienne
Carton 131, Dossier 1: Condition des soies, statistiques anciennes.
Carton 117, Dossier 1: Condition des soies, origines, demande pour la transfer.
Carton 104, Dossier 3: Cession de la Condition; traités de 1861 et 1872.
Carton 117, Dossier 3: Revision de traité de 1872; traité de 1890.
Carton 89, Dossier 2: Statistiques récents de la Condition des Soies jusqu'en 1909.
Carton 81, Dossier 3: Rubannerie (usages divers).
Carton 82, Dossier 7: Rubannerie (Outillage, Inventions), situation generale.
Carton 81, Dossier 2: Rubannerie (Piquage d'onces).
Carton 81, Dossier 4: Enquête parlementaire sur les industries textiles (1904); rubannerie.

Série P
Non-Coté: Matrice cadastrale de la commune de Marlhes

Newspaper
*Le Moniteur de Saint-Etienne*, 1903, 1905–06.


C. *Archives Communales de Marlhes (Loire), Mairie de Marlhes*
*Déliberations du Conseil Muncipal de Marlhes, 1789–1914, 5 vols.*

Etat Civil de Marlhes, 1815–1914:
Registres de naissance, 16 vols.
Registres de décès, 16 vols.
Registres de mariage, 7 vols.

II. Secondary Sources

Anderson, Michael. *Family Structure in Nineteenth Century Lancashire*. Cambridge: Cambridge University Press, 1971.
_____. "Urban Migration in Nineteenth Century Lancashire: Insights into Two Competing Hypotheses." In *Annales de démographie historique, 1971*, pp. 13–26. Paris: Mouton, 1971.
Ariès, Philippe. *Centuries of Childhood*. Translated by Robert Baldick. New York: Vintage, 1962.
_____. *Histoire des populations françaises*. Paris: Seuil, 1948.
"Aux origines de la révolution industrielle: industrie rurale et fabriques." Special issue of the *Revue du Nord* 240 (1979).
Barclay, George W. *Techniques of Population Analysis*. New York: John Wiley and Sons, 1958.
Barret, J. *Usages locaux du canton de Saint-Genest-Malifaux recueillis et mis en ordre par M. J. Barret, juge de paix du canton*. Versailles: E. Aubert, 1872.
Beaver, M. W. "Population, Infant Mortality and Milk." *Population Studies* 27(1973): 243–54.
Berkner, Lutz K. "Family, Social Structure and Rural Industry: A Comparative Study of the Waldviertel and the Pays de Caux in the 18th Century." Ph.D. dissertation, Harvard University, 1973.
_____. "Household Arithmetic: A Note." *Journal of Family History* 2 (1977): 159–63.
_____. "Inheritance, Land Tenure and Peasant Family Structure: A German Regional Comparison." In *Family and Inheritance: Rural Society in Western Europe 1200–1800*, edited by Jack Goody, Joan Thirsk, and E. P. Thompson, pp. 71–95. Cambridge: Cambridge University Press, 1976.
_____. "The Stem Family and the Developmental Cycle of the Peasant Household: An Eighteenth Century Austrian Example." *American Historical Review* 77 (1972): 398–418.
_____. "The Use and Misuse of Census Data for the Historical Analysis of Family Structure." *Journal of Interdisciplinary History* 5 (1975): 721–38.
_____, and Mendels, Franklin F. "Inheritance Systems, Family Structure and Demographic Patterns in Western Europe, 1700–1900." In *Historical Studies in Declining Fertility*, edited by Charles Tilly, pp. 209–24. Princeton: Princeton University Press, 1978.
Bloch, Marc. *Caractères originaux de l'histoire rurale française*. Oslo: H. Aschehough & Co., 1931.
Blum, Jerome. *The End of the Old Order in Europe*. Princeton: Princeton University Press, 1978.
Bois, Paul. *Paysans de l'Ouest. Des structures économiques et sociales aux options politiques depuis l'époque révolutionnaire dans la Sarthe*. Le Mans: Imprimerie M. Vilaire, 1960.
Bourgeois-Pichat, J. "The Population of France since the 18th Century." In *Population in History*, edited by D. V. Glass and D. E. C. Eversley, pp. 477–506. London: E. Arnold, 1965.

Braudel, Fernand. *Capitalism and Material Life, 1400–1800*. Translated by Miriam Kochan. New York: Harper and Row, 1973.

Braun, Rudolf. *Industrialisierung und Volksleben*. Erlenbach-Zurich and Stuttgart: Rentsch, 1960.

Chambers, J. D. *The Vale of Trent, 1670–1800: A Regional Study of Economic Change. Economic History Review Supplement* no. 3 (1957).

Chambre de Commerce de Saint-Etienne. *Enquête commerciale sur les traités de 1860*. Saint-Etienne: Theollier, 1971.

Chassagne, Serge. "La diffusion rurale de l'industrie cotonnière en France (1750–1850)." *Revue du Nord* 240 (1979): 97–114.

Chatellard, Claude. "La Misère à Saint-Etienne entre 1870 et 1914." Diplôme d'études supérieures, Université de Lyon, 1966.

Chayanov, A. V. *The Theory of the Peasant Economy*. Edited by Daniel Thorner, B. Kerblay, and R. E. F. Smith. Homewood, Ill.: Robert Irwin, Inc., 1966.

Christensen, Harold, ed. *Handbook of Marriage and the Family*. Chicago: Rand McNally, 1964.

Clerc, Gabriel. *Passementiers stéphanois en 1912*. Saint-Etienne: Theollier, 1912.

Coale, Ansley J. "The Calculation of Approximate Intrinsic Rates." *Population Index* 21 (1955): 94–97.

———. "The Decline of Fertility in Europe from the French Revolution to World War II." In *Fertility and Family Planning: A World View*, edited by S. J. Behrman, Leslie Corsa, and Ronald Freedman, pp. 3–24. Ann Arbor: University of Michigan Press, 1969.

———, and Demeny, Paul. *Regional Model Life Tables and Stable Populations*. Princeton: Princeton University Press, 1966.

Cobban, Alfred. *The Social Interpretation of the French Revolution*. Cambridge: Cambridge University Press, 1964.

Crozier, M. "Demande d'une loi sur les chemins ruraux; Rapport presenté au nom d'une commission nommée par la Section d'Agriculture." *Annales de la Société d'Agriculture de Saint-Etienne* 24 (1880): 50.

Daumard, Adeline, et al. *Les Fortunes françaises au XIXe siècle*. Paris: Mouton, 1973.

Dauphin, Cecile, and Pezerat, Pierrette. "Les consommations populaires dans la seconde moitié du XIXe siècle à travers les monographies de l'école de Le Play." *Annales: Economies. Sociétés. Civilisations* 30 (1975): 537–52.

Davis, James C. *A Venetian Family and Its Fortune, 1500–1900*. Philadelphia: American Philosophical Society, 1975.

Deane, P., and Cole, W. A. *British Economic Growth, 1688–1959*. Cambridge: Cambridge University Press, 1962.

De la Tour-Varan, J. A. *Notice statistique industrielle sur la ville de Saint-Etienne et son arrondissement*. Saint-Etienne: Theollier ainé, 1851.

Deprez, Paul. "The Demographic Development of Flanders in the 18th Century." In *Population in History*, edited by D. V. Glass and D. E. C. Eversley, pp. 608–30. London: E. Arnold, 1965.

De Vries, Jan. "Peasant Demand Patterns and Economic Development: Friesland 1550–1740." In *European Peasants and their Markets*, edited by

William N. Parker and Eric Jones, pp. 205–66. Princeton: Princeton University Press, 1975.

Dovring, Folke. *Land and Labour in Europe, 1900–1950.* The Hague: Martinus Nijhoff, 1956.

_____. "The Transformation of European Agriculture." In *The Cambridge Economic History of Europe,* vol. 6, part 2, pp. 604–72. Cambridge: Cambridge University Press, 1965.

Dufour, J. E. *Dictionnaire topographique du Forez et des paroisses du Lyonnais et du Beaujolais formant le département de la Loire.* Macon: Imprimerie Protat frères, 1946.

Du Maroussem, Pierre. *Fermiers montagnards du Haut-Forez.* Paris: Ouvriers des Deux Mondes, 1894.

Dunham, A. L. *The Industrial Revolution in France, 1815–1848.* New York: Exposition Press, 1955.

Duplessy, Joseph. *Annuaire du département de la Loire.* Montbrison: Cheminal, 1818.

"Enquête sur l'industrie laitière. Rapport présenté au nom d'une commission par M. F. Maire. Réponses pour l'arrondissement de Saint-Etienne." *Annales de la Société d'Agriculture* 28 (1884): 116–22.

Flandrin, Jean-Louis. "L'Attitude à l'égard du petit enfant et les conduites sexuelles dans la civilisation occidentale." In *Annales de démographie historique,* 1973, pp. 143–210. Paris: Mouton, 1973.

_____. *Familles: parenté, maison, sexualité dans l'ancienne société.* Paris: Hachette, 1976.

Fleury, M., and Valmary, P. "Les Progrès de l'instruction élémentaire de Louis XIV à Napoleon III d'après l'enquête de Louis Maggiolo (1877–1879)." *Population* 12 (1957): 71–92.

Fortier-Beaulieu, Paul. *Mariages et noces campagnards.* Paris: G. P. Maisonneuve, 1937.

Fournal, Etienne, and Gutton, Jean-Pierre. *Cahiers de doléances de la province de Forez.* 2 vols. Montbrison: La Diana, 1975.

Franklin, S. H. *The European Peasantry.* London: Methuen, 1969.

Gachon, Louis. *L'Auvergne et le Velay.* Paris: G. P. Maisonneuve et Larose, 1975.

Ganiage, Jean. *Trois villages de l'Ile-de-France.* I.N.E.D. Cahier No. 40. Paris: Presses Universitaires de France, 1963.

Garden, Maurice. *Lyon et les lyonnais au XVIIIe siècle.* Paris: Les Belles-Lettres, 1970.

Garrier, Gilbert. *Paysans du Beaujolais et du Lyonnais.* 2 vols. Grenoble: Presses Universitaires de Grenoble, 1973.

Gautier, Etienne, and Henry, Louis. *Crulai, paroisse normande.* I.N.E.D. Cahier No. 33. Paris: Presses Universitaires de France, 1958.

*Gazette nationale ou le Moniteur universel.* Reimpression de l'ancien *Moniteur.* Paris: Imprimerie Impériale, 1858.

Godechot, Jacques. *Les Institutions de la France sous la Révolution et l'Empire.* 2d ed. Paris: Presses Universitaires de France, 1968.

Goldschmidt, Walter, and Kunkel, Evalyn Jacobson. "The Structure of the Peasant Family." *American Anthropologist* 73 (1971): 1058–76.

Goode, William J. *World Revolution and Family Patterns.* New York: Free Press of Glencoe, 1963.

Goody, Jack; Thirsk, Joan; and Thompson, E. P., eds. *Family and Inheritance: Rural Society in Western Europe 1200–1800.* Cambridge: Cambridge University Press, 1976.

Goubert, Pierre. "Historical Demography and the Reinterpretation of Early Modern French History." In *The Family in History,* edited by Theodore K. Rabb and Robert I. Rotberg, pp. 16–27. New York: Harper and Row, 1971.

Gras, Louis-Jean. *Histoire de la rubannerie.* Saint-Etienne: Theolier, 1906.

———. *Histoire du commerce local et des industries qui s'y rattachent dans la région stéphanoise et forezienne.* Saint-Etienne: J. Thomas, 1908.

———. *Histoire économique de la metallurgie de la Loire.* Saint-Etienne: J. Thomas, 1908.

———. *Histoire économique générale des mines de la Loire.* 2 vols. Saint-Etienne: Theolier, 1922.

———. *Les Routes du Forez et du Jerez.* Saint-Etienne: Theolier, 1925.

Greenfield, Sidney. "Industrialism and the Family in Sociological Theory." *American Journal of Sociology* 68 (1961): 312–22.

Guillaume, Pierre. *La Compagnie des Mines de la Loire (1846–1854).* Paris: Presses Universitaires de France, 1966.

Guizot, François. *Democracy in France.* 4th ed. London: John Murray, 1849.

Habakkuk, H. J. "Family Structure and Economic Change in 19th Century Europe." *Journal of Economic History* 15 (1955): 1–12.

Hajnal, John. "Age at Marriage and Proportions Marrying." *Population Studies* 7 (1953): 111–36.

———. "European Marriage Patterns in Perspective." In *Population in History,* edited by D. V. Glass and D. E. C. Eversley, pp. 101–46. London: E. Arnold, 1965.

Hedde, Philippe. *Indicateur du commerce, des arts et des manufactures de Saint-Etienne, Saint-Chamond, et Rive-de-Gier.* Saint-Etienne: Gaudelet, 1832.

———. *Revue industrielle de l'arrondissement de Saint-Etienne, suivie de l'indicateur du commerce, des arts et des manufactures de Saint-Etienne.* Saint-Etienne: Janin, 1836.

Henripin, J. *La Population canadienne au debut du XVIIIe siècle. Nuptialité. Fécondité. Mortalité infantile.* I.N.E.D. Cahier No. 22. Paris: Presses Universitaires de France, 1954.

Henry, Louis. *Manuel de démographie historique.* Paris: Droz, 1967.

———. "Some Data on Natural Fertility." *Eugenics Quarterly* 8 (1961): 81–91.

———, and Fleury, Michel. *Nouveau manuel de dépouillement et d'exploitation de l'état civil ancien.* Paris: I.N.E.D., 1965.

———, and Houdaille, Jacques. "Fécondité des mariages dans le quart nord-ouest de la France de 1670 à 1829." *Population* 28 (1973): 873–922.

Higonnet, Patrice. *Pont-de-Montvert: Social Structure and Politics in a French Village, 1700–1914.* Cambridge: Harvard University Press, 1971.

Hollingsworth, T. H. "Historical Studies of Migration." In *Annales de demographie historique, 1970*, pp. 87–96. Paris: Mouton, 1970.

Holtman, Robert. *The Napoleonic Revolution.* Philadelphia: Lippincott, 1967.

Houdaille, Jacques. "Fécondité des mariages dans le quart nord-est de la France de 1670 à 1829." In *Annales de démographie historique, 1976*, pp. 341–92. Paris: Mouton, 1976.

Hufton, Olwen. *The Poor of Eighteenth Century France, 1750–1789.* Oxford: Clarendon Press, 1974.

Jones, E. L., ed. *Agriculture and Economic Growth in England, 1650–1815.* London: Methuen, 1967.

————. "Introduction." In *Agriculture and Economic Growth in England, 1650–1815*, edited by E. L. Jones, pp. 1–48. London: Methuen, 1967.

Kisch, Herbert. "The Textile Industries in Silesia and the Rhineland: A Comparative Study in Industrialization." *Journal of Economic History* 19 (1959): 541–64.

Knodel, John, and van de Walle, Etienne. "Breast Feeding, Fertility and Infant Mortality: An Analysis of Some Early German Data." *Population Studies* 21 (1967): 109–31.

Kriedte, Peter; Medick, Hans; and Schlumbohm, Jurgen. *Industrialisierung vor der Industrialisierung.* Gottingen: Venadenhoeck und Ruprecht, 1977.

Lachiver, Marcel. *La Population de Meulan du XVIIe au XIXe siècle.* Paris: S.E.V.P.E.N., 1969.

Landes, David S. *The Unbound Prometheus.* Cambridge: Cambridge University Press, 1969.

Laslett, Peter. *The World We Have Lost.* New York: Charles Scribner's Sons, 1965.

————, and Wall, Richard, eds. *Household and Family in Past Time.* Cambridge: Cambridge University Press, 1972.

Lehning, James R. "Demographic, Economic and Cultural Factors in the Decline of Marital Fertility: Some Evidence from the Département of the Loire." Unpublished paper presented to Annual Meeting of the Social Science History Association, 1978.

Leon, Pierre. *Géographie de la fortune et structures sociales à Lyon au XIXe siècle (1815–1914).* Lyon: Centre d'histoire économique et sociale de la région lyonnaise, 1974.

Le Play, Frédéric. *L'Organisation de la famille.* Paris: Tequi, 1871.

————. *L'Organisation du travail.* Tours: Mame, 1870.

Lequin, Yves. *Les Ouvriers de la région lyonnaise (1848–1914).* 2 vols. Lyon: Presses Universitaires de Lyon, 1977.

Le Roy Ladurie, Emmanuel. "L'Amenorrhée de famine (XVIIe–XXe siècle)." In *Le Territoire de l'historien*, pp. 331–48. Paris: Editions Gallimard, 1973.

Levine, David. "The Demographic Implications of Rural Industrialization: A Family Reconstitution Study of Shepshed, Leicestershire, 1600–1851." *Social History* 2 (1976): 177–96.

————. *Family Formation in an Age of Nascent Capitalism.* New York: Academic Press, 1977.

Levy-Leboyer, M. "La Croissance économique en France au XIXe siècle." *Annales: Economies. Sociétés. Civilisations* 23 (1968): 788–807.

Limousin, Antoine. *Enquête de 1848. Rapport des Rubaniers.* Saint-Etienne: Pichon, 1848.

Litwack, Eugene. "Geographical Mobility and Extended Family Cohesion." *American Sociological Review* 25 (1960): 385–94.

Locard-Denoel. "De l'état de l'agriculture dans l'arrondissement de Saint-Etienne et de la nécessité de l'améliorer." *Bulletin Industriel de Saint-Etienne* 12 (1834): 284–96.

Lockridge, Kenneth. *Literacy in Colonial New England.* New York: W. W. Norton and Co., 1974.

Lucas, Colin. *The Structure of the Terror.* London: Oxford University Press, 1973.

Martin, Germain. *Le Tissage de ruban à domicile dans les campagnes du Velay.* Paris: Sirey, 1913.

Meaudre, Jacques. "La Poussée urbaine à Saint-Etienne, 1815–1872." Diplôme d'études supérieures, Université de Lyon, 1966.

Medick, Hans. "The Proto-Industrial Family Economy: The Structural Function of Household and Family during the Transition from Peasant Society to Industrial Capitalism." *Social History* 3 (1976): 291–315.

Mendels, Franklin F. "Proto-Industrialization: The First Phase of the Industrialization Process." *Journal of Economic History* 32 (1972): 241–61.

———. "Industrialization and Population Pressure in 18th Century Flanders." Ph.D. dissertation, University of Wisconsin, 1970.

Merley, Jean. "La Contribution de la Haute-Loire à la formation de la population stéphanoise au milieu du XIXe siècle." *Cahiers de la Haute-Loire* (1966): 165–80.

———. "Eléments pour l'étude de la formation de la population stéphanoise à l'aube de la Révolution industrielle." In *Démographie urbaine*, pp. 261–76. Lyon: Centre d'histoire économique et sociale de la région lyonnaise, 1977.

———. *La Haute-Loire de la fin de l'Ancien Régime aux débuts de la Troisième République (1776–1886).* Le Puy: Cahiers de la Haute-Loire, 1974.

Merlin, Pierre. *L'Exode rural.* Paris: Presses Universitaires de France, 1971.

"Météorologie." *Bulletin Industriel de Saint-Etienne* 22 (1851): 157–61.

Minchinton, Walter. "Patterns of Demand, 1750–1914." In *The Industrial Revolution*, vol. 3 of *The Fontana Economic History of Europe*, edited by Carlo Cipolla, pp. 77–186. London: Collins/Fontana Books, 1973.

Mokyr, Joel. *Industrialization in the Low Countries, 1795–1850.* New Haven: Yale University Press, 1976.

Monter, Xavier de. *Notice sur l'usine hydraulique et à vapeur de la maison Colcombet frères et Cie.* Paris: Victor Goupy, 1873.

Morineau, Michel. *Les Faux-Semblants d'un démarrage économique.* Cahier des Annales no. 30. Paris: Librairie A. Colin, 1970.

"Notice sur l'industrie de l'arrondissement de Saint-Etienne au commencement de 1828." *Bulletin Industriel de Saint-Etienne* 6 (1828): 5–19.

Ogier, Théodore. *La France par cantons et communes.* Lyon: Ogier, 1852.

Parrish, William; and Schwartz, Moshe. "Household Complexity in 19th

Century France." *American Sociological Review* 37 (1972): 154–73.

Parsons, Talcott. "The Kinship System of the Contemporary United States." *American Anthropologist* 45 (1943): 22–38.

———, and Bales, Robert F. *Family, Socialization and Interaction Process.* Glencoe, Illinois: Free Press, 1955.

Peyret, Alphonse. *Statistique industrielle du département de la Loire.* Saint-Etienne: Delarue, 1835.

Ploton, J. "La Moulinage de la soie à Dunières, 1718–1914." Cahiers de la Haute-Loire (1966): 137–64.

Pouthas, Charles. *La Population française pendant la première moitié du XIXe siècle.* I.N.E.D. Cahier No. 25. Paris: Presses Universitaires de France, 1956.

Prost, Antoine. *Histoire de l'enseignement en France, 1800–1967.* Paris: A. Colin, 1968.

Redford, A. *Labour Migration in England, 1800–1850.* Manchester: University of Manchester Press, 1926.

Richet, Denis. *La France moderne: l'esprit des institutions.* Paris: Flammarion, 1973.

Rouchon, Ulysses. *La Vie paysanne en Haute-Loire.* 3 vols. Le Puy: Imprimerie de la Haute-Loire, 1933–40.

Saint-Genest, M. le Baron de. "Culture des montagnes, défrichements des terrains de bruyère et leur mise en prairie." *Annales de la Société d'Agriculture* 11 (1867): 84–92.

Salber, Eva J: Feileib, Manning; and MacMahon, Brian. "The Duration of Post-Partum Amenorrhea." *American Journal of Epidemiology* 82 (1966): 347–58.

Schnerb, Robert. *Deux siècles de fiscalité française, XIXe–XXe siècle.* Paris: Mouton, 1973.

Schnetzler, Jacques. "Un Demi-Siècle d'évolution démographique dans la région de Saint-Etienne (1820–1876)." *Etudes Foreziennes* 1 (1968): 157–90.

Segalen, Martine. *Nuptialité et alliance: le choix du conjoint dans une commune de l'Eure.* Paris: Maisonneuve et Larose, 1972.

Shanin, Teodor, ed. *Peasants and Peasant Societies.* Middlesex: Penguin, 1971.

Shorter, Edward. "Illegitimacy, Sexual Revolution, and Social Change in Modern Europe." *Journal of Interdisciplinary History* 2 (1971): 237–72.

———. *The Making of the Modern Family.* New York: Basic Books, 1975.

Shryock, Henry S.; Siegel, Jacob S.; and Associates. *The Methods and Materials of Demography.* 2 vols. Washington, D.C.: Government Printing Office, 1973.

Slicher von Bath, B. H. *The Agrarian History of Western Europe A.D. 500–1850.* Translated by Olive Ordish. London: E. Arnold, 1963.

Smelser, Neil J. *Social Change in the Industrial Revolution.* Chicago: University of Chicago Press, 1959.

Smith, Daniel Scott. "A Homeostatic Demographic Regime: Patterns in West European Reconstitution Studies." In *Population Patterns in the Past,* edited by Ronald Demos Lee, pp. 19–56. New York: Academic Press, 1977.

Smith, Victor. "Un mariage dans le Haut-Forez en 1873." *Romania* 9 (1880): 547–60.

Soboul, Albert. "The Persistence of Feudalism in the Rural Society of 19th Century France." In *Rural Society in France*, edited by Robert Forster and Orest Ranum, pp. 50–71. Baltimore: Johns Hopkins University Press, 1977.

Société Impériale d'Agriculture, Industrie, Sciences, Arts et Belles-Lettres. *Compte rendu du commice agricole de Saint-Genest-Malifaux tenu au 1 et 2 août 1863*. Saint-Etienne: Theolier, 1863.

Stone, Lawrence. *The Family, Sex and Marriage in England, 1500–1800*. New York: Harper and Row, 1977.

Sussman, George D. "Parisian Infants and Norman Wet Nurses in the Early Nineteenth Century: A Statistical Study." *Journal of Interdisciplinary History* 7 (1977): 637–53.

Tenand, D. "Les Origines de la classe ouvrière stephanoise." Diplome d'études superieures, Université de Lyon II, 1972.

Thabault, Roger. *Education and Change in a Village Community: Mazières-en-Gatine, 1848–1914*. Translated by Peter Tregear. New York: Schocken Books, 1971.

Thiollier, Lucien. "Rubanier." In *Association Française pour l'Avancement des Sciences, XXVI Session, Août, 1897*. Saint-Etienne: Theollier, 1897.

Thirsk, Joan. "Industries in the Countryside." In *Essays in the Economic and Social History of Tudor and Stuart England*, edited by F. J. Fisher, pp. 70–88. Cambridge: Cambridge University Press, 1961.

Tilly, Charles. "Food Supply and Public Order in Modern Europe." In *The Formation of National States in Western Europe*, edited by Charles Tilly, pp. 380–455. Princeton: Princeton University Press, 1975.

———, ed. *The Formation of National States in Western Europe*. Princeton: Princeton University Press, 1975.

———, ed. *An Urban World*. Boston: Little, Brown and Company, 1974.

———. *The Vendée*. Cambridge: Harvard University Press, 1964.

———, and Tilly, Richard. "Agenda for European Economic History in the 1970's." *Journal of Economic History* 31 (1971): 184–98.

Tilly, Louise A. "The Food Riot as a Form of Political Conflict in France." *Journal of Interdisciplinary History* 2 (1971): 23–58.

———, and Scott, Joan Wallach. *Woman, Work and Family*. New York: Holt, Rinehart and Winston, 1978.

Tocqueville, Alexis de. *The Old Regime and the French Revolution*. Translated by Stuart Gilbert. Garden City, N.Y.: Anchor, 1955.

Touchard-la-Fosse, G. *La Loire historique, pittoresque et biographique*. Nantes: Suireau, 1840.

Van de Walle, Etienne. "Alone in Europe: The French Fertility Decline until 1850." In *Historical Studies in Declining Fertility*, edited by Charles Tilly, pp. 257–88. Princeton: Princeton University Press, 1978

———. *The Female Population of France in the Nineteenth Century*. Princeton: Princeton University Press, 1974.

———. "Household Dynamics in a Belgian Village, 1847–1866." *Journal of*

*Family History* 1 (1976): 80–94.

————, and Preston, Samuel H. "Mortalité de l'enfance au XIXe siècle à Paris et dans le département de la Seine." *Population* 29 (1974): 89–107.

————, and van de Walle, Francine. "Allaitement, stérilité et contraception: les opinions jusqu'au XIXe siècle." *Population* 27 (1972): 686–701.

Van Gennep, Arnold. *Le Folklore de l'Auvergne et du Velay.* Paris: G. P. Maisonneuve, 1942.

Vialleton, H. "Famille, patrimoine, et vocation héréditaire en France depuis le code civil." In *Mélanges offerts à Jacques Maury*, pp. 577–91. Paris: Dalloz et Sirey, 1960.

Villermé, L. R. *Tableau de l'état physique et morale des ouvriers employés dans le manufacture de coton, de laine et de soie.* 2 vols. Paris: J. Renouard, 1840.

Vinson, Louis. *L'Industrie de ruban à Saint-Etienne. Essai sur son évolution probable et son avenir.* Saint-Etienne: Loire Republicaine, 1910.

Weber, Eugen. *Peasants into Frenchmen.* Stanford: Stanford University Press, 1976.

Wylie, Laurence. *Village in the Vaucluse.* Cambridge: Harvard University Press, 1974.

Yver, Jean. *Egalité entre héritiers et exclusion des enfants dotés: essai de géographie coutumière.* Paris: Sirey, 1966.

Zeldin, Theodore. *France, 1848–1945: Ambition, Love and Politics.* Oxford: Clarendon Press, 1973.

Zola, Emile. *La Terre.* Paris: Fasquelles, 1933.

# Index